Yakovlev Piston-Engined Fighters

Yefim Gordon and Dmitriy Khazanov

Original translation by Sergey Komissarov

Midland Publishing

Yakovlev's Piston-Engined Fighters
© 2002 Yefim Gordon and Dmitriy Khazanov
ISBN 1 85780 140 7

Published by Midland Publishing
4 Watling Drive, Hinckley, LE10 3EY, England
Tel: 01455 254 490   Fax: 01455 254 495
E-mail: midlandbooks@compuserve.com

Midland Publishing is an imprint of
Ian Allan Publishing Ltd

Worldwide distribution (except North America):
Midland Counties Publications
4 Watling Drive, Hinckley, LE10 3EY, England
Telephone: 01455 254 450   Fax: 01455 233 737
E-mail: midlandbooks@compuserve.com
www.midlandcountiessuperstore.com

North American trade distribution:
Specialty Press Publishers & Wholesalers Inc.
11605 Kost Dam Road, North Branch, MN 55056
Tel: 651 583 3239   Fax: 651 583 2023
Toll free telephone: 800 895 4585

© 2002 Midland Publishing
Design concept and layout
by Polygon Press Ltd. (Moscow, Russia)
Colour artwork © Sergey Yershov
Line drawings © Aleksey Alyoshin

This book is illustrated with photos
from the archives of Yefim Gordon,
the A. S. Yakovlev Design Bureau and
the Russian Aviation Research Trust

Printed in England by
Ian Allan Printing Ltd
Riverdene Business Park, Molesey Road,
Hersham, Surrey, KT12 4RG

All rights reserved. No part of this
publication may be reproduced,
stored in a retrieval system, transmitted
in any form or by any means, electronic,
mechanical or photo-copied, recorded
or otherwise, without the written
permission of the publishers.

Contents

Introduction	3
1. The Yak-1 – Yakovlev's First Fighter	5
2. The Yak-7 – The First Derivative	41
3. The Yak-9 – The Private of the Skies	61
4. The Yak-3 – The Last of the Line	103
5. Yaks Abroad	129
Data tables	135
Colour drawings	137

Title page: A mid-production Yak-1 flown by M. V. Avdeyev (Hero of the Soviet Union), then a squadron commander with the 8th Fighter Regiment of the Black Sea Fleet Air Arm. He went on to become CO of the 6th Guards Fighter Regiment.
Below: Red Banner Baltic Fleet Air Arm pilots L. P. Savkin and I. P. Koocherov sit in their Yak-1bs on quick-reaction alert.

Introduction

Just like in other countries, development of aviation in the Soviet Union did not proceed at an even pace. Years and even decades of calm, evolutionary development were at times superseded by a revolutionary rush forward. The latter was usually understood to imply aviation's transition to a qualitatively new level. Thus, the advent of monoplanes supplanting biplanes, and the emergence of jet-powered aircraft were accompanied by a radical improvement of flight performance, in particular, by a dramatic increase of maximum speed.

In late 1930s and early 1940s Soviet aviation was undoubtedly passing through a period of sweeping changes. Realising that the Soviet Union was qualitatively lagging behind the countries holding the leading positions in world aircraft and aero engine construction, the Soviet government demanded that aircraft of considerably improved performance be urgently developed and placed in series production. Such aircraft were created within the shortest time possible. Vladimir Mikhaïlovich Petlyakov's bombers, Sergey Vladimirovich Il'yushin's attack aircraft, fighters created by Semyon Alekseyevich Lavochkin and Aleksandr Sergeyevich Yakovlev were produced in numbers running into thousands, featuring dozens, if not hundreds, of different versions. It was these machines that made up the bulk of the Red Army Air Force inventory in the period between 1941 and 1945.

Chief Designer A. S. Yakovlev created the prototype of his Yak-1 fighter in close co-operation with aero-engine designer Vladimir Yakovlevich Klimov who consciously chose for his M-105 engine a layout permitting the installation of a cannon that would require no synchronisation; it could be fired irrespective of the engine's rpm.

The aircraft, as well as the subsequent types and versions created in the course of the war years, was of mixed construction, featuring a tubular truss fuselage with plywood and fabric skinning, the welded engine mount being an integral part of the fuselage; mated to it were wooden wings which initially were built in one piece. The monoplane fighter had many features that were novel for its time – for example, the armament comprising cannons and machine-guns, cantilever tail surfaces, a retractable undercarriage, a variable-pitch propeller etc. At the same time, even at the moment of its emergence this kind of airframe could not be considered either advanced or innovative. Nevertheless, these aircraft had a happy fate, as it turned out.

In the course of their quantity production the Yaks underwent continuous aerodynamic refinement; steps were taken to improve the view from the cockpit; new, more deadly weapons were introduced. Not so successful was the work on the installation of more powerful engines, and in production one had, for the most part, to make do with this or that version of the baseline M-105 production engine. Austere equipment, especially measured by the standard of Western countries, was characteristic of virtually all Yakovlev fighters; this applied primarily to gunsights, radio equipment and mechanisms intended to reduce the pilot's workload in flight.

In designing and developing his aircraft Aleksandr S. Yakovlev proved to be not only a talented designer but also a production process organiser well versed in the capabilities and problems of the Soviet aircraft industry. All the Yaks proved to be cheap and well adapted to quantity production; they could easily be manufactured by unskilled labour and did not require the use of strategic materials which might be scarce. They could also be flown by pilots of very modest skills who had undergone hasty training during the harsh war years.

In comparison with the sophisticated all-metal Mustangs with their excellent aerodynamics and monobloc wings, the multi-role Messerschmitts and Focke-Wulfs, the Yaks were less resistant to combat damage. But they proved to be very amenable exactly for the type of war that came to be waged at the Soviet front when the main efforts of aviation were devoted to support of ground troops and aerial combat usually took place at low and medium altitudes.

This accounts for the fact that series production of Yakovlev fighters undertaken by six factories (not counting two machines assembled by a seventh factory) totalled 35,737 machines of different models; of these, 449 were built during the first half of 1941 and 1,927 machines were completed after the end of the war in Europe.

Left: Vladimir P. Yatsenko's I-28 experimental fighter during State acceptance trials at NII VVS.

Right: Appropriately serialled 21 Red, Mikhail M. Pashinin's I-21 fighter prototype is seen here during manufacturer's flight tests. These two aircraft were unlucky competitors of the I-26.

Above: The first prototype Mikoyan/Gurevich I-200 (the future MiG-1 interceptor) wore a red lightning flash on the fuselage and had an enclosed cockpit.
Below: The unpainted third prototype I-200. Like the other two, it was devoid of national insignia; note the open cockpit.

Above: The cherry-red and highly-polished Lavochkin/Gorboonov/Goodkov I-301, the first prototype of the LaGG-3.

Chapter 1

The Yak-1

Yakovlev's First Fighter

I-26 Prototype Fighters

The I-26 aircraft (the I stood for *istrebitel'* – fighter) occupies a special place in Aleksandr S. Yakovlev's creative activities as a designer. The military customers had good reasons to voice many complaints and criticisms concerning this machine, especially in 1940-1942. Nevertheless, this fighter had a happy fate. It was put into large-scale production and became the progenitor of a family of piston-engined fighters (the Yak-7, Yak-9 and Yak-3) that achieved worldwide renown. While retaining the baseline type's general appearance, it included no less than 60 prototype and series-produced versions.

By the beginning of 1939 Yakovlev's team had accumulated considerable experience. Six years earlier he had been granted production facilities in Moscow; gradually they were built up into the Experimental Plant No. 115. It was at this plant that Yakovlev had built his trainer monoplanes: the AIR-9, -10, -12, -15, -16, -18, -14, and -20 which could be classed as high-speed aircraft by the standards of those days. The latter two types were built in large numbers and designated UT-1 and UT-2 respectively. One more aircraft, the twin-engined AIR-17 trainer, was scheduled for series production under the designation UT-3. Finally, before starting design work on fighters, the Yakovlev team had created the twin-engined 'Aircraft No. 22' (later known as the BB-22, Yak-2 and Yak-4) which was regarded by the authorities as a successor to the obsolete Tupolev SB (ANT-40) bomber.

Yakovlev's work on the design of a high-speed fighter had a special feature about it: the machine was proposed in several versions. While other design teams submitted one project each, Yakovlev presented four projects at once. These were the I-26 front-line (tactical) fighter for low and medium altitudes; the I-27 (alias UTI-26) fighter trainer for conversion training; the I-28 (Yak-5) high-altitude fighter for air defence; and the I-30 (alias I-26U) multi-cannon fighter.

In contrast to other design bureaux, the Yakovlev team submitted neither a preliminary design (PD) project nor a mock-up of the future machine. Already at that time the Chief Designer had connections in high places which enabled him to skip such 'formalities'.

The work on the I-26 proceeded at a quicker pace compared to other projects, and all employees of the design bureau were fully aware of its importance. After all, the success or failure of the 'firstling' would seriously affect the destinies of the other machines. Yet the I-26 was born in greater pains than its stablemates. This was quite natural; after all, the badly needed experience in matters pertaining to the construction of a modern high-speed fighter was being acquired in the process of the design work.

Yakovlev appointed K. Sinel'shchikov, a young engineer, as chief project engineer for the I-26. Under his direction design work on the new machine started in May 1939; nearly eight months later, the prototype was completed and rolled out of the Experimental Plant's assembly shop. This time frame could not be considered overly prolonged, bearing in mind the fact that the production facility was a converted factory that had previously manufactured beds; in mid-1939 only 44 machine-tools were available for the work on the fighter. By the beginning of 1939 the Design Bureau had 45 engineers and 152 workers on its payroll.

The fighter that emerged served as the prototype for all the numerous subsequent versions which basically repeated the original type. In its layout the I-26 was a single-seat mixed-construction monoplane. The fuselage featured a welded steel-tube framework. The forward fuselage housing the engine had duralumin skinning, while the aft fuselage had a fabric skin supported by a lining consisting of light planks. The wings featuring a Clark-YH airfoil section were a one-piece unit, with no provision for detaching the outer panels, and were of wooden construction. Duralumin was used in the construction of the tail unit, ailerons (which had fabric skinning) and flaps.

Many parts and units featured a basically new design and had experimental status. These included the future fighter's 'heart' – the engine. It was envisaged that that the prototype would be powered by the M-106 high-altitude engine of increased output; this would enable the I-26 to attain a maximum speed of 620 km/h (385 mph) at altitude, the landing speed being 120 km/h (74.6 mph). The service ceiling was estimated at 11,000 to 12,000 m (36,080 to 39,360 ft), and it was

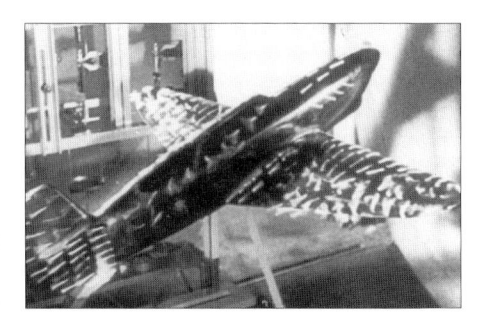

Top: A model of the I-26 in the TsAGI wind tunnel; note the wool tufts.
Above: The ill-fated I-26-1, the first prototype of the Yak-1. Note the red stripes on the propeller blades.

Above: the I-26-1 on wheels at a later stage of the manufacturer's flight tests. The fighter was painted cherry-red overall, except for the red and white striped rudder which was a trademark feature of Yakovlev aircraft in the pre-war years.

The first prototype had a rather pointed fin top and a boxy fairing atop the engine cowling housing the carburettor air intake.

expected that the fighter's manoeuvrability and climb rate would be outstanding for its time. Installation of the supercharged M-105 engine on the second prototype was expected to enhance the fighter's high-altitude performance.

However, these plans proved to be a product of wishful thinking – even the baseline M-105 engine (from which the M-106 was to be developed) existed only in prototype form by the time when construction of the I-26 prototype began. It should be noted that the engine developed under the direction of Vladimir Ya. Klimov was specially designed in such a way as to permit the installation of a cannon between the cylinder banks. The barrel of the 20-mm (.78 calibre) Shpital'nyy/ Vladimirov ShVAK cannon passed through the propeller hub, obviating the need for synchronisation and permitting the cannon to fire irrespective of the engine's and propeller's rpm. The cannon was supplemented by four synchronised 7.62-mm (.30 calibre) Shpital'nyy/Komarnitskiy ShKAS machine-guns arranged in pairs above and beneath the engine.

One might say the machine was built 'from scratch', with no prior fighter design experience to fall back on. As a result, the real fully-equipped airframe weighed 2,600 kg (5,733 lb) instead of the 2,300 kg (5,071 lb) estimated by the designers. To make the first flight possible, the fuel tanks of the I-26 were only partially filled and the cannon and machine-guns were not provided with ammunition. Yakovlev kept the promise he had given to Stalin; the I-26 was ready to fly by the beginning of 1940. On 13th January the Design Bureau's chief test pilot Yulian Piontkovskiy took the machine, which was fitted with a ski undercarriage for the occasion, into the air. This is how Yakovlev describes the historic moment: *'The blades of the spinning propeller merged into a single silver disc, and a cloud of dust rose behind the machine, indicating that the pilot had given the engine full throttle; the aircraft began its run. Finally, the fighter made a thunderous low pass over our heads and climbed steeply.*

Everybody heaved a sigh of relief. Piontkovskiy is confidently making a second circuit of the airfield. Everything is proceeding smoothly so far. The machine loses altitude and comes in for landing. The pilot performs a confident gliding manoeuvre, the aircraft touches down in the centre of the airfield and, after a short landing run, taxies to the hangar. Everybody, irrespective of rank and age, headed for the aircraft; the pilot was helped out of the cockpit and jubilantly thrown several times into the air. Even before Piontkovskiy had a chance to utter a word, I understood from the satisfied look on his face and his eyes shining with laughter that everything was OK.'

Piontkovskiy indeed had a high opinion of the fighter. However, concluding his report, he noted that the oil temperature had started to rise immediately after take-off; this alarmed him, compelling him to make an urgent landing.

The first series of flights showed that the machine was responsive, with low control forces, making the handling of the aircraft easy and simple. Its maximum speed at 5,000 m (16,400 ft) was 580 km/h (360 mph), which came close to the estimated figure. Only 5.2 minutes were needed to climb to this altitude.

Above and below: The wreckage of the I-26-1 after the crash in Moscow's Bol'shaya Maslovka Street on 27th April 1940. Yulian Piontkovskiy, Yakovlev's first chief test pilot, lost his life in the crash.

At the same time the I-26 suffered from a number of teething troubles caused by deficiencies both in design and production standards. It took a long time before the oil overheating observed in the first flight could be eliminated. After each flight the aircraft came back with traces of oil leaks on the side and lower panels of the engine cowling. Changes were repeatedly introduced into the oil system but failed to produce a radical improvement. After a flight of only two or three minutes at full throttle the pilot had to abort the mission. The engine was replaced five times, the propeller had to be changed even more frequently. Very soon the VISh-52 variable-pitch propeller (*vint*

Above and below: the identically finished I-26-2, the second prototype, during manufacturer's flight tests. Outwardly it differed from the I-26-1 in lacking the oblong carburettor air intake fairing and having a more rounded fin top.

Above and below: The I-26-2 following modifications intended to cure the engine overheating problem encountered in early test flights. The enlarged undernose oil cooler and recontoured water radiator bath are well visible.

Above: The M-105 engine of the I-26-2 with all cowling panels removed. The cowling design provided good access to the engine.

The tail unit and aft fuselage of the second prototype.

izmenyayemovo shahga), which turned out to be ill-suited for the type, gave place to the more suitable VISh-61P.

It transpired that many elements of the aircraft's structure were not strong enough. In particular, static tests revealed that the wing leading edges disintegrated when the load reached two-thirds of the calculated maximum figure. Undercarriage retraction was problematic and the wheels were not securely held by the locks, whether it be in the extended or in the retracted position. Apparently it was the defects of the moving elements of the undercarriage and the insufficient structural strength that caused the machine to crash on 27th April 1940. When performing its 43rd flight at low altitude, the aircraft made a flip roll, entering a spin, and crashed in Bol'shaya Maslovka Street in downtown Moscow near the Design Bureau's premises. Pilot Yulian Piontkovskiy was killed. Until then he had saved the Yakovlev fighter prototype fifteen times thanks to his swift and faultless judgement in critical situations. Piontkovskiy was succeeded by Sergey Korzin'shchikov as project test pilot.

The commission investigating the causes of the crash surmised that in the process of performing a roll the mainwheels had become unlocked spontaneously, the abrupt load causing a failure of the wing structure which was not strong enough. This reasoning sounds convincing to this day.

By the time when the I-26-1 crashed, the second prototype designated I-26-2 had already been completed. Its structure was strengthened; in particular, the wing leading edges were reinforced and the plywood skin was made thicker.

In his efforts to provide better cooling for the engine, the Designer had to relinquish the aerodynamically favourable position of the oil cooler. It was moved from its original location under the cylinder banks (ie, between the mainwheel wells) to a place under the engine sump (ie, under the extreme nose), which entailed an increase in the machine's drag. While the work on the machine was proceeding, the Government issued a directive stipulating that the M-107 engine – the most powerful of the liquid-cooled engines then available – be installed in the I-26. But it could not be implemented at the time because even the forerunner of this engine, the M-105, was still beset by teething troubles. (It may be noted at this stage that more or less normal operation of the M-107 engine (which was renamed VK-107 by that time in honour of its designer Vladimir Klimov) on the Yak-9U fighter was achieved only after the end of the war.

The VISh-61P propeller which had been selected to suit the M-105 engine during the first flights was also installed on the second prototype. Changes were introduced into the armament of the I-26-2: of the four machine-guns only the upper pair was retained, chiefly for CG reasons. The angle at which the aircraft sat on the ground was insufficient, and the aircraft tended to be 'nose-heavy' during landing runs, which incurred considerable danger of nosing over; the omission of the lower machine-guns was expected to alleviate this problem. With the alterations listed above, the I-26-2 acquired the features that were characteristic for the subsequent prototype and production versions.

Manufacturer's trials of the I-26-2 were brief. As early as 1st June 1940 it was submitted to NII VVS (*Na**oochno**-is**sled**ovatel'skiy institoot Voyenno-vozdooshnykh sil* – the Air Force Research Institute) for State tests. This was preceded in May by a Government directive requiring the I-26 to be put into large-scale production in Leningrad, Moscow and Saratov. This was an unprecedented event: the aircraft still had many defects to be eradicated, military engineers and pilots were only just beginning their part of the testing, and yet large-scale series production was already envisaged. Presumably this was not due solely to A. Yakovlev's abilities in 'promoting' his progeny (in April 1940, in addition to his previous posts, he was appointed Vice People's Commissar of Aircraft Industry with responsibility for prototype aircraft construction). More probably, the top echelon of the People's

Commissariat (Aleksey I. Shakhoorin, Pyotr V. Dement'yev and Pavel Voronin) became aware of the new fighter's potential and took the calculated risk in order to save time because the Second World War was already raging in Europe.

State trials of short duration conducted under the direction of engineer N. Maksimov brought no surprises. The machine demonstrated very high performance. Thus, the maximum speed attained at sea level was 490 km/h (305 mph), and at 4,800 m (15,744 ft), which was the second rated altitude, it reached 585.5 km/h (363.9 mph). The service ceiling was 10,200 m (33,456 ft), and a climb to 5,000 m (16,400 ft) took six minutes flat. The aircraft's structural strength remained insufficient, and it was tested at an all-up weight of 2,700 kg (5,954 lb) which was 100 kg (220 lb) lighter than the fully-equipped version. Despite this, the danger of the aircraft disintegrating was still present, and this had to be taken into account. A temporary ban had to be placed on most aerobatic manoeuvres. Due to G load limitations, test pilots Pyotr M. Stefanovskiy and A. Nikolayev performed a full-circle turn at the altitude of 1,000 m (3,280 ft) in 24 seconds (they figuratively described it as a 'pancake turn', since they avoided banking the machine). Coolant and oil overheating forced the pilots to reduce the engine's rpm during climb. The State trials revealed 123 defects of varying seriousness (unfortunately, about the same number of defects was found in the other prototype fighters – the I-301 and I-200 – which entered large-scale production before the war). Thus, the I-26 failed to pass the State trials. However, note was taken of the fact that the new fighter had proved to be about 100 km/h (62 mph) faster than the I-16 – the most numerous fighter in service at that time, and the I-26 was even easier to fly than Polikarpov's fighter. This promised great advantages.

When results of the testing of Yakovlev's first progeny were discussed by representatives of the People's Commissariat of Aircraft Industry and the Air Force, two issues came to dominate the discussion. Firstly, the fighter was not equipped with a generator and a rate-of-climb indicator. The bulky PAN-23 telescopic sight fitted originally was replaced by a ring-and-bead sight; this finally brought home the awareness of how primitive the aircraft's equipment was. The aircraft did not even have a communications radio receiver. This was a cause of concern for the leaders of NII VVS; Aleksandr Filin, chief of the Institute and an experienced engineer, noted quite rightly that a transmitter/receiver had to be installed even on prototype examples of fighters. The Chief Designer objected, however, being of the opinion that the purpose of testing was to evaluate the aircraft's flight and tactical performance and that a radio was not required for this. In the end, the commission ruled that the equipment suite of production fighters should be revised. Another point of doubt was the use of one-piece wings by Yakovlev. The absence of outer wing panel joints offered a weight reduction, but obviously it greatly hampered transportation and repairs of the fighter in field conditions.

Above: The I-26-2 during State acceptance trials at NII VVS.

Right: The windshield and reflector gunsight of the I-26-2.

The aircraft was immediately put into series production at Plant No. 301 in Moscow. In the summer of 1940 eighteen machines were manufactured there for the purpose of service trials, using I-26-1 drawings. Changes had to be introduced into the new fighter's units and systems in the process of construction. Thus, the design of the oil tank and its placement had to be changed three times, the shape of exhaust stubs was changed twice... Yet the numerous faults in the design of the engine, undercarriage and equipment were compounded by production defects. Service trials of the machine were conducted at Kubinka airfield near Moscow under the direction of engineer K. Chasovikov. Pilots of the 11th IAP (*istrebitel'nyy aviatsionnyy polk* – Fighter Air Regiment) who were the first in the Air Force to convert to the new fighter could begin flights only after the wing leading edges were reinforced.

The pilots took a liking to the machines and flew them confidently. It transpired that experienced pilots converting from the I-16 did not require any familiarisation flights on the UTI-26 '*sparka*' (the two-seat trainer version of the fighter). Although some defects were noted, the impression was that the I-26 was simple, docile in handling and that the machine had a bright future in store. In mock combat sessions the new machine displayed complete ascendancy over Nikolai N. Polikarpov's machines (the I-15*bis* and I-16). Yakovlev's aircraft was service-tested in the 11th IAP not only in daytime but at night as well. And, although the machines were not fitted with landing lights (a serious drawback for night flights), the pilots made trouble-free landings with the landing strip lit by a projector installed on the airfield.

A flight of five service-test batch I-26s took part in the traditional parade in Moscow on 7th November 1940, flying over Red Square, much to the admiration of the assembled public. Due attention was also paid to a comment made by test pilot A. Yakimov who, acting under order from People's Commissar of Defence Kliment Ye. Voroshilov (succeeded by that time by Timoshenko), checked the new fighter's performance. He said, 'This is not a combat aircraft but rather a kind of a lightplane – so simple and docile is it in flight.' But in the course of a prolonged operational service defects came to light which could not have been revealed during expeditious State trials. It was necessary to urgently reinforce

Above and below: Two more views of the I-26-2 during State acceptance trials. Note the radio set aft of the seat headrest, the lack of the gunsight and the characteristic hexagonal concrete slabs of the NII VVS hardstand at Shcholkovo airfield.

the undercarriage wheels and eliminate the jamming of the sliding cockpit hood in a dive and the tendency of the tailwheel to collapse on landing.

In the meantime, the third prototype – the I-26-3 – was ready for State trials. On this machine the Design Bureau staff and the Chief Designer managed to eradicate many of the defects noted earlier. In particular, they succeeded in bringing the airframe strength to the required level. This enabled the fighter to attain in a dive an indicated airspeed of 635 km/h (395 mph), which had been considered dangerous earlier, and perform aerobatics at maximum permissible G loads. The anticipated good manoeuvrability of the fighter was corroborated: a full-circle turn at the altitude of 1,000 m (3,280 ft) could be performed in 20 to 21 seconds and the fighter gained 800 to 1,000 m (2,624 to 3,280 ft) in a climbing turn from that altitude.

The improvements had to be paid for: the all-up weight rose by 100 kg (220 lb). It was expected that the front-line fighter would become still heavier after the installation of the necessary equipment, in particular, the radio set. However, this did not adversely affect the I-26's easy handling. In October-November 1940 NII VVS test pilots P. M. Stefanovskiy, A. Koobyshkin, A. Proshakov, K. Groozdev and A. Nikolayev checked the machine's behaviour in different flight modes. The work was conducted under the direction of leading engineer A. Stepanets who subsequently headed most of the teams engaged in testing Yakovlev fighters and did much for improving the quality of prototype and production machines. At the beginning of December a report was signed, stating that the I-26-3 had passed the trials with satisfactory results. However, defects noted during testing were still numerous. The main defects included imperfections in the design of the fighter's undercarriage, pneumatic system and powerplant (oil overheating and unstable running of the engine at cruising rpm) and the absence of the necessary special equipment (radio set, landing light, onboard generator etc.).

The war is imminent

Series production of the fighter got under way in the late autumn of 1940. In addition to the small Plant No. 301 in Moscow which had already gained some experience in the construction of Yakovlev aircraft, production of the machine was started at Plant No. 292 (former 'Saracombine' plant producing agricultural machinery) in Saratov. It discontinued work on the I-28 fighter designed by Vladimir P. Yatsenko (not to be confused with Yakovlev's aircraft bearing the same designation!) and switched over completely to mastering production of the promising I-26; in December 1940 the latter was allocated the designation **Yak-1** reflecting the name of its Chief Designer.

According to the Government's plans, the two abovementioned plants, supplemented by Plant No. 126 in Komsomol'sk-on-Amur which also joined in the Yak-1 programme, were to deliver 220 machines by the end of that year. However, the latter enterprise, being overburdened with work on the Il'yushin DB-3f bomber, was unable to start production of the fighter. Besides, Aircraft Plants Nos. 301 and 292 suffered from a chronic shortage of propellers, engines, radiators and other units, which hampered the expansion of production.

Launching Yak-1 production in Saratov was also accompanied by a multitude of problems. In accordance with the rules adopted in the Soviet Union at that time the plants engaged in aircraft production used the loft-floor-and-template method. It consisted in providing the plant with big plywood sheets upon which full-size layouts of the main units and parts of the future machine were marked. Templates were made by copying the outlines on the loft-floor panels; they were used for manufacturing the jigs and tools and, later, the parts themselves. When alterations were introduced into the drawings, this necessitated changes in the whole production process. As witnessed by reports of the Design Bureau, the Chief Designer approved 7,460 (!) changes in the drawings of its first fighter in the period between June and December 1940 alone. Besides, for a long time the Plant's workers could not master the welding of the fuselage truss and the woodworking jobs associated with wing construction; lack of experience and breaches of production procedures led to a large amount of defective products. Despite this, on 3rd October 1940 Plant 292 test pilot Colonel P. Shootov took the first production Yak-1 into the air.

In the period between the end of 1940 and early 1941, series production was marked by a gradual build-up of the monthly output, although the tempo of this build-up was not as high as the top management of the aircraft industry might wish. The plan for 1940 was not fulfilled. By the end of 1940 military representatives had taken delivery of 48 Yak-1s in Moscow and 16 in Saratov. While in December 1940 one aircraft per day was rolled out (and not always accepted by the Air Force because of defects), in April of the following year this figure rose to two per day, reaching three per day before the outbreak of the war, despite the cessation of Yak-1 production at Plant No. 301 since April. Production costs per one Yakovlev fighter made up 158,000 roubles in 1941, while those of one Bf 109F were 103,000 Reichsmark (the labour costs of one Soviet machine were approximately 50% lower than those of the German machine).

Production flaws were gradually ironed out; still, one could not claim that the machine was above criticism. Critical remarks accompanied all the tests of production machines at the beginning of 1941. Among the defects noted were oil leaks through piping joints, uneven fuel consumption from the port and starboard fuel tanks, and water and oil overheating.

At that time almost all design changes were accompanied by an increase in weight. The Yak-1 c/n 04-06 (ie, fourth aircraft in Batch 6) tested in February-March 1941 weighed as much as 2,858 kg (6,302 lb). Many defects of the aircraft were eradicated: the main gear doors were strengthened, the carburettor air inlet was redesigned, the wing root fairings and the numerous hatch covers became more tight-fitting. The oil cooler was made less protruding, which helped make the aircraft more streamlined. Analysis of the materials of numerous tests indicates that the following performance figures obtained during tests were typical for the Yak-1 in 1941: speed at sea level, 480 km/h (298 mph); speed at the second rated altitude of 4,950 m (16,236 ft), 577.5 km/h (358.9 mph). Time to 5,000 m (16,400 ft) was now 5.7 minutes. The aircraft performed a full-circle turn at the altitude of 1,000 m (3,280 ft) within 20 to 21 seconds. The fighter's landing speed was 137 km/h (85 mph), and cruising range reached 700 km (435 miles).

Preparation for – and participation in – the May Day parade of 1941 became a crucial test for the newly produced machines; 40 Yak-1s were assigned for this mission. The pilots of the previously mentioned 11th IAP, which was part of Moscow's anti-aircraft defences, performed 162 missions in all. There were no fatal crashes or serious accidents with the Yaks, but all sorts of technical failures ran into dozens. Especially disturbing were the cases of disruption of the fuel system's filler tubes – the risk of a fire was great.

From mid-May onwards the 11th IAP was fully equipped with 62 Yak-1s (that was the regular complement at that time); the pilots of this regiment had made a worthy contribution to eradicating the defects of the first production Yaks. Before the war this regiment became a sort of Academy for the flying personnel and ground crews of other units; flight and squadron commanders from these units received their training there.

Based in the vicinity of Baku, the 45th IAP commanded by Major I. Dzoosov became the second regiment in the Air Force to convert to Yakovlev's fighter. 78 Yaks were sent to the Transcaucasian region in April 1941, which made it possible not only to equip the said unit to full strength, but also to establish a training centre for the Transcaucasian area.

Above and below: The fifth production I-26 (c/n 0105) manufactured by the Moscow aircraft factory No. 301 and delivered to NII VVS. The aircraft did not exactly conform to the manufacturing drawings.

Above: The second production I-26, c/n 0102, after suffering a landing accident on 9th October 1940 when the undercarriage collapsed after touchdown.

Small numbers of production Yak-1s supplemented the inventory of other units literally a few days before the outbreak of the war. The main part of flyable Yaks were stationed in the Moscow area, but 105 fighters of this type succeeded in reaching the five western military districts situated along the border. Only the pilots of the 20th IAP based at Sambor (Kiev Special Military District) had enough time for gaining a modicum of mastery over the new fighter – 70 pilots learned to fly the fighter in visual meteorological conditions, and seven pilots mastered flying in the night-time and in clouds.

Service introduction of the Yak-1

As a result of delays with deliveries of new Yaks to Air Force service units in the western borderside military districts, in June 1941 the majority of these new machines was flown only by some of the commanders of regiments and smaller units. Just about one month more, and the process of conversion, at least the initial one, would have been completed. Among those who fully mastered the new fighter was Major B. Soorin, Commander of the 123rd IAP. On 22nd June, repulsing the air raids of the German aviation against the headquarters of the 4th Army in Kobrin, the regiment commander took his machine to the air four times, claiming the destruction of three enemy aircraft, but was killed in action in the evening of that day.

The pilots of the Naval Air Arm (AVMF – *Aviahtsiya Voyenno-morskovo flota*) also converted to the Yak-1. In the Black Sea Fleet air arm it was Lieutenant Yu. Shitov from the 9th IAP who was to gain the first victory while flying this fighter type, shooting down a Romanian reconnaissance aircraft. By the outbreak of the war his unit (commanded by Major K. Malinov) was presumably the biggest in the Black Sea Fleet air arm, with nearly 90 combat aircraft on strength, including three Yak-1s. Subsequently the complement of the 9th regiment was curtailed, while the number of Yaks in it rose steadily.

Most of the Yaks which opposed the invasion of the Luftwaffe at the borders of the Soviet Union met a tragic fate. But, as a matter of fact, all types of fighters, bombers and attack aircraft suffered enormous losses. However, unlike the I-16s and the SB bombers, the Yaks of the 91st and 123rd IAPs suffered losses mainly on the ground not only during the first day of the war but until the end of June; if they had a choice, Soviet pilots preferred to fly their missions on older types which they had thoroughly mastered.

After just a few days of combat no Yaks remained in the inventory of the Air Force of the Western and South-Western fronts. Pilots of the 20th IAP gained fame in fierce combat against German airmen at the South-Western

Front. During three days alone (10th to 12th June), while committed to action at distant approaches to Kiev, the unit increased its score by 26 downed enemy aircraft. In those days many aces from JG3 and I/JG53 meeting their Soviet adversaries over Zhitomir, Berdichev and Fastovo, had a chance to gauge the strong and weak points of the new Soviet machine. Despite the fact that 38 Yaks were repaired and sent into battle again, only six of the 63 machines of this type remained on strength with the 20th IAP by 27th July; of these, only two were flyable while the others required 'treatment'.

The only replenishment of the Soviet Frontal aviation at that time was represented by five Yak-1s which arrived (together with 29 MiG-3s) at Idritsa airfield on the northern flank of the Western front, being a part of a group of test pilots led by Lieutenant-Colonel P. Stefanovskiy. On 10th July Lieutenant V. Kozhevnikov, piloting a Yak, scored his first victory; while on a mission in a group, he shot down a Henschel Hs 126 artillery spotter. Shortly thereafter the unit, also known as the 402th IAP, was transferred to the 57th Air Division and continued to fight against the enemy at the North-Western Front.

On this strategic direction the new Yak-1s were concentrated mainly in the 158th IAP. Initially the regiment was based near Pskov, later it joined Leningrad's air defence units. Among its pilots mention must be made of A. Chirkov who shot down an enemy aircraft on 23rd June 1941 (this was the first victory in the skies of Leningrad). Initially Chirkov flew the I-16; later he successfully converted to the Yak-1, increasing his score to seven enemy aircraft in mid-August. It was his initiative to conduct air combat by a pair (instead of a flight of three aircraft, as had been the usual practice in the Soviet Air Force).

In the late summer and in the autumn Yakovlev's fighters shouldered their main burden in Moscow area. As of 10th July 1941, 133 Yak-1s made up approximately one sixth of the fighter aviation element which defended the capital in the ranks of the units of the 6-th IAK (*istrebitel'nyy aviatsionnyy korpoos* – Fighter Air Corps) of Air Defence. Their high level of combat readiness is borne out by the fact that only nine fighters were in disrepair. The Yaks could also boast the Air Corps' first victory: on 2nd July 1941 Lieutenant S. Goshko of the 11th IAP chased an enemy reconnaissance aircraft. When the Yak's armament jammed, the pilot rammed the enemy aircraft in the vicinity of Velikiye Looki and landed his aircraft safely. The German Heinkel's crew, which was killed in the attack, included a military journalist who had embarked on collecting materials about the 'devastating blows inflicted by *Luftwaffe* pilots on Russian cities'.

Yak-1s in the final assembly shop of the Saratov aircraft factory No. 292.

The outbreak of the war posed an acute problem – it was necessary to organise a steady conversion of the flying personnel to new aircraft types, including the Yak-1. Quite obviously, the conversion centres that had been set up at production factories and in the 11th IAP were already unable to cope with the needs of the Red Army's Air Force. Most of the flying personnel and ground crews who had lost their aircraft during the first days of combat were sent to the rear. There it was necessary to quickly work up a unit for dispatching the airmen to the front again. For this purpose Reserve Air Regiments, or ZAPs (*zapasnoy aviatsionnyy polk*) were set up. One of the first reserve units, the 8th ZAP, which specialised in the conversion training to the Yak-1, was deployed in Bagai-Baranovka near Saratov at the beginning of July 1941.

The story of the 273rd IAP can be considered typical. In mid-July the unit's CO, Captain I. Suvorov, and another five pilots arrived in Oryol where the 6th ZAP was based. The regiment was tasked with achieving opera-

Yak-1 fuselages on the conveyor belt assembly line

tional status in the shortest time possible and mastering the Yak-1 fighter. Twenty pilots from the 49th and 163rd IAPs and another seven from the ZAP were placed under Suvorov's command; all of them had previously flown the I-16, and none of them had any idea of Yakovlev's machine.

The entire conversion process took 11 days, during which 32 pilots logged almost 128 flying hours. On 27th July the pilots passed an 'exam' designed to check their knowledge of the materiel and of the basic piloting techniques; the commanders evaluated the accomplishments of most pilots as 'good'. Apparently the demands towards the pilots were not very stringent, since the conversion to the Yak-1 in the 273rd IAP was accompanied by one fatal crash and one non-fatal accident. Such incidents happened again in the period between 28th July and 3rd March 1941, when this unit was on duty in the Air Defence system of the town of Oryol.

German bombers usually made their sorties over the Soviet rear areas at night and the regiment had no pilots that had received instrument flying training. Attempts to intercept enemy reconnaissance aircraft in daytime proved unsuccessful, too. From 3rd August onwards the 273rd IAP started defending the city of Toola where important Soviet arsenals were situated. As for the regiment's first victory, it was gained in the skies of the South-Western front to which a number of Air Regiments were transferred from other sectors and from the rear at the end of August due to a worsening of the tactical situation at this direction. On 27th September Lieutenant L. Ufimtsev rammed a Heinkel He 111 over the town of Romny and was killed in the act.

The combat effectiveness of the Yak-1 would have been higher, had it not been for some annoying defects of the machine. When the 158th IAP, before its transfer to the rear from the already besieged Leningrad, handed its surviving Yak-1s over to the 123rd IAP (commanded by Major B. Romanov), it transpired that the number of aircraft in disrepair was twice as big as the number of those in good order. The latter unit had not had time to complete conversion to the new machine before the war and continued the conversion training in July. Judging by comments from the flying personnel and ground crews, preparing the machines for flight was a complicated and time-consuming task. Many troubles stemmed from the M-105P engines. They were more reliable than the AM-35As installed in the MiG-3 fighters, but there were cases of magneto and speed governor failures and cases when oil was ejected through the output shaft of the reduction gearbox. Metal chips accumulated in the oil cooler of one of the engines during the second sortie; the engine jammed and the pilot had to seek a place for an urgent forced landing in order to avoid more serious consequences.

On the eve of the German offensive against Moscow the Yak-1s made up 10% of the fighters in the front-line aviation. Gradually, as the airframe's and engine's defects were eradicated and teething troubles were cured, it became clear that the Yak-1 had greater chances of success in combat against German fighters compared to other aircraft of the Red Army's Air Force. Here is the appraisal given to it at that time by Luftwaffe experts: *'The Yak-1 fighter is presumably the best Soviet fighter. It had a better speed and rate of climb compared to the MiG-3 and came close to the performance of the Bf 109F, but was inferior to the latter in speed. It was appreciably more difficult to hit the Yak-1 from behind than the MiG-3. It retained a good rate of climb up to 6,000 m (19,680 ft), but its manoeuvrability fell off at that altitude. For this reason the pilots dived from high altitudes to lower ones where they accepted combat.'*

The abovementioned 20th IAP actively joined battle within the Air Force of the Bryansk front, where Guderian's 2nd Tank Group was waging an offensive intended to by-pass Moscow. The regiment was based at Karachayevo airfield together with the 4th IAP which had the MiG-3s on strength. One of the pilots of the latter unit, G. Zimin (later awarded the title of Hero of the Soviet Union and promoted to Air Marshal) wrote that, after having seen the Yak-1 for the first time and having sat in its cockpit, he felt *'a well-meaning*

This view of Yak-1 fuselages undergoing assembly clearly shows the engine bearer design.

envy towards the neighbours'. Both regiments made part of the 11th Composite Air Division (SAD – *smesh*annaya aviatsi*on*naya di*vee*ziya) led by General G. Kravchenko – a Soviet ace who had gained fame during the hostilities at Khalkhin-Gol (the Nomonhan incident) in Mongolia. The command took every effort to ensure that the pilots could make full use of the Yak-1's combat potential, and results were not slow in coming. In September, in one of the night sorties alone, Captain G. Konev succeeded in shooting down two Junkers bombers.

A high level of flying skills and bravery were characteristic for Captain K. Titenkov, a squadron commander from the 11th IAP. After the first German air raid had been repulsed in the evening of 21st July 1941, he was recommended for decoration with the Order of Lenin; the text of the recommendation contained the phrase: *'He is capable of flying new types of aircraft both in day- and nighttime.'* This fact was very important at that time because experienced fighter pilots capable of flying night missions could be counted on the fingers of one hand. And Titenkov did not merely fly sorties; he downed an He 111 in his Yak-1 during his very first encounter with the enemy. Two days later the brave pilot destroyed a Ju 88.

Sadly, the combat career of this outstanding airman did not last long. By 10th October 1941 when Titenkov was killed in the crash of his Yak-1 (c/n 2525) in adverse weather conditions, he had scored four personal victories and two shared 'kills' in 172 combat sorties. This success is all the more impressive since five of the six claimed victories are confirmed by German documents. It has been established on the basis of materials from *Bundesarchiv* that the Soviet pilot shot down the following aircraft: an He 111P from 4/KG55 (c/n unknown, tactical code G1+BM) on the night of 22nd July, Ju 88D-1 WNr. 1253 from 4(F)/14 on 24th July, He 111P-3 WNr. 3183 from *Wekusta* 26 on 20th August, Bf 110D-1 WNr. 3810 from 2(F)/122 on 24th September and Bf 110E-2 WNr. 4513 from 4/ZG 26 on 7th October. At that time the Yaks had neither communications equipment nor navigation aids, which only accentuates Titenkov's outstanding skills. The Yaks still had no landing light either.

Half a year's experience of operational service made it possible to arrive at some conclusions. Let us look at the documents of the 6th IAP of the PVO (**P**rotivovoz**dooshn**aya obo**ron**a – Air Defence). On the eve of the New Year of 1942 the regiment's command undertook a thorough analysis of the combat experience, evaluating the advantages and disadvantages of the new fighter. According to the report submitted by Chief of Staff Colonel Komarov, 150 Yak-1s were phased into service at different times; of these, 80 were subsequently transferred together with their units to other fronts, primarily to the Leningrad area, where a very complicated situation arose in the autumn of 1941. Of the remaining 70 Yaks, 42 were lost in aerial combat, 14 machines fell victim to anti-aircraft fire, and seven Yak-1s were written off as non-combat losses (one crashed on take-off, another due to pilot error during landing approach and five more were lost due to engine failures). Worthy of note is the fact that 89% of losses are combat losses. (In comparison, it may be pointed out that under similar circumstances 74 MiG-3s out of the 209 that remained in the PVO system were lost in aerial combat and 37 MiGs had to be written off as a result of various accidents; combat losses accounted for only 67% of the overall attrition.)

Yak-1s nearing completion.

The first improvements of the basic type

There was no shortage of defects and complaints. They were not so dangerous in flight as was the case with the first MiG-3s, and did not cause such a serious deterioration of performance as in the case of the LaGG-3, but they did cause quite a few vexations.

The moving elements of the undercarriage remained unsatisfactory, as before. Bumps and jerks occurred during retraction; sometimes the undercarriage legs got stuck in an intermediate position and would not retract fully. Besides, not infrequently the undercarriage collapsed during landing; as for the tailwheel, its failures were caused mainly by the insufficient castoring angle.

The armament of the Yak-1 also provided its share of troubles. Many pilots considered

The final assembly shop of plant No. 292 in 1943. The aircraft were towed through the shop, tail first, by means of a special floor-mounted conveyor; the numbers denote the assembly stations.

Above: This view gives an idea of the scale of Yak-1 production in Saratov. Note that the improved Yak-1b 'bubbletop' version had superseded the original 'razorback' version of the Yak-1 by 1943.

Still minus propeller, one of the first production Yak-1b's is pushed out into the open at aircraft factory No. 292.

it to be inadequate and prone to jamming. The cockpit got excessively hot, and oil leaking from the breather sprayed on the cockpit windshield, which hampered the piloting – the fighter had to be flown with the sliding canopy hood in the open position.

As early as the summer of 1941 the M-105P engine installed in the Yaks began to be supplanted by its improved version – the M-105PA. The latter had reinforced crankcase and connecting rods and was provided with a floatless carburettor which enabled the pilot to perform inverted flight for some time and enter a dive with negative g-loads. There were also other changes. However, not all defects (in particular, the spill of oil from the breather) could be eliminated.

Despite serious problems which accompanied Yakovlev's fighters at that time, during the first month of the war the Soviet government adopted several important decisions calling for the expansion of the series manufacture of the Yaks. Thus, on 24th June Plant No. 292 was prescribed to deliver 1,350 combat machines to the front instead of 1,100, as stipulated earlier. It was envisaged that production of the Yak-1 should be mastered at aircraft factories in Leningrad (Plant No. 47) and Engels (Plant No. 492). Besides, in the summer of 1941 the People's Commissar of Aircraft Industry approved a programme of Yak production at the new Aircraft Plant No. 448 in Tbilisi and its branch in Kutaisi (Plant No. 131). However, the harsh wartime conditions prevented these plans from being implemented.

Meanwhile, the staff of the Yakovlev OKB (*opytno-konstrooktorskoye byuro* – design bureau) and of Plant No. 292 in Saratov did not halt their efforts aimed at improving the fighter's airframe. In November 1941 a Yak-1, c/n 2029, successfully passed tests at NII VVS. It featured a number of design improvements. These included a supplementary hydraulic power cylinder which ensured smooth and bump-free retraction and extension of the undercarriage, and a simplified non-retractable tailwheel. A new easily detachable propeller spinner was introduced, as were a trim tab on the rudder, a landing light, and a radio, the installation of which was accompanied by shielding and electrical bonding of the engine and the airframe. A special breather vent tank was added to eliminate the tell-tale oil spill problem.

Besides, the reliability of the armament was improved. Unfortunately, this was accompanied by an increase of the all-up weight to 2,934 kg (6,469 lb) and some deterioration of performance. Maximum horizontal speed was 468 km/h (291 mph) at sea level and 560 km/h (348 mph) at 4,800 m (15,744 ft), that is to say, it proved to be 12 to 17 km/h (7.4 to 10.6 mph) less than that of the early Yak-1s. The time required to reach 5,000 m (16,400 ft) rose to 6.8 minutes, ie, an increase of more than one minute. The manoeuvrability of the machine remained good – the time of performing a full-circle turn at low altitude was 19 to 20 seconds. In the course of a combat turn the fighter gained some 900 m (2,952 ft). The introduction of engine boost at take-off made it possible to reduce the landing run by 5% and compensate for the Yak's increased take-off weight.

The abovementioned Yak-1 c/n 2029 became the first example of this type to be fitted with a communications radio at the production plant. Approximately 1,000 machines built earlier did not have even the simplest radio receiver. Subsequently, in the course of several months radio equipment was installed in one Yak-1 out of every ten. This was due to the Chief Designer's firm conviction that, as long as the quality of radio communication was still unsatisfactory, the radio did nothing but add extra weight to the airframe.

Even prior to that, in October-November 1941, the Yaks were provided with rocket armament. Here note must be made of the initiative displayed by Major A. Negoda, commander of the 562nd IAP. He performed four to five sorties after one refuelling, strafing the enemy's forward lines with the new 82-mm RS-82 rockets (RS – *raketnyy snaryad*, rocket projectile). This was possible because the for-

Above and below: Yak-1 '16 White' (c/n 0406) during checkout trials at NII VVS. Such trials were held from time to time to make sure that production aircraft conformed to the Air Force's specifications.

An early-production Yak-1 built by plant No. 292; note the characteristic shape of the upper main gear door segments.

Above and below: Yak-1 '30 White' (c/n 0218) which was modified according to the decision of a joint NKAP and Air Force commission. The crudely hand-painted tail number was obviously temporary.

Yak-1 c/n 0105 in a rather unusual (and well-weathered) camouflage.

ward line of defence passed about 10 km (6 miles) from the regiment's airfield in Khimki near Moscow. The German anti-aircraft defences were hard put to it to repulse effectively the attacks of Soviet fighters which made a surprise appearance at extremely low altitudes.

By that time the 562nd IAP had accumulated appreciable combat experience. The regiment's pilots downed eight enemy machines in aerial combat and destroyed one German aircraft on the ground during strafing sorties. The Soviet losses comprised 13 machines that were shot down or damaged, nine pilots were killed in action. Two Yaks made forced landings, but eight machines (including those from other regiments) were repaired by the technical personnel.

In all, 195 Yaks were fitted with rocket armament at the Plant by the end of 1941; another 953 fighters were retrofitted with this armament by the late spring of the following year. The installation of six RS-82 projectiles on the machine found a positive response from the flying personnel; as a result, rocket armament began to be fitted to the fighters directly at the front. Although the external stores increased the all-up weight by 65 kg (143 lb) and decreased the maximum speed by some 30 km/h (18mph), firing these projectiles against aerial targets (especially during head-on attacks) produced a strong psychological effect on the enemy. In the event of a direct hit (which happened extremely rarely) the enemy aircraft simply disintegrated in the air.

In the course of combat it became clear that there was really no need to score a direct hit by all means. The projectiles were provided with fuses for self-destruction, and explosions at close range inflicted serious splinter damage on enemy machines. Even German bombers, despite their high survivability, were often unable to continue their mission after being damaged by splinters. However, the absence of a guidance system in the RS projectiles and imperfections in their design led to a great dispersal of the rockets and the probability of hitting a manoeuvring air target remained low.

At the end of the autumn the task of preparing a 'winterised' version of the Yak-1 came to the fore. It was a standard fighter in which the wheel landing gear was replaced by a retractable ski undercarriage. In addition, heating was provided for some units of the powerplant (piping, radiators, oil tanks, breather tank etc.); a system for diluting oil with gasoline was installed; the water radiator was filled with antifreeze solution; a thick cushioned cover was placed on the engine cowling to prevent the engine from getting overcooled when the aircraft was parked on the airfield, especially during a frosty night. To make the aircraft less noticeable against the snowy background, a coat of washable white paint made of a chalk and glue solution was applied over the summer camouflage. In the winter version the Yak-1 became 70 to 80 kg (154 to 176 lb) heavier and 30 to 40 km/h (18.7 to 24.9 mph) slower at all altitudes.

The Yaks were operated intensively from snow-covered field airstrips without clearing away the snow. No other new fighter type was so extensively used on a ski undercarriage. Up to 25th February 1942, 830 Yak-1s were built in this version. One of the reasons for this was that ski undercarriage simplified landings on uneven airfields covered with a thick layer of snow. A fighter fitted with skis was more stable during the landing run and did not bounce. A strip of only 250 m (820 ft) was needed for take-off, and the landing run, with the use of brakes and landing flaps, was only 275 m (902 ft). The angle at which the aircraft sat on the ground was considerably increased, which reduced the danger of a nose-over in the case of a sharp decrease in speed.

However, intensive operation of the Yak-1 on skis during the winter of 1941-1942 revealed that the undersurface of the skis was not sufficiently abrasion-resistant; it endured 80 take-offs and landings at the most. Pilots of the 236th IAP noted that the skis of a parked fighter got stuck, as if by suction, to the surface and the aircraft could be moved only after it had been swung at the wingtips and the tail by the ground crew.

Above and below: Soon after production entry the fixed rear portion of the canopy was redesigned, the result looking rather like the LaGG-3 or the North American P-51A/B Mustang. The shape of the upper main gear doors was also changed at this stage. Here, Yak-1 c/n 1569 is seen during trials.

This winter-camouflaged mid-production Yak-1 was damaged by German fighters and made a belly landing. The engine has snapped off on impact and the aircraft looks like a write-off.

Above and below: On 31st October 1940 the engine of this brand-new Moscow-built Yak-1 (a very early-production aircraft still called I-26, c/n 0209) cut at the altitude of 5 m (16 ft) during a test flight. Test pilot Maj. S. G. Plygoonov managed a forced landing during which the port mainwheel strut collapsed.

Another close call for the same factory test pilot S. G. Pygoonov. This Yak-1 (I-26, c/n 0107) suffered a landing gear collapse during the take-off run on 14th September 1940.

Efforts to provide Plant No. 292 'Saracombine' with high-productivity jigs and tools and introduction of continuous flow-line assembly of the aircraft and its parts had their effect: even before the outbreak of the war the production of combat machines acquired a regular tempo. Whereas four fighters were delivered per day in June, at the end of October 1941 the daily output reached eight machines. The time required for the manufacture of some assemblies was considerably reduced. For example, the assembly of the fuselage was effected in the course of nine days instead of 14, and the final assembly in the course of three days instead of seven.

Concentration of efforts on the series production of the relatively well-developed Yak-1 fighter left no choice but to finally give up the plans for switching over to manufacturing the improved Yak-3 (I-30). The government directives on launching series production of the Yak-1 in Tbilisi and Kutaisi likewise failed to be implemented. All the work on this fighter was concentrated in Saratov.

At first no steps were taken to organise a sufficiently stringent control over the fighter's all-up weight. Almost all changes introduced into the design led to an increase of the airframe weight. From early August 1941, however, this drawback was partially remedied. Thanks to Yakovlev's initiative, designers and production engineers began to receive remuneration literally for every gram of weight that was saved. In mid-August 1941, starting with the 29th production batch, the weight was brought down to 2,917 kg/6,432 lb (without external stores and radio) which became characteristic for the Yak-1.

The first six months of the war showed that the Yak-1 was the most satisfactory among the fighter types that had been put into series production before the war. However, Yak-1s did not occupy a notable place numerically among other fighters. On the eve of the Soviet counteroffensive near Moscow, on 5th December 1941, the service units of the Red Army Air Force had only 83 Yak-1s on strength (about 8% of all fighters), and of these only 47 were considered serviceable. This can be explained in part by the wide use of machines of obsolete types and by serious difficulties in replenishing the heavy losses sustained during the first six months of the war.

Production fighters at the front

At the beginning of 1942 the Yak-1 was the best Soviet fighter as regards overall performance. New fighter units were being trained at an accelerated tempo in the rear. In January six Air Regiments equipped with Yakovlev's fighters could be simultaneously sent to the front for the first time, which constituted a sizeable contribution to enhancing the combat capabilities of the Soviet aviation. Two regiments were sent to reinforce the 146th and 47th Air Divisions. These were, respectively, the 20th IAP (commanded by Major A. Starikov; the unit was retrained for combat on the Yak-1 for the third time already) and the 236th IAP commanded by Major Antonov, who had passed conversion training for the second time in a ZAP. In the course of the counteroffensive conducted by Soviet troops near Moscow, the former of the mentioned units supported the troops of the 50th Army providing cover for airfields in the area of

Kaluga from which the 4th Airborne Corps began its assault operations, and the latter successfully conducted operational activities in co-operation with the troops of the 20th Army when penetrating the enemy defences at the Lama River.

The number of pilots mastering the new machine grew steadily. While only 156 pilots could fly the Yak-1 by 22nd June, by 1st February 1942 their number increased to 637. Gradually pilots flying the Yak-1 came to participate in combat on all fronts, with the exception of the Karelian front. A certain decline in the activity of Luftwaffe fighters enabled the Soviet airmen to feel confident of their own capabilities. Front-line conferences were held in a number of units for the purpose of exchanging combat experience, selecting the optimum operational tactics and assessing the quality of the materiel.

Thus, pilots of the Air Force of the Kalinin front analysed the special features of winter operation of the Yak-1s. Airmen of the 237th IAP had a good opinion of the machine, yet they also noted some drawbacks, most of which were associated with the undercarriage design. When airborne, the undercarriage legs were not always securely held by their uplocks, especially during violent manoeuvres; cracks appeared in the front portions of the skis after 20 to 30 landings, and the undercarriage breaker struts failed in the event of landing with a high sink rate. The regiment's ground crews called attention to the difficult access to units of the powerplant during an engine change and the persistent spraying of oil on the cockpit windshield because of the insufficient sealing of the reduction gear output shaft.

In the meantime, optimistic reports came from the South-Western Front: the 296th IAP commanded by Major N. Baranov, which was the only Air Regiment in the Air Force of the Front at that time to be equipped with the Yak-1s, attained exceptionally successful results in combat. According to operational reports, on 9th March 1942 seven Yaks led by Captain B. Yeryomin successfully fought a battle against 25 German aircraft, among which there were 12 Bf 109Es with bombs intended for an attack mission. The attack undertaken by 'Stalin's falcons' was swift and sudden. Very good use was made of rocket projectiles carried under the wings – they wreaked havoc among the German pilots, preventing them from dumping their bomb load in time. The six Bf 109Fs that were on the scene were of little help, since they had failed to notice the attacking Soviet fighters. *'As a result, five Bf 109s were shot down together with two Ju88s. The most striking thing about it is the fact that our airmen suffered no losses'* – said the concluding lines of the Soviet report.

Above and below: Yak-1 c/n 3055 equipped with retractable skis and six RO-82 launch rails for 82-mm RS-82 unguided rockets. Note that the front portions of the skis are carefully streamlined.

Above: Head-on view of the same aircraft, showing to good effect the RS-82 installation. The rockets were used with good results not only against ground targets but against enemy bomber formations as well.

It proved impossible to find confirmation of considerable losses of the German aviation in their documents referring to 9th March. Nevertheless, the successful use of Soviet fighters came under discussion in the State Defence Committee, and instructions were issued to give a wide coverage in the newspapers to the Soviet airmen's feat. At the initiative of A. Yakovlev, newspapers mentioned for the first time the type of the aircraft that had taken part

Above: A Yak-1 with special skis onto which the fighter was rolled for take-off from snow-covered airfields. These 'overshoes' fell away when the aircraft lifted off, to be used by the next aircraft.

Above and below: A production 'razorback' Yak-1 with aerodynamic refinements based on TsAGI recommendations. Note the modified rear portion of the canopy and the faired engine exhaust stubs.

in the battle: 'Yakovlev-1'; that was done with a view to promoting public acquaintance with the aviation materiel. Earlier, combat aircraft were referred to figuratively: 'our steel birds', 'Stalin's falcons' or 'hawks with Red Stars'.

'At that time confidence in the capabilities of our armament was very much needed by everyone – from a worker at an aircraft factory and a pilot to the General Designer and the Army Command – B. Yeryomin later noted – Hence the swift and broad response.' All the participants of the air battle were awarded Orders of the Red Banner, and the *Pravda* newspaper published their photos.

In the spring of 1942 the Soviet Government took the decision to begin setting up new formations – Air Armies (VA – vozdooshnaya armiya). By 10th May 1942 the 1st VA established on the basis of the Air Force of the Western front had 36 Yak-1s in good condition and 9 machines in disrepair at its disposal. In addition to the already mentioned regiments, fighters of this type were also on the strength of the 32nd, 66th, 516th IAPs and other units. At that time the units were weakened by prolonged combat activities; as a rule, they had five to eight Yak-1s instead of the full complement of 20 machines.

At the end of the spring of 1942 a number of new Air Regiments was converted to the Yaks. One of them was the 1st Guards Red Banner IAP (the former 29th IAP). This unit was considered to be one of the most famous in the Soviet Union.

Over the years, pilots of nationwide fame – Valeriy Chkalov, Sergei Gritsevets, Anatoliy Serov and others – had served in the 1st Soviet fighter squadron (?) which later formed the basis of the 29th IAP. The regiment distinguished itself in combat against the Luftwaffe while still flying I-16s; later it fought on Hawker Hurricanes. In May 1942 a group of pilots led by their commander, Lieutenant-Colonel A. Yoodakov, flew their mounts to an airfield in the rear, where they immediately set about familiarising themselves with Yakovlev's firstling. The airmen were elated over the machine; a short while later seven fighters demonstrated complex group aerobatics over the airfield.

The most famous Soviet fighter-pilot Aleksandr I. Pokryshkin flew combat sorties on a Yak-1 from mid-May till 9th August 1942 (at that time he was Senior Lieutenant with the 16th Guards IAP). This unit received well-used and fairly battered Yak-1s from other regiments fighting at neighbouring sections of the front; this was probably the reason for the very reserved comments from the pilots. Previously, Pokryshkin had thoroughly studied the MiG-3 and actually taken a liking to it; yet he noted that the Yak-1 was easier to fly and more forgiving and had more potent armament. Thanks to these advantages the famous ace achieved eight victories during a period of incessant air battles that lasted for almost three months, when he downed three Bf 109s, three Ju 88s and two Bf 110s.

The 16th Guards IAP fought at the southern flank of the Soviet-German front. In the late spring the German aviation (especially fighters) considerably stepped up its activities there, and the Soviet airmen were in a tough situation. Yak fighters took part in combat in the areas of the Kuban' and Don rivers, and in the Crimea. Thus, airmen of the 45th IAP making part of the 3rd Special Air Group commanded by Colonel I. Dzoosov fought especially hard combats repelling the enemy's onslaught on Sevastopol'. According to official information, in June 1942 Soviet airmen made 186 combat sorties and achieved 22 victories, even though the enemy enjoyed air superiority (according to information from German sources, six or seven 'kills' of German aircraft can be confirmed; according to Soviet sources, own losses amounted to eight Yak-1s and two pilots lost). Lieutenant N. Lavitskiy achieved special success, with seven 'kills' to his credit. When Wehrmacht troops stormed the blazing city of Sevastopol', eleven Yak-1s of the 45th and 247th IAPs left the Crimea on the night of 1st July, landing safely on airfields in the Krasnodar Area.

The retreat of the Soviet troops in the south was accompanied by the loss of a considerable amount of materiel. As noted earlier, the Yak-1 fighters posed problems in maintenance and transportation because of their one-piece wing structure. Nevertheless, there were cases when Soviet military personnel displayed exceptional perseverance and sense of duty trying to preserve the materiel.

Thus, technician Mal'tsev from the 220th IAD (*istrebitel'naya aviatsionnaya diveeziya* – Fighter Air Division) received an order to evacuate a machine belonging to Lieutenant A. Vitkovskiy from the place of a forced landing. The fighter had landed near the front-line in swampy terrain and needed repairs in factory conditions. Enlisting the help of the local population to make a road of brushwood, Mal'tsev loaded the fighter onto the platform of a truck and took it to aircraft repair shops in Uriupinsk. However, enemy troops were approaching that place, too. The Yak-1 had to be transported further east, camouflage being required to protect it from enemy air strikes. Mal'tsev managed to ferry the fighter over the Don river on a raft; his adventures lasted for more than a week.

New versions

The staff of the Design Bureau and Chief Designer Alexander Yakovlev continued to seek possibilities of improving their machine. Their fighter was still inferior to its main opponent in air combat – the German Bf 109F. The task became all the more urgent when the Soviet intelligence reported that that the F-2 version had been supplanted on the production line by the F-4 version featuring an engine of greater output and better altitude performance and improved armour protection and armament (in actual fact, the first Bf 109F-4s went into action at the Eastern front for the first time in August of 1941). According to G. Barkhorn, a German ace, 'Friedrich the fourth' (as the Bf 109F-4 was popularly known in the Luftwaffe) marked a peak in the development of the Messerschmitt machine as far as controllability and agility were concerned. The new model further increased the advantages of the German machine over the Yak-1 with

Above: A pilot poses in the cockpit of his Yak-1, 2 White. Note that the lower segments of the main gear doors have been removed to stop them from being fouled by mud during operations from muddy airstrips in the spring and winter.

Above: This Yak-1b, 17 Red, was flown by Yves Bizien of the 'Normandie-Niémen' regiment. It bears the inscription *'To the defenders of the Stalingrad Front from the collective farm workers of the Krasnoyarsk District of the Saratov Region'*, meaning it was paid for by fund-raising. The upper propeller blade appears to be damaged.

Above: Capt. P. I. Pavlov of the 21st IAP (Red Banner Baltic Fleet air arm) taxies out for take-off in his 'razorback' Yak-1 after the alert has been sounded, 1942.

Above and below: Yak-1 c/n 3560 was converted into the *etalon* (production standard-setter) for 1942 with a teardrop canopy and cut-down fuselage spine. Note the moulded frameless windshield; the aircraft had a Yak-7 oil cooler, as it had been planned to install an M-105PF engine which was ultimately never fitted.

The Yak-1 *etalon* for 1943 during checkout trials at NII VVS.

regard to rate of climb and other performance characteristics, while retaining a parity in manoeuvrability. The Bf 109F-4 retained also the superiority in speed. The latter point proved to be very important; the German pilots had the ability to impose a dogfight on the Yaks if they wished it and break off the engagement, should the situation turn to their disadvantage.

While the German machines were progressively fitted with engines of steadily rising power, in the case of the Yak-1 substituting the M-105PA for the M-105P had not added a single extra horsepower to the machine. Its designers were well aware of the fact that introduction of a new engine was an unrealistic option at that time. Therefore the idea cropped up of uprating the available engine.

The story of how the boosted version of the M-105PA came into being is very unusual. In April 1942 a mixed team comprising specialists from the engine factory and NII VVS and led by Military Engineer (3rd rank) B. Nikitin, was sent on a mission to the 236th IAP of the Air Force of the Western Front (commander Major P. Antonets). At its own initiative the team made arrangements for seven Yak-1s with the M-105PA engines to be subjected to trial operation with the boost pressure increased from 910 mm Hg to 1,050 mm Hg.

This resulted in a considerable improvement of performance. The pilots of the regiment willingly flew the modified aircraft. The Air Force was faced with the prospect of immediately enhancing the combat capabilities of all Yak-1 fighters then in service by simple and expeditious means. Introduction of the increased boost pressure, as it seemed initially, did not require any modification of the M-105PA engine and could be effected in front-line units by their own technical staff without impairing the employment of the aircraft in combat operations.

However, operational use of boosted engines brought some unpleasant surprises. It turned out that in summer weather the fighter could fly with the radiator shutter fully closed (to achieve maximum speed) for no more than two minutes, after which the temperature of water and oil rose above the permissible limits. For the same reason it proved impossible to perform a continuous climb with the boosted engine. It was necessary to level off several times in order to bring the temperature condition of the engine back to normal. The increase of the water and oil temperature was further aggravated because the radiator core tubes became clogged with oil which was spilled from the breather or leaked from engine piping joints.

All this came to the knowledge of the authorities. The Commander of the Air Force issued an order requiring two of the seven modified Yaks to be transferred to NII VVS for research purposes. The test results were as follows: with the engine running at the same nominal revs and under other conditions identical to those of the usual Yaks, the increased supercharging pressure enabled the 'new' fighter to attain a maximum horizontal speed that was approximately 20 to 25 km/h (12.4 to 15.5 mph) higher at altitudes from sea level to 3,500 m (11,480 ft). Time to

5,000 m (16,400 ft) was reduced by one minute, and the time needed for a banking turn at 1,000 m (3,280 ft) by one second. Take-off performance was also improved. At the same time water and oil in the boosted engine got overheated. To keep their temperature within acceptable limits, the engine revs had to be reduced from the nominal 2,700 rpm to 2,400 – 2,500 rpm, which, in effect, nullified all the advantages afforded by increasing the boost pressure.

On the basis of the results of these tests the People's Commissariat of Aircraft Industry tasked Chief Designer A. S. Yakovlev with redesigning the engine cooling system and taking measures to prevent oil spill from the breather, as well as introducing engine seals. Also, the engines themselves were to be perfected. The main improvements that were to be effected by engine constructors included reinforcement of the crankcase and piston pins and increasing the diameter of borings in the carburettor nozzles.

The production version of the boosted engine was assigned the designation M-105PF. Its readjustment, as compared to the M-105PA, entailed not only an increase of power but also a decrease of altitude performance. Thus, the output at the first rated altitude became 1,260 hp at 700 m (2,296 ft) instead of 1,100 hp at 2,000 m (6,560 ft), without taking into account the dynamic pressure, and at the second rated altitude the power rose from 1,050 hp at 4,000 m (13,120 ft) to 1,180 hp at 2700 m (8,856 ft). At altitudes in excess of 4,000 m (13,120 ft) the characteristics of boosted and unboosted engines proved to be identical.

In June 1942 a Yak-1 (c/n 15-69) with a boosted M-105PF engine and increased oil cooler area passed tests at NII VVS. Despite the modified oil cooler, the temperature condition of the powerplant deteriorated. At a take-off weight of 2,917 kg (typical for a Yak-1 without a radio), the fighter attained 510 km/h (317 mph) at sea level and 571 km/h (355 mph) at the second rated altitude of 3,650 m (11,972 ft); it needed 6.4 minutes to climb to 5,000 m (16,400 ft), performed a full-circle turn at low altitude in 19 to 20 seconds and gained 980 m when climbing in a combat turn. However, to ensure normal operation of the aircraft the engine revs at low altitude had to be limited to 2,550 rpm.

It proved possible to reduce the Bf 109F's ascendancy at low altitude, as demonstrated by mock combat between the Yak-1 M-105PF and the Bf 109F, conducted at NII VVS for training and test purposes. At 1,000 m (3,280 ft) the Bf 109F had a marginal advantage in vertical and horizontal manoeuvrability. The German fighter succeeded in getting on the tail of its 'adversary', but only after four or five turns. At the altitude of 3,000 m (9,840 ft)

Above and below: Saratov-built 'bubbletop' Yak-1 c/n 04111 during tests at NII VVS. The aircraft wears winter camouflage, though this is not very obvious because the machine is covered all over in soot and oil from the engine!

both fighters fought on equal terms; in effect, aerial combat became restricted to head-on attacks. It was to the Yak's advantage if its 'adversary' could be lured to higher altitudes. Already at 5,000 m (16,400 ft) the Yak-1 came to possess greater manoeuvrability and its pilot could impose his will on the enemy.

It must be taken into account, though, that when the Bf 109F was evaluated at NII VVS the supercharger system of the Daimler-Benz DB 601N engine did not ensure the maintenance of a constant degree of supercharging. On the other hand, when the German engines functioned normally, the Messerschmitt fighter, possessing better engine performance at high altitude, was not inferior, but, on the contrary, considerably superior to the Yak-1 M-105PF at 5,000 m (16,400 ft) and higher. Besides, NII VVS had tested the Bf 109F-2, while, as noted earlier, it was the Bf 109F-4 with the more powerful DB 601E engine that had become Germany's main fighter type by the summer of 1942. The Yak-1 M-105PF was markedly inferior to it on many counts.

Yak-1 fighter (modified)

Another direction of work in the Yakovlev OKB (Design Bureau) was concerned with improving the vision, armour protection and armament of the production Yak-1. To achieve this, considerable alterations, based on the available experience, were incorporated in one example of the fighter in June 1942. The following design features were adopted.

To improve rearward vision the upper fuselage decking behind the cockpit was cut down and the cockpit canopy was given a streamlined teardrop shape. The moulded visor gave place to a visor formed by optically flat glazing panels which lessened the distortion of objects observed by the pilot.

To enhance the protection of the pilot's head, a bulletproof windscreen and a rear bulletproof glass panel were installed. The pilot was also protected by an armoured headrest and armoured armrest.

Changes in the armament consisted in replacing two 7.62-mm ShKAS machine-guns by one 12.7-mm UBS machine-gun (also synchronised), while the 20-mm ShVAK cannon

Top: This photo illustrates the standard shape of the oil cooler bath and supercharger air intake.
Centre: The oil cooler and supercharger intake modified in accordance with TsAGI recommendations make an interesting comparison.
Above: The fifth version of the oil cooler bath developed by TsAGI.
Below and bottom: Yak-1 c/n 1047 was lightened and equipped with an all-round vision teardrop canopy.

was retained. The OPB-1 telescopic gunsight was replaced by a ring-and-bead VV-1 sight; this was done in response to insistent demands from front-line units dissatisfied with the poor quality of the telescopic gunsight.

Additionally, the modified fighter featured alterations to the control stick which was made similar to that of the German Bf 109. The stick had push-buttons for actuating the armament; this permitted the pilots to fire their weapons without diverting attention from piloting during violent combat manoeuvres. On 1st July 1942 A. Yakovlev reported to the Government that the work on modifying the Yak-1 had been completed. The fighter was immediately submitted for State trials. NII VVS test pilots A. Proshakov, P. M. Stefanovskiy, A. G. Kochetkov, L. M. Koovshinov and V. Khomyakov assessed the new features as excellent. The report on the results of the State trials said that *'the forward view and visibility to the sides and rearwards through the bulletproof glass and the transparent aft part of the canopy are good and can be regarded as the best compared to all Soviet fighters'*. It was recommended that these alterations be incorporated in production machines and the aircraft tested be regarded as an *etalon* (production standard-setter).

Time was needed to implement in production the improvements described above. Only in September 1942 did Plant No. 292 begin to build the modified Yak-1s. This aircraft with the UBS-12.7 machine-gun and improved-vision cockpit canopy was sometimes called Yak-1b (with a lower-case 'b'), especially in the documents of front-line units (It should be noted that, in contrast to other Yak models, the versions of the Yak-1 were not assigned official suffix letters). Right from the start they were powered by M-105PF engines. By the end of 1942 the number of machines of this version reached 959 out of that year's total production of the Yak-1 (3,474).

In the period of December 1942 – January 1943 the Yak-1b aircraft were passing operational service tests in the 32nd Guards IAP of the 210th IAD at the Kalinin Front and in the 176th IAP of the 283rd IAD at the Stalingrad Front. During this time 58 new fighters flew up to 700 combat sorties, performing 38 dogfights and shooting down 25 enemy aircraft, as claimed by the units, for the loss of six Yak-1bs. The new fire control system and the cockpit hood with improved view to aft were appreciated by the flying personnel and were recommended for introduction on all fighters. The airmen also approved the other changes effected by the Design Bureau.

The lightened version of the fighter

The Bf 109 retained its main advantage over the Yak-1 – superior vertical manoeuvrability which was due to lower power loading. The Soviet designers sought to strip the enemy of this advantage by further lightening the Yak-1.

In March 1942, in response to the Chief Designer's instructions, the OKB staff intended to achieve a radical lightening of the airframe. This work had experimental status at the time. Ten airframes were completed as interceptors. The list of measures aimed at reducing the all-up weight comprised 25 items. The most important of these included deletion of the ShKAS machine-guns with their ammunition supply, deletion of one of the two compressed air bottles and dispensing with the use of self-sealing coat on fuel tanks.

The weight saving achieved totalled 162 kg (357 lb). One of the fighters was flight-tested by the OKB's chief test pilot Pavel Fedrovi who spoke highly of the aircraft. All ten lightened Yak-1s were delivered to the 12th Guards IAP of the 6th IAK of the Moscow air defence system and were used as interceptors.

The OKB reverted to this experience in September 1942. Twenty lightened Yak-1s were manufactured specially for the Stalingrad Front. At an all-up weight of 2,780 kg (6,130 lb) these machines were marginally faster than the usual Yaks. Importantly, vertical manoeuvrability was appreciably improved. The lightened Yak-1s formed a part of the complement of the 512nd IAP (commanded by Hero of the Soviet Union, Lieutenant-Colonel N. Gerasimov) and the 520th IAP (commanded by Major S. Cheerva).

Experience gained in air battles showed that, when piloted by well-trained airmen, these aircraft were quite a match for the Bf 109F-4 and Bf 109G-2 at low and medium altitudes. While a standard production Yak-1 required on average 26 sorties per one German aircraft shot down, the lightened version scored one 'kill' in 18 (according to Soviet reports). The latter version also boasted lower own losses. Lightened Yaks caught up with the Bf 109s during climb, but it was in the banking turns that they were particularly superior to the adversary. Deletion of the machine-guns did not seriously diminish the effectiveness of attacks because German aircraft, especially bombers, were destroyed primarily by cannon fire.

512th IAP pilots I. Motornyy and V. Makarov, who were sent by their command to the Saratov Plant to take delivery of the first lightened Yak-1s for their unit, engaged in a dogfight during their ferrying flight, claiming two Bf 109G-2s shot down. After landing at a field airstrip on the bank of the Volga River, they said: 'On the lightened Yak we shall down any Messerschmitt in a vertical manoeuvre'.

The results of the work on lightening the Yak-1 were subsequently used by the Yakovlev OKB in the development of other fighters, especially the Yak-3. But at that time, in September 1942, it was decided to refrain from committing the lightened Yak-1 to large-scale production. While the reduced weight of fire was not of crucial importance for experienced fighter pilots, the Soviet top command considered it too heavy a price for ordinary airmen and the lightened version of the Yak-1 was not built in quantity by Plant No. 292.

The fighter-bomber version of the Yak-1

In May 1942 the Yak-1 was once more subjected to alterations. In keeping with a Government decision, rocket projectiles carried under the wings were dispensed with in order to regain the speed that was so necessary in combat against the Messerschmitts. At the same time, it was decided that the Yaks be used in a new capacity – the fighter-bomber role. For this purpose two bomb racks with sway braces and shackles were mounted under the wings. Each of them could carry one 25 to 100-kg (55 to 220-lb) bomb. A lever installed in the cockpit enabled the pilot to drop this deadly load.

Pre-flight maintenance of a ski-equipped Yak-1.

With the bombs the aircraft could be used as a high-speed fighter-bomber, and without bombs – as a tactical fighter. Installation of bomb racks and attachment of bombs increased the all-up weight and spoiled the aerodynamics of the machine, adversely affecting its performance and handling qualities. The speed reduction was especially serious, reaching 30 km/h (18.6 mph). The Yak-1 became heavy and sluggish in handling. After the bombs had been dropped the performance improved, but, since the bomb racks still were there, it remained lower than without this equipment.

In the opinion of the Air Force command, installation of bomb armament on the Yak-1

Yak-1s in standard dark green/black camouflage at a frontline airfield. The second aircraft in the row has had its lower main gear door segments removed.

Above: Lidia Litvyak, a famous female fighter pilot, poses on the wing of her Yak-1. She gained ace status, shooting down 12 enemy aircraft, before being killed in action near Oryol on 1st September 1943.

Above: Technicians push a late-production Yak-1 into a sheltered position after a sortie.

was unwarranted because it had been effected without due regard to the real capabilities of the M-105PA engine, the power of which was clearly inadequate for this task. Also, the pilots of front-line units were dissatisfied with the bomb racks; they often said they were carting around a useless load. As the best type of Soviet fighter aircraft at that time, the Yak-1 was intended primarily for the interception of enemy attack aircraft and for aerial combat, not for bombardment and attack missions. Nevertheless, bomb racks on production machines were retained until the end of series production.

Bitter fighting at the fronts in the second half of 1942

Let us mentally return again to the Eastern front. The main events of the summer of 1942 took place over its southern sector where the Germans flung new air groups and *Geschwader* into the fray. Again, as had been the case in the summer of 1941, the Luftwaffe firmly maintained air superiority. All types of Soviet aircraft suffered heavy losses under these circumstances. To ease the situation of the Red Army troops in that area, the Soviet command launched a number of counter-offensives on other fronts.

One of the toughest battles raged from 30th July 1942 onwards in the sky and on the ground near the town of Rzhev. The Soviet aviation committed considerable forces to activities in that area. Among the 489 fighters that went into action over the Western front, there were 72 Yak-1s (44 of them in serviceable condition) in the 1st Air Army and 13 Yak-1s (nine of them operational) in the units of army aviation. At first 'Stalin's falcons' had luck on their side, but then Luftwaffe aces, first of all those of JG51 'Mölders', succeeded in taking over the initiative.

Soviet commanders of ground troops repeatedly voiced their criticism towards airmen. The latter appeared over the heads of Soviet soldiers and commanders for only a few minutes, responded poorly to commands from the ground, and allowed German attack aircraft to bomb important targets near the front and in the rear of the Red Army with virtual impunity.

Colonel L. Kooldin, deputy commander of an Air Army, took to the air in a Yak-1 with a view to assessing the situation personally, but he was shot down and killed in a dogfight. In all, during August of 1942 the aviation of the Western and Karelian Fronts (the latter was providing cover for the offensive against Rzhev from the north) lost 61 Yak-1 (one loss for only 19 combat sorties); of these, 37 fighters of this type were lost in air battles.

The situation was not better in the south where the airmen of the 8th Air Army, committed to action on the South-Western Front, had to stand the most severe test. German technicians painting new bars on the vertical tails of their Messerschmitt fighters to mark the 'kills' had every reason to feel satisfied. Soviet documents confirm that hardly a day passed without heavy losses. Thus, the 8th Army lost 5 Yak-1s on each of the three days – 8th, 10th and 13th August, and on 12th August seven Yakovlev fighters were shot down.

In the 273th IAP, out of the 15 Yak-1s that were on strength by the beginning of August, and the 19 machines that came as a replenishment, 14 fighters had to be written off for various reasons in the course of a month; in the 515th IAP 27 Yaks out of 37 were lost during the same period. Some air regiments, such as the 211th IAP, lost their operational capability in the course of three days at the front and had to be sent to the rear for reorganisation.

This calls for some comment. In 1974, many years after the victorious end of the war, Yakovlev published his book, originally called *Notes of an Aircraft Designer*, in a new edition called *A Life's Goal*. The book is written in a vivid and colourful manner and makes good reading, but not infrequently it gives a biased presentation of important elements in the history of Soviet aviation. Thus, the Chief Designer speaks much about successes, but says nothing about the failures – his own and those of his colleagues. Nevertheless, he feels compelled to dwell on the heavy losses in battles over Stalingrad. One of the chapters of the book is eloquently called *The Yaks burn*.

Presumably the heavy losses sustained by the Soviet aviation are mainly associated not with the shortcomings of this or that aircraft (for example, the Yaks) but with the poor training standard of the average Soviet pilot and the small number of flying hours accumulated by him before being sent to the front. In the summer of 1942 a flying school cadet was transferred to a ZAP (Reserve Air Regiment) after logging 70 to 80 hours on trainers and having barely mastered the essential piloting techniques; there he was given the opportunity to perform 15 to 20 flights, which was by no means enough for mastering a fighter, even such a simple one as the Yak-1. When the Soviet pilot arrived at the front he immediately became a potential prey for German aces who had performed hundreds of combat sorties.

Sure enough, there were also Soviet pilots who were very well trained and who proved to be a real danger for the enemy. Thus, on 6th August Lieutenant (Senior Grade) Mikhail Baranov from the 183rd IAP, expertly conducted aerial combat against a group of enemy aircraft while providing cover for a group of Soviet attack aircraft. He dam-

**Above: Several female pilots fought in the 586th IAP. Here, left to right: G. Boordina, T. Pamyatnykh, V. Khomiakova and V. Lisitsina discuss a dogfight performed (obviously successfully) by Khomiakova.
Below: The aviatrices pore over a map of the battle area, planning the next mission.**

A Yak-1b pilot receives his Communist Party membership certificate after proving his worth in combat.

31

Above: A still from a Soviet documentary film showing a Yak-1b (foreground) and a late-model Yak-9 (note the aft-positioned cockpit) in flight; such pictures are quite rare.

Above: French pilots fought alongside Soviet airmen, and the French 'Normandie-Niémen' regiment gained fame. Here, the unit's pilots discuss a mission with a Soviet colleague.

The Yak-1s of the *Normandie-Niémen* regiment sported tricolour spinners and a French roundel superimposed on a white lightning flash. This one is pictured at Monastyrshchina in October 1943.

aged a Ju 87, compelling it to make a forced landing in the territory held by Soviet troops, and downed two Bf 109s, one of which was destroyed by ramming. After this the brave pilot parachuted to safety in a sector held by Soviet marines. Baranov's score rose to 18 personal and six shared 'kills'. At that time no other pilot could equal Mikhail's effectiveness in combat; in a few days he was awarded the Gold Star of Hero of the Soviet Union.

However, most of the Soviet pilots were young, with no combat experience, and could not successfully oppose the German aces. The top command of the Red Army Air Force sought to remedy the situation by sharply increasing the production of combat materiel and expediting the training of a growing number of new combat pilots for the front. In the autumn of 1942 when the Soviet forces were hard put to it, the workers of Plant No. 292, unwilling to disrupt the steady production tempo, would no longer seek shelter when the air raid alarm was sounded as German bombers approached Saratov. In the autumn of 1942 the further simplification of production process and curtailment of the use of materials that were costly or in short supply, made it possible to reduce labour costs of the manufacture of one Yak-1 2.2 times compared to mid-1941. At that time the Soviet fighter was three to four times cheaper than its main opponent, the Bf 109G-2.

Israel Levin, Director of the Saratov Aircraft Plant, recalls that on 2nd September 1942 he received a Government telegram with instructions from the Supreme Command requiring him to send all the aircraft produced to the Stalingrad Front. On 6th September he received a telephone call from Stalin who, concluding the conversation, said: 'The situation in the Stalingrad area is very difficult. Fighters are badly needed. Take measures to increase the production'.

Workers and engineers spent 24 hours a day in the workshops of Plant No. 292, and they succeeded in overfulfilling the strenuous plan of fighter production. 336 Yaks were completed in September 1942 (compared to 168 machines a year before); in the following month this number reached 338. The constant replenishment of the Soviet Air formation by new aircraft contributed to changing the situation at the front – first of all on the banks of the Volga where, without any exaggeration, the outcome of the war was being determined during those months.

A successful counteroffensive launched by the Soviet troops on 19th November 1942 made it possible to achieve a radical change in the situation in the Stalingrad area. The weakening of the Luftwaffe and the need to spend much effort on delivering supplies to the encircled 6th Army commanded by Field-Marshal von Paulus permitted the Red Army

Air Force to win and firmly maintain air superiority.

Soviet airmen demonstrated many an example of successful actions in which they made use of new combat tactics. Thus, on 28th November 1942 three Yak-1s from the 293rd IAP met four Ju 52/3m transports while flying an interception mission after being summoned by the command post of the 287th IAD in the area of the Srednyaya Akhtuba River (Middle Akhtuba, one of the Volga's tributaries). The Ju 52s, loaded with foodstuffs, were on their way to the encircled troops, but they lost their bearings, and all of them were shot down in the course of several minutes.

One more case of the enemy aircraft losing their way took place at the end of December. Twenty Junkers transports escorted by Messerschmitt fighters made their appearance directly over the Bolshiye Chapoorniki airfield where considerable forces of the Soviet aviation were based. But the waves of the transport aircraft were passing at such low altitude that the fighter flights on quick-reaction alert could not take to the air to intercept them. At that time a group of fighters from the 201st IAD was returning to base after a 'hunt-and-kill' mission against targets of opportunity. Instead of landing, four Yak-1s led by Lieutenant (Senior Grade) L. Dyoma immediately engaged the enemy. Bursts of cannon and heavy machine-gun fire hit the enemy aircraft one by one. The Soviet fighters turned away from the Junkers transports at absolutely minimum distances, sometimes passing between the wings and stabilisers of the enemy machines. The combat lasted no more than twenty minutes, in the course of which the enemy lost 15 aircraft, and two damaged Ju 52/3ms made forced landings on the Soviet airfield.

Improved version of the Yak-1 fighter

The work on perfecting the fighter went on incessantly right from the start of the series production. Improvement of the aircraft's aerodynamics, along with measures designed to reduce the all-up weight, was one of the main areas of the OKB's activities during the whole period of the series production of the Yak-1. This work was conducted in conformity with plans and, as a rule, at the OKB's own initiative. But sometimes exigencies of life compelled the Design Bureau to resort to urgent measures.

One of such time intervals when the work acquired the character of a crash programme was the period of autumn and winter of 1942. A dire situation arose during the air battle over Stalingrad; it was caused, in particular, by the advent of new German fighters – Bf 109G-2s fitted with engines of greater power and better altitude performance which gave them

Above: A lot of combat aircraft were paid for by public donations. This one was paid for by collective farm workers of the Lysaya Gora ('Bald Mountain') District of the Saratov Region.

Above: This Yak-1 was donated to Maj. Shishkin (HSU) by the 'Signal of the Revolution' collective farm located in the Voroshilov District of the Saratov Region.

Pilots discuss a successful mission beside another donated aircraft fighting on the Stalingrad Front.

Above: Yak-1 c/n 3299 served as the prototype for the M-106P engine installation.

Production Yak-1s powered by the M-106P engine were outwardly identical to their M-105-powered brethren

considerable ascendancy in air combat. On 13th October 1942 Chief of the Main Directorate of the People's Commissariat of Aircraft Industry S. Shishkin submitted to People's Commissar A. Shakhoorin a report on the evaluation of the German fighters based on comments from the fronts. The document noted that the Bf 109G-2 possessed only marginally greater speed compared to Soviet fighters but enjoyed a considerable advantage in rate of climb and, consequently, in the vertical manoeuvre.

The leaders of the country demanded that performance of Soviet fighters be enhanced. This applied, above all, to the Yak-1 fighter. It was envisaged that the work would be concentrated on improving aerodynamics and installing the more powerful M-106 engine with a single-speed supercharger.

Aerodynamic improvements were effected in accordance with the Government decision adopted in December 1942. Under the terms of this document, production Yak-1s were to attain, at their maximum power rating, a speed not less than 525 km/h (326 mph) at sea level and 590 km/h (367 mph) at 3,750 m (12,300 ft), ie, be 15 to 20 km/h (8.9 to 12.4 mph) faster compared to the actual performance of Yak-1 fighters at the end of that year. The work conducted under Yakovlev's direct control comprised the following: completely sealed bulkheads were installed in the fuselage; the tailwheel was made retractable once again; the engine cowling and the wing root fairings were redesigned in accordance with the recommendations of theoretical aerodynamics; a debris guard wire mesh screen installed in the water radiator intake was deleted; the exhaust stubs were fitted with fairings and the shape of the stubs was altered so that they provided a measure of additional thrust; the shape of the water radiator and oil cooler ducts was altered; finally, the aircraft's overall surface finish was improved.

The Yak-1 fighter with the M-106 engine

It was presumed that that the work on the installation of a new, more powerful engine promised still greater advantages. Besides, the Yakovlev OKB had thoroughly refined the airframe to adapt it to the installation of the M-106. Many novel features were incorporated in the structure with a view to improving the aerodynamics and reducing the weight. Thus, the wings had metal spars, the lightened tail unit also acquired a metal framework. Two fuel tanks holding 400 lit. (88 Imp gal) were installed in the outer sections of the wings; two circular-shaped oil coolers patterned on those of the I-26-1 were installed in the wing centre section. The latest achievements of aviation science, in particular, recommendations from TsAGI (*Tsen**trahl'nyy** **a**ero- i **ghid**rodina**mich**eskiy insti**toot*** – the Central Aero- and Hydrodynamics Institute) were used in selecting the shape of the oil coolers.

In its armament and equipment the experimental fighter differed little from its production stablemates. It also featured a similar engine cowling design.

The M-106-1sk was a modified version of the M-106 that had been recommended for installation on fighters as far back as the beginning of 1941. At that time the engine was supposed to develop 1,350 hp for take-off, to have the same rating at 2,000 m (6,560 ft) and deliver 1,250 hp at 4,000 m (13,120 ft). Now, the engine was redesigned under the direction of Vladimir Ya. Klimov: it was made lighter; reliability was increased by installing a single-speed supercharger designed by V. Dollezhal'. An increased boost pressure (1,175 mm Hg instead of 910 mm Hg in the M-105) ensured greater power output; it was approximately 150 to 200 hp greater than that of the M-105PA and 'PF at altitudes of 4,000 m (13,120 ft) and higher.

Importantly, the M-106 differed from its predecessor in having a lower compression rate, a greater output of the main oil pump, a stronger crankshaft etc. Yet, the dry weight of the M-106 remained virtually the same as that of the M-105PF; this obviated the need for calculating anew the aircraft's CG position.

Thus, the main advantage of the M-106 over the M-105PF lay in its ability to deliver greater power while retaining the same weight and overall dimensions. Another advantage was associated with the character of variations in the power output depending on the altitude. The M-105 had a two-speed supercharger, and the need to switch the speeds entailed a fall in the power output at 1,800 to 2,000 m (5,904 to 6,560 ft). German pilots flying the Bf 109 knew this handicap of the Soviet engine and tried to impose combat on the Yakovlev fighters exactly at these altitudes. The Messerschmitt fighters had turbo-couplings which switched over automatically; thus, they suffered no loss in speed. In the M-106 engine, thanks to the single-speed supercharger, the power output increased smoothly from sea level to the rated altitude, and then decreased depending on the changes in atmospheric pressure.

Testing of the Yak-1 M-106 conducted in January 1943 showed that the fighter possessed excellent performance. At the weight of 2,757 kg (unprecedentedly low for aircraft of this type) the fighter attained a speed of 557 km/h at sea level and 630 km/h at 3,400 m (11,152 ft). The fighter needed only 4.5 minutes to climb to 5,000 m (16,400 ft). It seemed that a brilliant future was in store for the machine. However, these hopes were shattered. Pilot A. Kokin noted that the water radiator and oil coolers on this aircraft ensured adequate cooling of the engine at nominal power only when the ambient temperature at sea level was not higher than 15° C. Otherwise, the machine could not be flown at the nominal engine power rating.

The testing was conducted by engineer K. Mkrtychan who had actively participated in the development of the prototype Yak-1 M-106. Flight tests showed that the M-106 engine had not been developed to the standard required for normal operation: its running was accompanied by vibration, detonation, emission of smoke and ejection of oil through joints. It became clear that the aircraft could not stay airborne for a long time.

Almost contemporaneously with this work, engineers of LII (*Lyotno-issledovatel'skiy institoot* – Flight Research Institute) installed the M-106 on a production Yak-1. The speed went down by approximately 20 km/h (12.4 mph) as compared to the prototype fighter with the same engine, and the time to 5,000 m (16,400) rose by 1.1 minute. However, engine operation proved unsatisfactory on the LII-modified aircraft as well.

Despite the setbacks, the Yak-1 M-106 was ordered into series production. By 18th February 1943 the Saratov Plant manufactured 47 aircraft. The work on the M-106-powered fighter was considered to be the most important in the first quarter of that year. Of all the machines completed, only 32 were officially accepted by the military customer. In spite of all the efforts, they could not be tested during the winter, and subsequently, the engines on the majority of these machines either were replaced by the M-105PF, or underwent readjustment. Several Yak-1 M-106s were operated in the 148th IAP (commanded by Lieutenant-Colonel G. Zaitsev) with the supercharging pressure decreased. A basically sound concept ended in a failure in 1943, entailing a considerable loss of work time, equipment and materials.

A flight of Yak-1s of the Red Banner Baltic Fleet's 3rd GvIAP on quick-reaction alert.

Yakovlev's firstling soldiers on until the end of the war

In the biggest air battles of 1943 the Yak-1 fighter, alongside with its Yak-7B and Yak-9 stablemates and the La-5 fighter, constituted the main types of front-line machines. Yak-1s also made up a considerable part of the Soviet aviation reserves – the Air Corps of the Supreme Command. Thus, the 3rd IAK (Fighter Air Corps) commanded by General Yevgeniy Ya. Savitskiy played an important part in the springtime air battles in the Kuban' River area. The commander of the Air Corps, subsequently promoted to Air Marshal and made twice Hero of the Soviet Union, recalled: *'Shortly before the transfer to the south I was summoned to Moscow where I received the combat assignment and was given the possibility to choose the fighter type on which I would like to join combat. I did not need time for reflection: I had long ago decided for myself that the Yak-1 was what I needed.'* In all, by 20th April there were nearly 200 Yakovlev fighters of different models in the six regiments that made up the Air Corps.

The first blow dealt by the German aviators in the course of the colossal battle at the Kursk Bulge was sustained by airmen of the 2nd and 16th Air Armies. By 5th July 1943 these formations had 659 Yak-1s and Yak-7Bs in their inventory. Thus, the 1st Guards Fighter Air Division (IAD) commanded by Colonel Kroopenin had 54 Yak-7Bs at its disposal, and the 273rd IAD commanded by Colonel I. Fyodorov operated 81 Yaks of different types. The Yak-7B was the main type, while Yakovlev's 'firstling' was the mount of, for example, Hero of the Soviet Union Captain I. Zoodilov (Yak-1 c/n 17140), Lieutenant A. Borovykh from the 147th IAP (Yak-1 c/n 27141) who was later twice awarded the highest distinction of the country, and others. It was these formations that bore the brunt of the combat over the northern flank of the battle and suffered the greatest losses. Suffice it to say that by the morning of 7th July only 27 Yak-1s remained in the 1st Guards IAD, and only 17 fighters were available in the 273rd IAD; the number of serviceable machines in the regiments could be counted on the fingers of one hand.

The Soviet airmen were up against not only all types of enemy aircraft, including the new Fw 190A-5 and Bf 109G-6 which were fitted with more powerful engines, heavier armament and increased armour protection, but also the most skilled and experienced crews of the Luftwaffe. But the German aviation maintained air superiority for only a few days. Fresh units were committed to action in the area and corrections were made to combat tactics; this enabled the Soviet to check the enemy's onslaught.

Materials on the test results of Yak-1 c/n 07127 (seventh aircraft in Batch 127), which could be considered typical for mid-1943, make it possible to assess the merits and shortcomings of the machine. First of all, leading engineer M. Pronin noted that many proposals aimed at perfecting the aerodynamics and armament and improving the handling qualities had been implemented in this machine. At the weight of 2,884 kg (6,359 lb), a maximum speed of 521 km/h (324 mph) was attained at sea level and 591 km/h (367 mph) at the second rated altitude of 4,100 m (13,448). The climb to 5,000 m (16,400 ft) took 5.5 minutes. These figures matched those stipulated by the Government directive.

Some serious shortcomings were also noted. Thus, there was a case when the Yak-1's sliding cockpit canopy disintegrated after being torn off in a dive to an indicated airspeed of 660 km/h (410 mph). Fuel feed from the port and starboard fuel tanks remained uneven. The range of two-way radio communication with the ground was improved – it surpassed 50 km (31 miles) at 1,000 m (3,280 ft), but the level of noise still remained very high. Test pilots Yu. Antipov and V. Khomiakov noted that the bulletproof windshield was not sufficiently transparent and that oil was still leaking through the various seals of the engine crankshaft. Excessive effort was

Above and below: Two views of the I-28 (Yak-5) fighter prototype. The fighter was powered by a supercharged M-105PD engine, hence the enlarged chin-mounted oil cooler.

required for actuating the elevator and ailerons, and pilots quickly got tired because of excessive heat in the cockpit.

Yakovlev continued the work on perfecting his 'firstling' till the end of series production. For instance, excellent results were obtained during checkout tests of Yak-1 c/n 46139 in May 1943. At an all-up weight of 2,864 kg (6,315 lb) the aircraft attained a speed of 539 km/h (335 mph) at ground level and 605 km/h (376 mph) at the second rated altitude of 4,100 m (13,448 ft), a climb to 5,000 m (16,400 ft) took 5.7 minutes, and the Yak-1 gained 1,050 m (3,444 ft) during climb in a combat turn.

Apparently, this was the limit of what could be obtained from this type of fighter. In this form this aircraft could successfully oppose all types of German production fighters at low and medium altitudes where most of the dogfights took place. One must keep in mind the well-established production process at Plant No. 292 and small deviations in the performance of different examples of production Yak-1s at that time.

The Plant functioned like well-adjusted clockwork. However, on the night to 24th June 1943 a group of German bombers forced their way to Saratov through the air defences and bombed the factory; considerable workshop area was destroyed in the resulting fire. By 13th September of that year, at the cost of incredible efforts, the Plant's personnel succeeded in restoring the volume of production completely to the pre-bombardment level. Yet the number of the Yak-1s delivered to the Soviet Air Force was reduced by at least 500 machines.

By the time when production of the Yak-1 was finally discontinued in July 1944 in favour of the Yak-3, 8,666 production machines had been assembled at aircraft factories. The final machine was officially accepted by military representatives in October of that year. Plant No. 292 in Saratov manufactured 192 batches, while circumstances compelled Plant No. 301 in Moscow to limit its production run to only six batches.

Owing to lack of replenishment the number of Yak-1s in front-line units gradually declined. Of the 5,810 fighters that were in the inventory of active Air Armies by the beginning of 1945, 735 were of the Yak-1 type (76 of them in disrepair). They did not stand idle: 79 machines of this type had been lost in combat by Victory Day; in 1945 one aircraft was lost in every 83 sorties (the total attrition of Yak-1s caused by enemy action amounted to 3,336 machines in the period of 1941 to 1945).

The Yak-1s soldiered on till the end of the war in the Naval Aviation and in the PVO units. Thus, various establishments in the rear, primarily near Zhitomir, Kiev and Smolensk, were protected by nearly 300 Yak-1s in the winter and spring of 1944, while by the middle of the year this number was reduced to 272. Among the machines assigned to this difficult service there were some modified aircraft which were fitted with radio compasses and special equipment for night flights – 385 such fighters were built in 1943-1944. Starting in the second half of 1944, however, they were gradually supplanted in the PVO units by Hawker Hurricanes, Curtiss P-40 Kittihawks and Supermarine Spitfires.

Mention must be made of the fact that Yak-1s fought in the ranks of the French 'Normandie-Niémen' regiment which received 14 fighters of this type in March 1943. Before re-equipping with Yak-9s in June of that year, the unit destroyed nine German aircraft for the loss of four Yak-1s and four pilots. The Polish 1st Fighter Regiment 'Warszawa' (Warsaw) had 34 Yak-1s on strength by July 1944, but its participation in combat activities was limited: by the end of January 1945 only one Fw 189 was shot down, while six own machines were lost due to various causes. Besides, the Soviet 586th Air Regiment composed entirely of woman pilots fought on Yak-1s from the winter of 1942 onwards; initially it was assigned to the air defence of Saratov. Now these pages of aviation history are well known.

I-28 (Yak-5) high-altitude fighter prototype

Whereas previous prototype aircraft were created for operation at low and medium altitudes, the I-28 – also known as 'aircraft 28', I-26V (*vysotnyy* – high-altitude) and I-28V – was intended for use by the PVO system. It was the first time Chief Designer A. Yakovlev embarked on the development of a high-altitude fighter.

As distinct from other designers who made use of high-altitude engines, Yakovlev placed his bet on the use of the prototype M-105PD engine fitted with the E-100 supercharger designed by V. Dollezhal'. The supercharger's impeller drive was provided with a hydraulic coupling which made it possible to smoothly change the rpm as the flight altitude increased. A similar device was incorporated in the Daimler-Benz DB 601E engine which had been designed in Germany at that time. The German engine's second rated altitude was 5,100 m (16,728 ft) versus the M-105PD's 6,650 m (21,812 ft); on the other hand, the DB 601E had 10 to 15% higher power ratings. But, most importantly, the Daimler-Benz designers had created and fully developed an automatic supercharger speed control system, while in the Soviet engine the impeller's rpm were controlled manually. This caused much inconvenience for the pilot during flight and prevented the engine power from being fully used.

The prototype I-28 was completed within three months and made its first flight on 1st December 1940 with P. Ya. Fedrovi at the controls. The high-altitude fighter differed structurally from the I-26 in having the undercarriage borrowed from the UTI-26 (Yak-7UTI) and being provided with automatic slats of considerable span. The wing span was reduced from 10,0 m (32 ft 9.7 in) to 9.74 m (31 ft 11.5 in), the wingtips being less rounded.

The design performance of the I-28 included a speed of 515 km/h (320 mph) at sea level and 650 km/h (404 mph) at the altitude of 9,000 m (29,520 ft) with the engine running in boosted mode; it was to climb to 5,000 m (16,400 ft) within 5.2 minutes and reach a service ceiling of 12,000 m (39,360 ft). Besides, since the power output changed smoothly between the first and the second supercharger speeds, the I-28 was expected to possess a significant advantage in speed over the I-26 and I-301 fighters within the range of altitudes between 3,500 to 4,000 m (11,480 to 13,120 ft), because engines lacking the hydraulic coupling were afflicted by the so-called 'drops in power output'. Consequently, there was every reason to hope that that the I-28 would also prove to be a good tactical fighter.

However, the engine proved troublesome from the outset. It emitted fumes, vibrated, spluttered and ejected oil spills. The very first flight ended in a forced landing. Attempts to establish the I-28's actual performance characteristics proved unsuccessful. The engine underwent modifications and was tested in February-March 1940, but this brought no success to the aircraft (which in the meantime was redesignated Yak-5, 1940 model). In the first half of 1941 the OKB concentrated all its efforts on the development of the Yak-1, resuming work on high-altitude aircraft in 1942 with the Yak-7 production fighter.

I-30 (Yak-3 1941 model) fighter prototype

The I-30 aircraft was built as the last of the prototype machines; in consequence, it incorporated all the experience accumulated by the OKB. Small wonder that it possessed a large number of design improvements and operational advantages over its predecessors. These included the use of easily detachable propeller spinner, ejector exhaust stubs and a modified control stick

The photos on this page depict the first prototype I-30 (I-30-1). Note the four-section flaps visible in the centre photo; as was often the case with Yakovlev prototypes, the fighter was totally devoid of markings.

patterned on that of the German Bf 109. The I-30's wings had metal spars and featured detachable outer panels housing two additional ShVAK-20 cannons which fired outside the propeller disc. The weapons' overall weight of fire amounted to 4.28 kg/sec, which was considerably superior to the firepower of other Soviet front-line fighters and was fully in accordance with the requirements posed by military pilots.

The engine mount featured breaks which simplified engine replacement in field conditions. Also incorporated were some successful design features evolved on previous aircraft, such as a forward shift of the CG and an undercarriage patterned on that of the Yak-7, as well as slats of similar design to those of the Yak-5. This time the designers paid sufficient attention to the machine's special equipment. Pilots assessed it as meeting the specification requirements for a tactical fighter. Reliable two-way radio communication between the aircraft and the ground was ensured within a range of 200 km thanks to the extremely thorough electric bonding and shielding.

Piloted by Pavel Fedrovi, the I-30 fighter made its first flight on 12th April 1940, powered by an M-105PD engine featuring the E-100 supercharger. Unfortunately the high-

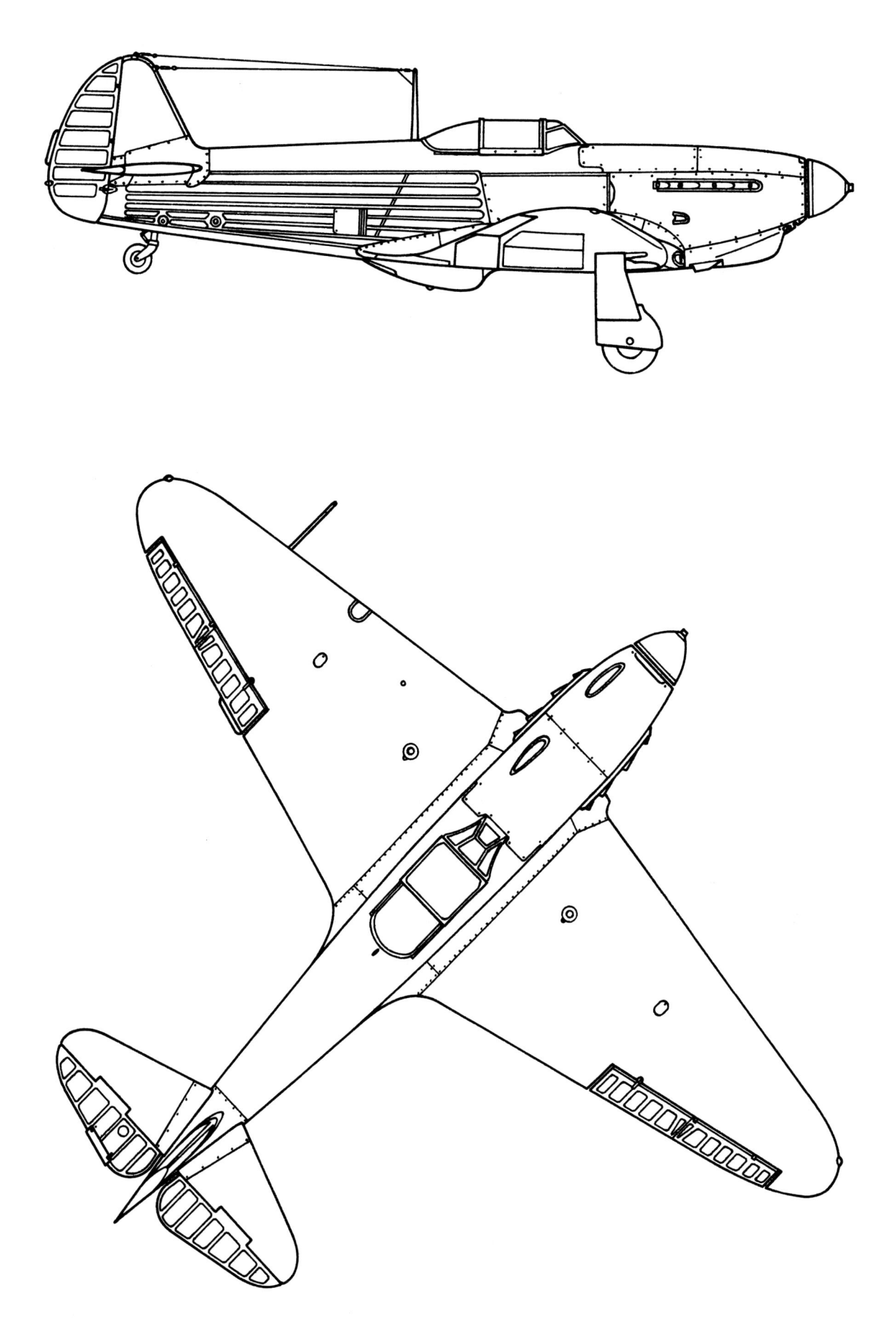

A four-view drawing of a Yak-1b.

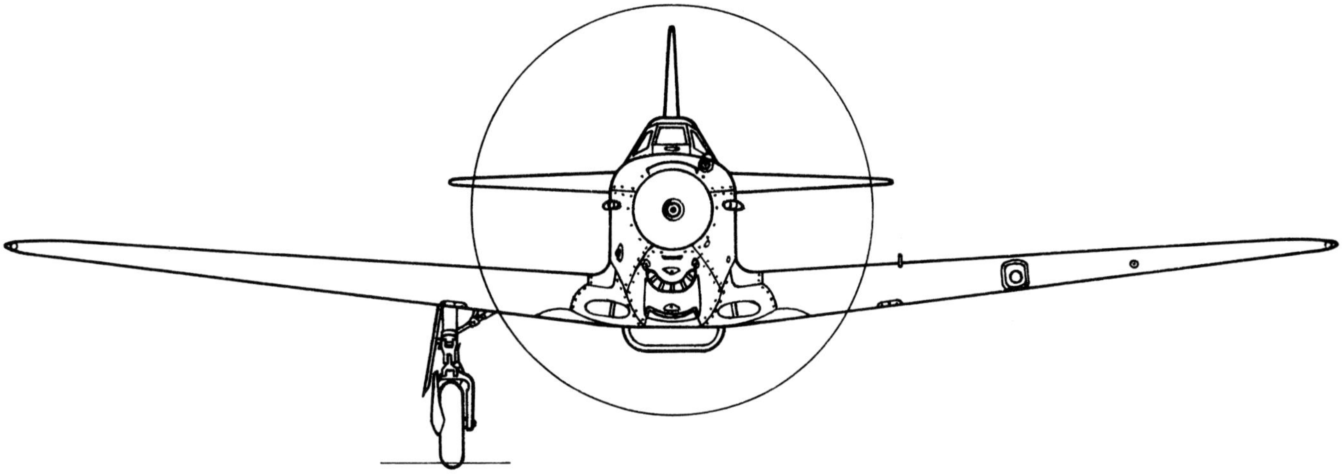

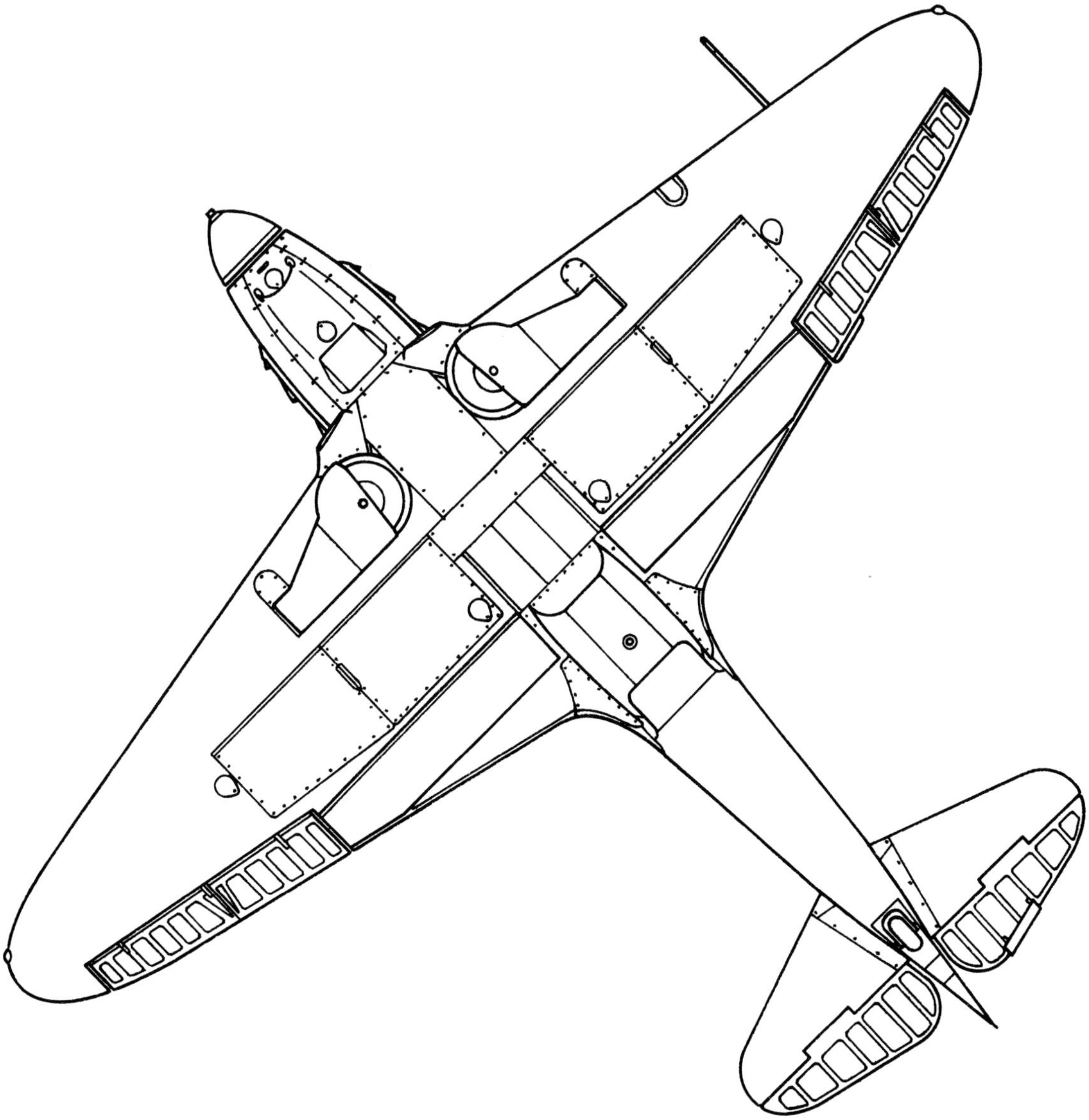

Above: Another view of the I-30-1

Above and below: The second I-30 prototype after a crash-landing. The aircraft was declared a write-off.

altitude engine was not yet fully developed before the war, and an engine of the old M-105P model had to be installed in the aircraft. With this engine the aircraft passed State trials on 3rd July 1941 (pilot A. Nikolayev, engineer A. Stepanets). At an all-up weight of 3,310 kg (7,299 lb) it attained a maximum speed of 476 km/h (296 mph) at sea level and 571 km/h (355 mph) at the second rated altitude of 4,900 m (16,072 ft); time to 5,000 m (16,400 ft) was 7.0 minutes and the service ceiling was 9,000 m (29,520 ft).

The high gross weight caused an increase of the landing speed to 142 km/h (88 mph). However, the landing run remained almost unchanged thanks to the possibility of using wheel brakes effectively. The provision of slats on the I-30 brought down the fighter's minimum pre-stall speed and, in effect, precluded the possibility of the aircraft entering a spin even in the case of grave piloting errors.

Increasing the fuel load from 305 to 383 kg and introducing a service tank improved the fuel feed system and enabled the fighter to cover a maximum distance of 975 km (606 miles) in high-speed flight mode. Summing up his impressions, fighter pilot Stepan P. Sooproon, who had flown the fighter, told A.Yakovlev: 'With such fighters we need not fear any Messerschmitts!'. This conversation took place during the first days of the war when the renowned Soviet ace was leaving for the front as the Commander of a fighter regiment.

As early as 21st April 1941 the Government issued a decision requiring the Moscow aircraft factory to halt the production of the Yak-4 and switch to the I-30 which was allocated the designation Yak-3. By the time the war broke out a number of incomplete airframes had been manufactured.

On 21st April 1941 a decision was taken to launch the production of the Yak-3, 1941 model (I-30), also in Saratov. Chief Designer A. S. Yakovlev had no doubts that the Yak-1 would be superseded by its more perfect stablemate. At pre-war conferences, when faced with numerous complaints concerning the Yak-1 (in particular, regarding the absence of a radio), the Chief Designer invariably reacted by saying that all the shortcomings would be eliminated on the Yak-3 (I-30).

In the meantime, A. Yakovlev's OKB continued the development of the prototype I-30 – the Yak-3 *'dooblyor'* (second prototype) was completed in May 1941. The cockpit layout evolved on it was recommended as standard for all fighters of the Red Army Air Force. Obviously envisioning large-scale production, Yakovlev reverted to one-piece wooden wings without slats. Powered by the M-105PD, the *'dooblyor'* was damaged in an accident at LII and struck off charge.

The work on the first prototype I-30 was not yet completed at the outbreak of the war. One of the documents stated: *'The Yak-3 powered by the M-105P engine possesses potent and well-developed armament; it is easy to fly and can easily be mastered by war time medium-skilled pilots. As such, it is recommended for introduction into service with the Red Army Air Force.'*

Many members of the OKB staff believed that the setback with the second prototype would not affect the destiny of the new promising aircraft. Still, production of the Yak-3 (I-30) failed to materialise. At first its phasing into production was postponed to 1942 and then the decision to launch series production was cancelled altogether. This was due to various reasons, notably the scarcity of aluminium caused by the industry's redeployment to the eastern regions of the USSR and by the loss of a number of enterprises which remained on the territory occupied by the enemy. Furthermore, the mass-produced Yak-1 had no special need for slats, being sufficiently easy in handling without them; and, lastly, the phasing of a new aircraft into production would inevitably have entailed a reduction in the output of series-manufactured machines – something that was ill-affordable during the course of the war.

Chapter 2

The Yak-7

The First Derivative

Prototype UTI-26 fighter trainer

As noted earlier, the Yakovlev OKB, as distinct from other design teams, prepared three more combat aircraft in parallel with the I-26 fighter,.

The first of them was the machine designated UTI-26 (*oochebno-trenirovochnyy istrebitel'* – fighter trainer), also referred to in various documents as the UTI-26-4, UTI-1, UTI-27 and so on. The Design Bureau started work on this aircraft at the beginning of 1940. The Government authorised this work by adopting an appropriate directive. It was presumed that the Yakovlev OKB was in a better position to tackle this task than other design teams, bearing in mind Yakovlev's rich experience in designing trainer aircraft. Furthermore, the assumption was that the new aircraft would have substantial commonality with the I-26 prototype, which lessened the risk of a failure: one could not jeopardise the re-equipment of the Air Force units with new-generation fighters.

That happened to be the case. Indeed, the first UTI-26 was basically similar to the I-26 fighter. It differed in having two cockpits (for the trainee and the instructor) placed in tandem under a common canopy and in featuring dual controls. No intercom was fitted at first, and the instructor could communicate with the trainee by means of a rubber hose. The provision of a second cockpit required the wings of the UTI-26 to be moved somewhat aft.

On 23rd July 1940 pilot Pavel Ya. Fedrovi took the fighter trainer into the air. After a few development flights the machine was submitted for State trials. They were conducted by engineer A. Stepanets and pilots Pyotr M. Stefanovskiy and A. Koobyshkin in the period from 28th August till 19th September.

On 30th August an incident occurred: the undercarriage collapsed during taxying due to faulty design. On the whole, most of the criticism levelled at the UTI-26 were directed at this element of the airframe. It was pointed out that locks were unreliable, the wheels were not strong enough to cater for the all-up weight, and the mainwheel struts were set at an insufficient angle for preventing nosing-over; this, in effect, precluded the use of wheel brakes during the landing run, especially when the instructor was not in the rear seat. All these defects had to be rectified. There was nothing new in these complaints – they had already been voiced with regard to the I-26.

However, the presence of such defects appeared inadmissible in a fighter trainer intended for primary training in flying schools or for taking ill-trained pilots of service units on familiarisation flights. Besides, 11th IAP pilots who had flown the aircraft noted that in certain flight modes, including landing, the required deflection of the elevator from the neutral position was exceedingly small, which meant it was all too easy to apply excessive elevator input; this made the use of the aircraft as a trainer very problematic.

Nevertheless, on 25th September the military customer recommended the UTI-26 into series production, since it was the only type available for transition to the I-26, I-200 and I-301 fighters that were already in series production. It was decided that the work on perfecting the aircraft would be continued on the second prototype.

Above and below: The UTI-26-1, the first prototype of the future Yak-7 which was originally conceived as a trainer but ultimately evolved into a real combat aircraft. The aircraft is shown here during manufacturer's flight tests.

41

The UTI-26-1 'unbuttoned' for maintenance during manufacturer's flight tests.

Known as the UTI-26-2, the second prototype differed from its predecessor primarily in having an altered ratio between the sizes of the elevator and stabilizer, the total area of the horizontal tail remaining unchanged. It also featured changers in the undercarriage design; bigger wheels were fitted to match the machine's all-up weight, and the fulcrums of the mainwheel struts were relocated, making it possible to increase the angle intended to prevent nose-overs. However, these measures created new problems even as they eliminated old ones: the wheels' plane of rotation noticeably deviated from the aircraft's direction of movement, thus creating an additional load on the undercarriage pivots.

Certain alterations in the fighter's structural layout caused a forward shift of the CG, which improved stability. This was confirmed by test pilots who put the aircraft through an intensive flight test programme right from the first days of 1941. Virtually all of them, including NII VVS Chief A. Filin, got the opportunity to fly the new aircraft, performing at least 260 aerobatic manoeuvres in it. It makes sense to cite here a report on the tests of the UTI-26-2: *'The aircraft possesses good controllability and sufficient stability in piloting, has pleasant handling qualities and performs aerobatic manoeuvres easily. The visibility is quite satisfactory, the presence of a canopy obviates the need for using goggles. The aircraft enters a spin only in the case of a considerable loss of speed and recovers easily. It forgives even grave piloting errors with no serious consequences. The aircraft possesses a very broad range of safe speeds.'*

As for performance characteristics, they were close to those of the I-26. At a weight of 2,750 kg (6,064 lb) the fighter trainer attained a maximum speed of 500 km/h (296 mph) at sea level and 586 km/h (364 mph) at 4,500 m (14,760 ft). The aircraft climbed to 5,000 m (16,400 ft) within 5.5 minutes. The machine needed 310m (1,017 ft) for the take-off run and as many as 750 m (2,460 ft) for the landing run; the latter figure was due to insufficiently strong wheels making abrupt braking dangerous. The landing speed was 125 km/h (77,7 mph).

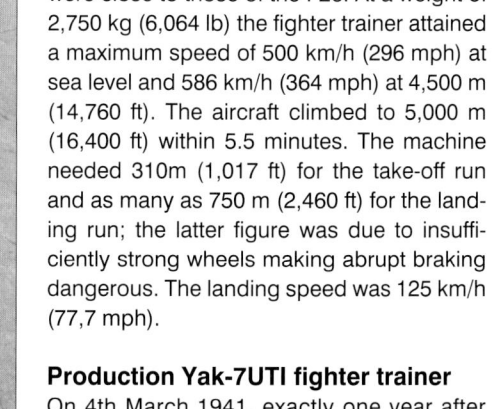

Production Yak-7UTI fighter trainer

On 4th March 1941, exactly one year after the adoption of the directive calling for the development of the machine, the UTI-26

A rare top view of the UTI-26-1 during State acceptance trials.

was put into series production under the designation Yak-7UTI at Plant No. 301 which, until then, had manufactured the Yak-1. When manufacturing drawings were transferred to the Plant, some changes were introduced: since a fighter trainer was supposed to perform take-offs and landing without retracting the undercarriage, the tailwheel was made non-retractable; the engine speed was limited to a figure that was substantially lower than the nominal rpm; and only the port ShKAS machine-gun was retained. The all-up weight of production machines was nearly 2,800 kg (6,174 lb), and performance was close to that of the production Yak-1s of the period.

On 18th May 1941 P. Ya. Fedrovi test-flew the first production Yak-7UTI from the Central Airfield in Moscow (the present Khodynka). Deliveries of these aircraft to the Air Force units commenced literally right before the outbreak of the war, but the machines were operated mainly in the regiments deployed in western areas. These aircraft played an important role in expediting the conversion of Soviet pilots to the new-generation fighters.

Taking into account the operational experience with Yak trainers, in early August 1941 engineer Cherepov (an employee of Plant No. 301) came up with an important proposal: motivated by the wish to simplify production and thus increase the output, he suggested that production Yak-7s be built with a fixed undercarriage. In his opinion, this was fully in conformity with the character of work performed by the aircraft and their pilots. Right away, in August, the suggestion was implemented in series production.

On the 87 aircraft manufactured before 20th July that were operated by various Air Force units, the most serious complaints concerned the mainwheel leg pivots which failed by the dozens. The parts were reinforced, but even that did not immediately cure this annoying defect.

Yak-7R tactical reconnaissance aircraft prototype

One of the first adaptations of the Yak-7UTI was directed at adapting it for the tactical reconnaissance role. Following instructions from Chief Designer Aleksandr S. Yakovlev, two production aircraft were fitted with an AFA-I aerial camera and an RSI-4 radio set. To enable the latter to function, shielding and electric bonding was performed on the aircraft; the pilot's seat was provided with an armoured back and the canopy glazing was altered. The aircraft was armed with an engine-mounted 20-mm ShVAK cannon. When the Yak-7R ([*samolyot*-] *razvedchik* – reconnaissance

Four more views of the UTI-26-1 at NII VVS during State acceptance trials. These views show well the clean lines of the aircraft, an impression enhanced by the extensively glazed canopy.

Above and below: A Batch 22 Yak-7B (c/n 2203) during checkout tests at NII VVS; note the one-piece main gear doors attached to the oleo struts that were characteristic of late-production Yak-1s and Yak-7s alike. The rear cockpit transparency has been deleted but the cockpit is still functional, allowing a passenger (usually the aircraft's technician) to be carried in case of need.

aircraft) had been given an approval from the Research Institute of Specialised Services, a recommendation was issued to build a small batch of such machines.

Yak-7 tactical fighter

In August 1941 another transformation of the fighter trainer was effected under the direction of leading engineer K. Sinel'shchikov at Plant No. 301. This time it was converted into a 'real' fighter. A standard production Yak-7UTI, c/n 04-11, was taken off the assembly line and subjected to the following alterations: an armoured seat back was installed in the rear cockpit, the gun camera was deleted, the fuel tanks were provided with self-sealing coating and an inert gas pressurization system employing a bottle with carbon dioxide. The fighter was armed with the engine-mounted 20-mm ShVAK cannon with 120 rounds and two synchronised 7.62-mm ShKAS machine-guns with a total of 1,500 rounds, as well as six rails (three under each wing) for 82-mm (3.22-in.) RS-82 unguided rockets. The latter were fired by means of electric bomb release mechanism placed in the pilot's cockpit. The canopy of the rear cockpit and the tailwheel remained unchanged, so that the fighter virtually did not differ in external appearance from the two-seat Yak-7UTI.

The designers reported the results of their work to Yakovlev. The Chief Designer was sceptical about the idea, but then changed his mind and gave his approval. When he had informed the government that the conversion trainer had been evolved into a fully capable fighter, the work received support from the People's Commissariat of Aircraft Industry. Two directives issued by the People's Commissariat in August stipulated that already from 15th September onwards the Yak-7UTI was to be built 'to Yak-1 standard', referring to the identical armament. Here a curious occurrence took place: errors slipped into the texts of the directives. According to these texts, Plant 301 in Moscow and then, after evacuation, Plant 153 in Novosibirsk were to manufacture Yak-1 fighters! In actual fact the Yak-1 was never built there, but fighters manufactured at these plants were entered into statistical reports under this designation. In reality, the collective of the Plant built 186 Yak-7s in Moscow (51 of them with armament) and 21 in Novosibirsk (including 11 fighters).

Right from the outset favourable comments came in concerning the Yak-7 fighter. Thus, the document on the acceptance of the aircraft by the Design bureau's technical commission stated that the Yak-7 single-seat fighter was a better machine than the Yak-1. The size of the undercarriage wheels was in full conformity with the all-up weight which came close to three tonnes (6,150 lb). The detachable engine mount fitted to the Yak-7 facilitat-

A lineup of Yak-7s at a tactical airfield. These fighters were paid for by donations from Young Communist League members of Novosibirsk; hence each aircraft carries the legend 'Novosibirskiy komsomol'.

ed repairs and made it possible to relatively easily adapt the aircraft to a different engine. The main undercarriage legs were set at a higher angle intended to preclude nose-overs, which lessened the danger of the machine turning turtle after a resolute application of wheel brakes. The second cockpit which was retained on the Yak-7 could be used for carrying maintenance personnel and cargoes during redeployment of air units, for bringing pilots back from the places of forced landings or for installing a long-range fuel tank; almost all of these options were subsequently implemented. The acceptance document stated: *'These special features of the Yak-7 made it a promising machine and made it possible to develop a number of versions'* (sic; the use of the past tense in the quotation is incongruous – translator's note).

As for performance, the characteristics of the Yak-7 proved to be very similar to those of the Yak-1 fighter. At an all-up weight of 2,960 kg (6,527 lb), which was 160 kg (353 lb) higher than that of the Yak-7UTI, the Yak-7 fighter attained a maximum speed of 471 km/h (293 mph) at sea level and 560 km/h (348 mph) at 5,000 m (16,400 ft). The altitude of 5,000 m could be reached within 6.8 minutes. (All performance figures are quoted for the fighter without external stores and with the cockpit hood closed). Manoeuvrability turned out to be somewhat inferior to that of the Yak-1; 24 seconds were needed for a full-circle banking turn at 1,000 m (3,280 ft) and the Yak-7 gained 750 m (2,460 ft) during climb in a combat turn.

The handling qualities of the fighter were highly assessed. Referring to the Yak-7's spinning characteristics, A. Lazarev, a Plant No. 153 test pilot, noted that spin recovery was 'exceedingly simple – no tricks, once the rudder pedals and the control stick in the transverse plane have been put into the neu-

Another view of the same unit's Yak-7s as the crews go to the flight line, preparing for the day's work. Not all of the fighters sported the red arrow near the engine exhaust stubs.

Yak-7B c/n 2241 was another example subjected to checkout tests at NII VVS.

tral position, the aircraft instantly ceases rotation and enters a dive'.

In September 1941 a Yak-7 armed with unguided rockets successfully passed trials. It transpired that, thanks to the fighter's good stability, projectile dispersal during attacks against ground targets was somewhat less than in the case of the LaGG-3 and the Yak-1, and the rocket hits were much more closely grouped than in the case of the MiG-3.

In October 1941 all enterprises, including Plant No. 301, had to be evacuated from Moscow, which was detrimental to the deliveries of aircraft to front-line units. In the meantime, the work on perfecting the fighter continued unabated. Right before the transfer to Novosibirsk designers succeeded in completing a 'winterised' example of the Yak-7 that was to serve as a standard for production; it incorporated features similar to those of the 'winterised' Yak-1 described in Chapter 1.

The work on fitting heavier armament to the Yak-7 was under way – it envisaged the installation of two synchronised ShVAK cannon; the evacuation prevented the completion of this work.

During the late autumn of 1941 a very strained situation arose in Novosibirsk. Plant No. 153 which had been built there before the war could not cope with the task of manufacturing LaGG-3 fighters; as if that were not enough, after the transfer of the Yakovlev OKB to Siberia work started on setting up a second continuous flow assembly line there for the production of the Yak-7 fighter. At the same time trains coming from the USSR's western areas delivered personnel and equipment, barracks for housing the personnel and auxiliary premises were built. Four different aircraft enterprises happened to be placed on the same territory. Each collective had its own director and chief engineer, and they wished to exercise control over their subordinates

and the equipment. The government tasked A. S. Yakovlev with uniting everybody and everything into a single enterprise before too many cooks spoiled the broth.

'I imagined for a minute what could have happened if, under the conditions of a capitalist society, the interests of four private firms had clashed in a similar situation, – Yakovlev recalled. – *And here our system and our people made it possible to solve an incredibly complex organisational and technical task within the shortest space of time.'*

Simultaneously the Chief Designer succeeded in getting the united Plant relieved of the LaGG-3 manufacture programme so that all efforts could be concentrated on the production of his Yak-7. Brigade engineer Leshookov, a representative of the State Defence Committee in Novosibirsk, advocated a different point of view: first of all, he maintained, it was necessary to improve the Yak-7 fighter because the latter had no tangible advantages over the LaGG-3 as yet, and it would be advisable to manufacture both types in parallel. However, Yakovlev made use of his influence on Stalin to secure for himself the control over the entire Plant No. 153 which, after the evacuation, became one of the biggest in the Soviet aircraft industry.

Yak-7 fighters saw combat employment for the first time during the counteroffensive started by Soviet troops near Moscow. In early December one of the squadrons of the 172nd IAP equipped with Yak-7s (the other two were equipped with LaGG-3s and Yak-1s) escorted a group of 65th ShAP (Attack Air Regiment) Il'yushin Il-2 attack aircraft and itself attacked enemy ground troops in the area of Teriayeva Sloboda and Rooza when the Soviet troops were liberating the town of Volokolamsk. Only eight Yak-7s were in the entire inventory of the Soviet aviation at that time, three of them being fully operational.

Yak-7M fighter prototype

A very unusual modification of the Yak-7 was effected in August 1941. It was undertaken not in Moscow or in Novosibirsk, where the Yak-7 was being manufactured at the time, but in Saratov. A group of Yakovlev OKB engineers was rendering assistance to Plant No. 292 in getting Yak-1 production under way. Today it is difficult to say what prompted the initiation of this work, but many elements that had been evolved on the prototype I-30 fighter were incorporated into the design of the fighter trainer. As a result, a version emerged which was designated Yak-7M (*modifit-seerovannyy* – modified).

The aircraft was stripped of all equipment in the rear cockpit and of the sole ShKAS machine-gun which was replaced by three

Another Yak-7B seen during checkout tests at NII VVS. Curiously, the aircraft wears summer camouflage, even though the tests were held in winter.

20-mm ShVAK cannon. One of them was a hub-mounted weapon, while the other two were mounted in the wings outside the propeller disc area and did not require synchronisation. Thanks to this weapons fit the Yak-7M was superior to all Soviet and German fighters in weight of fire. The most serious alterations concerned the wings. Wing span was marginally reduced from 10.0 m (32 ft 10 in.) to 9.74 m (31 ft 11.5 in.), and the wingtips were made more angular because the leading edge housed slats of a fairly large span. Installation of cannons and their ammunition boxes necessitated a reduction of the capacity of outer wing tanks. The wing structure was strengthened and the flaps area was increased. To compensate for the forced reduction of fuel capacity, a supplementary 80-litre (17.6 Imp gal) fuel tank was installed behind the pilot's armoured seat back.

In October 1941 the Yak-7M was transferred for trials to NII VVS; it immediately attracted the attention of leading engineer A. Stepanets and pilot V. Khomiakov who headed the team engaged in testing Yakovlev fighters at the time. They noted that, despite the all-up weight being increased to 3,160 kg (6,968 lb), the handling of the machine was appreciably simplified thanks to the installation of slats. The danger of the aircraft flipping into a spin due to pilot error was virtually eliminated. Stability, especially lateral stability, was improved. All this justified the conclusion that flight safety had been considerably enhanced. The minimum admissible speeds were reduced by 30 to 40 km/h (18.6 to 24.8 mph) as compared to production Yak-1s and Yak-7s both when performing different aerobatic manoeuvres and during pancaking.

Test firing of the cannons revealed that they functioned faultlessly in all flight modes. Dispersal of the shells proved to be within acceptable limits. For the purpose of aiming the cannons were so adjusted that their fire converged in one point at the distance of 400 m (1,312 ft). After the necessary development and test firing it became clear that the armament of the Yak-7M could be used very effectively against both aerial and ground targets. In its overall performance the Yak-7M fighter was marginally inferior to the Yak-1 and Yak-7, mainly because this particular machine had been operated for a long time, had suffered a minor accident and underwent the modification simultaneously with the repairs that had to be made to the fuselage and wings.

The Yak-7M fighter was recommended for series production. However, this enticing proposal made by NII VVS could not be put into effect during the winter of 1941-1942 – the new machine would have necessitated too radical changes in the production process that were not feasible at that time.

Above: A rather rare shot of a winter-camouflaged Yak-7B

Above: This Yak-7B is armed with six 82-mm RS-82 unguided rockets on underwing racks. The picture was taken during trials at the Soviet MoD's Artillery Weapons Proving Ground (NIPAV).

Above: Close-up of the starboard triplet of RO-82 launch rails on the Yak-7B shown above.
Below: RS-82 rockets with their propeller-like fuse vanes under the wing of the Yak-7B.

Top and above: Because of the variance in weight and performance characteristics from batch to batch, checkout tests had to be held rather frequently. Note the old-style black-outlined insignia on this Yak-7B.

Yak-7A production fighter

The Yak-7 underwent serious alterations in 1942. Whereas at the beginning of the year it still retained all the features of its predecessor – the fighter trainer, at the end of the year it was transformed into one of the best fighters of its time. This was accompanied by an appreciable increase in the number of machines manufactured. While the output of Yakovlev fighters totalled a mere six to seven machines during the winter months of 1942 (Plant No. 153 was still continuing production and deliveries of the LaGG-3), the production tempo reached six to seven Yak-7s per day in August of the same year.

In early January 1942 a Yak-7, c/n 14-13, was transferred to NII VVS for joint manufacturer's and State tests (its c/n – Batch 14, 13th aircraft in the batch – reveals that Plant No. 153 continued the sequence of batches initiated at Plant No. 301 after the amalgamation of the two plants). The machine was test-flown with both wheel and ski undercarriage. The tests revealed that the performance of the machine was still marginally inferior to that of the UTI-26. In the 'summer' version it attained a maximum speed of 476 km/h (296 mph) at sea level, this figure rising to 550 km/h at 5,000 m (16,400 ft). This altitude could be reached within 6.8 minutes.

When fitted with skis and sprayed with the winter chalk-based paint over the summer camouflage, the Yak-7 lost some 30 to 40 km/h (18.6 to 24.8 mph) in speed. Rate of climb, range and field performance also deteriorated, while the landing run was reduced by approximately 150 m (492 ft) owing to the considerable friction of the skis on the snow.

The design of the skis proved to be successful. They were manufactured at Plant No. 153 entirely from auxiliary materials. The ski had a wooden construction and featured a framework consisting of spars, transverse frames, lugs and a runner. Wide use was made of the Siberian larch which grew in the forests of the Novosibirsk region. The framework of the ski was supplemented by plywood skinning, sheet aluminium being used for the edging on the sides. Mounted on the upper side of the ski was the so-called 'cabane' with 'paws' made from Cromansil alloy tubes. The ski mounted on the non-retractable tail strut featured a similar design. To evaluate the operational qualities of the skis, test pilots made nearly three hundred successful landings; no anomalies were revealed.

In accordance with A. Yakovlev's directions leading engineers from different organisations – A. Stepanets from NII VVS, P. Limar from LII, K. Tarootin from Plant No. 153 – joined forces to further develop the fighter as a standard for series production. As a result, with a wheeled undercarriage the fighter attained 495 km/h (308 mph) at sea level and 571 km/h (355 mph) at 5,000 m (16,4000 ft), climbing to this altitude within 6.4 minutes.

From the beginning of 1942 onwards the fighter was series-produced in Novosibirsk under the designation Yak-7A. Various improvements were envisaged and introduced into the design gradually, mainly in the spring of that year. The principal improvements included installation of a two-way radio with aerial mast and wire aerial. A partially retractable tailwheel was introduced and the fixed strut joining the upper part of the tail skid with the fuselage frame was replaced by a pneumatic actuator for tailwheel retraction; additional gear doors were introduced to close the mainwheel wells completely when the undercarriage was retracted. The sliding hood of the rear cockpit was replaced by a hinged plywood hood that swung open to starboard; when closed, it ensured a smooth transition between the canopy of the pilots cockpit and the rear decking of the fuselage.

Ammo belt link collectors were installed instead of link chutes; this made it possible to eliminate the openings in the cowling and save the belt links for subsequent re-use. A lever controlling the engine boost was installed to shorten the take-off run. The inert gas pressurization system for the fuel tanks was altered and the instrument panel layout was changed.

When all the changes had been incorporated, the Yak-7A proved to be one of the fastest Soviet production fighters; even if it was somewhat inferior to the Yak-1 in manoeuvrability, the armament was equally capable.

At the beginning of the summer of 1942 several dozen Yak-7As were operated by the aviation of the Volkhov and the Western Fronts. Referring to the merits of the Yak-7A, Lieutenant Filatov wrote in his letter addressed to Gheorgiy M. Malenkov, Secretary of the Central Committee of the Communist Party: *'The tactics employed by German pilots in air combat are based on making use of their advantages in speed and rate of climb – they try to force us to fight in the vertical plane. It is necessary by all means to increase the maximum speeds of our fighters. Besides, Yak-7 pilots have poor visibility to aft; it is necessary to provide the fighter with a fully glazed all-round vision canopy because the metal framing reduces the observable zone by about 30%.'*

The comments that came from the front were predominantly favourable. Here is an excerpt from a letter dated 13th July 1942 that was sent to A. Yakovlev by Major A. Morozov, commander of the 283rd IAP which had several Yak-7As on strength:

'My wingman and I were conducting a dogfight with eight Bf 109Fs. Despite his numerical superiority, the enemy could do nothing to us, because the Yak-7A enabled us to perform all the manoeuvres at will, and the vaunted fascist carrion vultures (that was a common allusion to Luftwaffe aircraft among Soviet people at the time – *translator's note*) *could not make a firing pass at us, no matter how they tried …*

The pilots of my regiment who are flying this aircraft have literally lost their hearts to it; it's no use trying to lure them to some other fighter type, and the pilots of the neighbouring units look at us with envy.'

Yak-7B production fighter

The letter to A. Yakovlev which had been quoted above also noted some shortcomings of the Yak-7, however. Among these Major Morozov noted the fighter's inadequate armament, insufficient speed and 'rather weak' (ie, not sufficiently powerful) engine.

It was these shortcomings that the team of the Yakovlev OKB persistently sought to eradicate. Results of this work were embodied in the M-105PA-powered Yak-7B which differed from its predecessor in having heavier armament and some aerodynamic refinements.

Two normal-calibre machine-guns were replaced by UBS-12.7 large-calibre machine-guns, while the engine-mounted 20-mm ShVAK cannon was retained. Besides, in overload configuration six RS-82 rockets or two 25- to 100-kg (55- to 220-lb) bombs could be carried underwing.

TsAGI recommendations concerning aerodynamic refinements were fully incorporated in the Yak-7B. Besides, improvements were effected to the carburettor air inlets with a view to using the ram air pressure to a fuller extent and achieving higher rated altitudes. The aircraft got a better surface finish, perfected radiator and oil cooler ducts were installed.

Despite the presence of an aerial mast with its aerial and the installation of new armament, which spoiled the clean contours of the upper part of the engine cowling, compounded by the increase of the all-up weight by nearly 100 kg (220 lb) over the Yak-7 and Yak-7A, the Yak-7B's performance proved to be somewhat higher than that of its predecessors.

After the replacement of the 7.62-mm ShKAS by the 12.7-mm UBS the Yak-7B's weight of fire fully met the requirements of front-line units, and this fighter could be used more effectively than the Yak-1 and the Yak-7 for engaging both air and ground targets. Its salvo weight of 2.72 kg/sec was more than 1.5 times greater than the Yak-1's and Yak-7A's,

Top and above: One of the first Yak-7Bs built by the Novosibirsk aircraft factory No. 153 seen at NII VVS during additional State acceptance trials.

1.35 times greater than that of the late-production LaGG-3 and 3.5 times greater than that of the Bf 109F (as tested in the Soviet Union).

The report on the results of the State trials of the Yak-7B noted: *'…In comparison with the Yak-1 aircraft which has built up a good service record at the front, the Yak-7B aircraft features a more perfected and promising design. During the period of its series manufacture the Yak-7 has been progressively improved and fitted with new, more capable armament and special equipment with no adverse effect on its performance and combat capabilities. This positive phenomenon is due to the efficient handling of the questions of providing the fighter with new armament and equipment and to the OKB's persistent work on improving the performance of production aircraft.'*

Excellent results were obtained during the tests of the Yak-7B conducted by LII for the purpose of evaluating the balanced character of controls in different flight modes. For example, in the opinion of test pilots, the La-5 was inferior to the Yak fighter: the former possessed insufficient directional stability, too 'light' ailerons and, on the contrary, too high stick forces from the elevators. The Bf 109E received a reasonably positive evaluation, yet its ailerons and tail surfaces were not quite so effective as those of the Soviet fighter.

Having compared the Yak-7B with indigenous and German fighters, as well as with British and American fighters that were delivered under the Lend-Lease arrangement, the institute arrived at the conclusion that this aircraft was among the best with regard to stability and controllability. Upon completion of the State trials the State Committee of Defence adopted a decision requiring Plant No. 153 to switch its assembly line from producing the Yak-7A to the manufacture of the Yak-7B. Already in April 1942 the first production Yak-7B was completed in Novosibirsk.

Contemporaneously, Plant No. 21 in Gor'kiy and Plant No. 82 (which had returned to Moscow from evacuation) began tooling up for the production of this fighter. Yakovlev had succeeded in 'squeezing' S. A. Lavochkin and his LaGG-3 fighter out of the former of the two factories (one of the biggest in the Soviet Union), but after the successful development of the promising La-5 powered by the M-82 air-cooled engine Lavochkin regained control over Plant No. 21; only five Yak-7Bs assembled in Gor'kiy passed accep-

Above and below: This late-production Moscow-built Yak-7B, c/n 4101, was modified with a cut-down rear fuselage decking and bubble canopy. It is seen here during State acceptance trials.

Above and below: Another modified 'bubbletop' Yak-7B. This aircraft differs from Yak-7B c/n 4101 in having a recontoured water radiator bath.

tance and were delivered to front-line units.

As early as May 1942 the first three Yak-7Bs were assembled at the Moscow plant from shipsets delivered from Novosibirsk. By the end of July of that year 27 fighters had been built; 11 of them were pronounced combat-ready and were promptly sent to front-line units. They proved to be noticeably inferior in quality to their stablemates from Novosibirsk. Especially many complaints were voiced concerning the production standard of the armament. Thus, Yak-7B c/n 820307 (ie, Plant No. 82, Batch 3, 7th aircraft in the batch) which was operated by the 4th IAP proved to have a malfunctioning ShVAK-20 cannon.

Series-produced aircraft from all factories were immediately sent to the front. To improve aerodynamics, the rocket armament was deleted at the end of May 1942, but the bomb racks were retained. The first phenomenon encountered in the front-line units of the South-Western Front was an inadmissible forward shift of the CG caused by the greater weight of the armament. The use of wheel brakes during landing became dangerous. To prevent nosing-over, a supplementary 80-litre (17.6 Imp gal) fuel tank was installed in the rear cockpit from the end of May 1942.

Pilots often expressed their displeasure with having this tank, which lacked self-sealing into the bargain, behind their backs. Its presence increased the all-up weight and led to deterioration of flight performance, especially of the vertical manoeuvrability; besides, it entailed an increased fire hazard. In consequence, personnel of front-line units began removing the supplementary tanks without bothering about official approval.

Pilots of the 434th IAP were among the first to receive the M-105PA-powered Yak-7B. This unit enjoyed a special status because it was subordinated not to the commander of the 8th Air Army in whose sector it was operating, but to Chief Inspector of the Red Army Air Force Colonel Vasiliy I. Stalin, the Leader's son. The regiment commanded by Hero of the Soviet Union Major I. Kleshchov had experienced and well-trained airmen in its ranks. Surprisingly, the flying personnel included four girls: K. Nechayeva, K. Blinova, A. Lebedeva, O. Shakhova. Already in the first battles with the enemy they showed that they could fight on a par with men.

Having started combat sorties on 13th July, the regiment made 827 individual sorties by 3rd August 1942 and shot down (according to official Soviet information) 55 enemy aircraft – more than what was scored by some fighter air divisions during the same period – for the loss of three Yak-7Bs and one pilot. Hero of the Soviet Union Lieutenant V. Alkidov was classed as missing in action for some time. But fate was merciful to him: though taken prisoner by the Germans, he managed

This rare picture shows a 'bubbletop' Yak-7B in the TsAGI wind tunnel during tests of the canopy jettison system. Note that the engine is running and the wheels have been removed in order to secure the aircraft in the tunnel.

to escape and return to his own forces. However, as a consequence of the wounds he had sustained, he was unable to resume flying.

Comparative trials of the Yak-1 and the Yak-7B were conducted in the 202nd IAD, but the pilots failed to reach a consensus: each of the two machines had its adherents. Having analysed the combat experience accumulated in the 146th and 181th IAPs, Commander of the 234th IAD Yaroslavtsev came to the conclusion that the Yak-7B was superior to all other types flown by Soviet pilots earlier. However, as he noted, *'the Yaks have an excessively long landing run; the fighter is 'nose heavy' and, most importantly, it lacks some 30 to 50 km/h* [18.6 to 31 mph] *to gain an advantage over the contemporary Bf 109F.'*

In the summer of 1942 an important direction of work on perfecting the Yak-7B lay in uprating its engine. The Yakovlev OKB actively took part in experiments with increasing the boost pressure from barometric 910 to 950 mm, and then to 1,000 and 1,050 mm and with determining the influence of the engine boost on the maximum speed and other performance of the aircraft.

The results of these experiments proved very promising; they formed the basis for the adoption of a Government decision which tasked Vladimir Ya. Klimov (chief designer of the M-105 engine) with transferring the engine from the normal to the boosted mode within the shortest time possible.

To ensure reliable running in boosted mode, the piston pins were reinforced and the carburettor was readjusted. At that time the production M-105PF engine had no other differences from the M-105PA.

In addition to the engine modification, a number of other measures were effected on the Yak-7B aircraft (from the 22nd batch onwards) in accordance with Yakovlev's instructions. They were aimed at improving the aerodynamics and reducing the all-up weight, mainly by lightening some elements of the structure without compromising the strength and impairing the aircraft's operational qualities.

The main alterations included lightening of the fuselage framework, deletion of wiring to rocket projectile guide rails, a change in the incidence of propeller blades at low pitch. As a result, the M-105PF-powered Yak-7B (Yak-7B M-105PF) proved to be 30 to 35 kg (66 to 72 lb) lighter than its predecessor with the same armament and equipment. Tests conducted on Yak-7B c/n 2241 at NII VVS showed that a maximum speed of 514 km/h (319 mph) was attained at sea level, reaching 570 km/h (354 mph) at the second rated altitude of 3,650 m (11,972 ft). The time need to climb to 5,000 m (16,400 ft) was 5.8 minutes, and a banking turn could be performed during 19 to 20 seconds. In a combat turn beginning at 1,000 m (3,280 ft) the Yak-7B gained 950 to 1,000 m (3,116 to 3,280 ft) in altitude. In the opinion of NII VVS experts, such performance characteristics enabled the fighter to wage combat successfully with the Bf 109 at low and medium altitudes.

In the summer of 1942, Yak-7B M-105PF fighters fought intensive battles with the Luftwaffe units near Stalingrad. On 20th August a whole air division – the 288th IAD – equipped with the last batches of Yakovlev's machines was committed to action. Making use of the Yak-7B's advantages, the 4th IAP staffed with the most experienced pilots, shot down (according to pilot reports) 29 German aircraft, mostly Bf 109s, in the course of six days between 7th and 12th September for the loss of only nine machines.

The results scored by other regiments of the division proved to be more modest, with higher losses of their own. Commander of the 288th IAD Lieutenant-Colonel Konovalov was of the opinion that the Yak fighters of his formation were inferior in performance to German fighters. In his letter addressed to Stalin he noted that it was impossible to obtain under field conditions the characteristics obtained during tests at NII VVS, especially the maximum speeds stated in test reports. He asked that urgent measures be taken to ensure a real improvement of flight performance.

A commission was immediately sent to the division's regiments, establishing that the potential of the fighters was indeed not used to the full at the front. For the purpose of convenience the factors causing reduction of speeds were divided into two groups: those depending on the pilot and those outside the pilot's control. It transpired that many airmen flew their fighters in combat with the canopy hood open or even removed and with fully open radiator shutters; they piloted their machines at substantially lower engine speeds relative to the maximum revs (2,700 rpm) and so forth. Naturally, as a result the fighters flew at speeds that were 40 to 50 km/h (24.9 to 31 mph) slower than those indicated in the reports of military test pilots, and could not perform vertical manoeuvres energetically.

One of the factors classed as being outside the pilot's control was the indifferent attitude of the tech staff to the condition of the aircraft's external surface. Technicians cut various openings in the skinning of the engine cowling instead of carefully sealing all airframe joints. Poorly fitting wheel well doors, hatches and maintenance access covers (this was especially often the case after repairs in field conditions) led to a considerable increase of drag and, in consequence, to a reduction of speed.

Urgent work was undertaken on the 288th IAD so as to show the ground personnel how the Yaks should be properly maintained. One of the aircraft that had been repaired several times and had logged no fewer that 60 hours was 'treated' by specialists who eliminated some obvious causes for the reduction of speed. After this the machine showed at the hands of fighter pilot A. Zaitsev a speed of 495 km/h (308 mph) at sea level instead of 467 km/h (290 mph) before the improvements. The results were on hand. But time was required to make them available to all front-line units.

Yak-7 tactical reconnaissance aircraft

During the period described here the Yakovlev OKB concentrated its attention on perfecting the production machines. However, possibilities were found for creating new prototype versions. One of the results of such work was a reconnaissance fighter derived from the Yak-7B.

As far back as August 1941 two prototype aircraft had been built at Plant No. 301 in Moscow on instructions from Chief Designer A. Yakovlev. These were Yak-7s in a reconnaissance version, equipped with AFA-IM aerial cameras and an RSI-4 radio. At that time they were not ordered into production because of the acute need for the single-seat Yak-7 fighter.

The photo-reconnaissance version of the Yak-7B was essentially similar to the mentioned Yak-7 prototypes. It was intended for conducting reconnaissance from altitudes between 300 and 3,000 m (984 to 9,840 ft). A sample of aerial photography equipment was built at plant No. 82 in 1943; this plant also manufactured nearly three hundred Yak-7s fitted with aerial cameras.

Provision was made on the production Yak-7B fighters for a place with appropriate fittings for the installing the AFA-IM camera and its mount. Therefore, conversion of the fighter for photographic reconnaissance missions could be effected by front-line units in field conditions in accordance with the technical manuals that went with the aircraft.

Yak-7-37 fighter

The Yak-7-37 was an important derivative of the Yak-7B M-105PA fighter, obtained by replacing the standard 20-mm ShVAK cannon with a 37-mm cannon designed by Boris Shpital'nyy. Installation of this weapon had previously undergone development on the LaGG-3.

With a weight of fire reaching 4.15 kg/sec (9.15 lb/sec), the Yak-7-37 packed a considerably greater punch than all other known fighters that were taking part in combat activities.

In connection with the installation of the new armament some changes had to be introduced into the design of the Yak-7. The cockpit was moved 400 mm (15.6 in) aft and the rear cockpit was deleted in order to provide accommodation for the cannon's breech in the engine bay and to preserve the CG within acceptable limits. The size of the modified fighter's tailwheel was increased. To reduce the danger of entering a spin at low speeds

Left: The Yak-7-37 was a derivative of the Yak-7B armed with a 37-mm Shpital'nyy Sh-37 cannon firing through the propeller hub. The long barrel of the Sh-37 is noteworthy in this view.

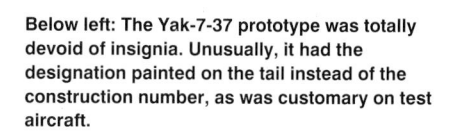

Below left: The Yak-7-37 prototype was totally devoid of insignia. Unusually, it had the designation painted on the tail instead of the construction number, as was customary on test aircraft.

Below: The engine of the Yak-7-37 with the cowling removed, showing the ammunition box of the Sh-37 cannon nestling between the cylinder banks.

and critical angles of attack, the Yak-7-37 was fitted with slats.

Following brief trials conducted in April-May 1942, the decision was taken to build a small batch of Yak-7-37s, since the type was of some interest for the Red Army's Air Force. In August 1942 a batch of 22 Yak-7-37s featuring no slats was built in Novosibirsk; these machines were sent for operational trials to the 42nd IAP at the North-Western Front.

In 12 group air battles in which Yak-7-37s participated, ten enemy aircraft were shot down at the cost of four own machines lost and another three damaged. The MPSh-37 cannon (*motornaya pushka Shpitahl'novo* – Shpital'nyy engine-mounted cannon) proved to be a reliable weapon. A shell hitting an enemy aircraft's fuel tanks caused an explosion, and a hit in the wing would tear a hole measuring more than one square metre (10.6 sq ft). Scoring a hit with just one shell was usually enough to destroy the enemy aircraft.

Fragmentation/incendiary or armour-piercing/incendiary/tracer shells with an initial speed of 900 m/sec (2,950 ft/sec) made it possible to effectively engage not only aerial targets but also ground targets (armoured vehicles, light tanks) and even small ships. The tests were pronounced a success, and Yakovlev decided to continue the work on installing the 37-mm cannon between the cylinder banks on a fighter of improved design.

Yak-7 M-82 fighter prototype

The Yak-7 M-82 occupies a special place among among the purely experimental versions of the Yak fighter. It was one of the first programmes for perfecting the aircraft which was initiated as far back as August 1941. Yakovlev OKB documents show that the work on the installation of the Shvetsov-designed M-82 nine-cylinder radial (which was very popular in the Soviet Union at the beginning of the war) was undertaken largely for research purposes and was necessary for Yakovlev in the same degree as for other designers (for example, Semyon A. Lavochkin, Artyom I. Mikoyan, Mikhail I. Goodkov and others. This was due primarily to the fact that Yakovlev's designs were relatively lightweight and could also forthwith be successfully operated with the liquid-cooled M-105 engines.

When the design work on the Yak-7 M-82 commenced, the fighter was expected to possess the following basic performance characteristics: a maximum speed at sea level of 515 km/h (320 mph) with the engine boosted; a speed of 615 km/h (382 mph) at the rated altitude of 6,400 m (20,990 ft); a climb time to 5,000 m (16,400 ft) of 5.5 minutes. This performance could enable the machine to compete comfortably with other Yakovlevs, as well as Lavochkin fighters. However, when the firm's chief test pilot Pavel Ya. Fedrovi began flight tests of the new fighter, it became clear that the machine was a failure.

The M-82 engines that were available to the OKB were from the first batches; they had many production flaws and, in consequence, were plagued by malfunctions. Four engines had to be replaced successively on the aircraft during the tests. Still, it proved impossible to ensure satisfactory engine operation at the second supercharger speed.

Besides, the expected speed increase failed to materialise. Tests revealed that top speed at sea level was only 501 km/h (311 mph), ie, much lower than the estimated figure. This was mainly due to a discrepancy between the propeller diameter and the engine power. The mainwheel legs were too short to allow a propeller of the required diameter (3.2 m/10 ft 6 in) to be installed, and the fighter barely avoided scraping the surface of the airfield with the propeller blade tips when a propeller of 2.8 m (9 ft 2 in) diameter was installed.

Development of the Yak-7 M-82 was discontinued in May 1942.

Yak-7PD high-altitude fighter prototype

Development of the Yak-7PD represented a sequel to the work initiated in 1940 when the I-28 (Yak-5) was designed. This time it was not a new-build prototype but rather a conversion of a production airframe which was mated to an experimental M-105PD engine. The latter featured the E-100 supercharger designed by V. Dollezhal'; the supercharger was developed at TsIAM (*Tsentrahl'nyy institoot aviatsionnovo motorostroyeniya* – the Central Aero-Engine Institute). At the same time, in the late summer of 1942, the Yakovlev OKB fitted an airframe of the 22nd batch with an improved carburettor air intake, concurrently modifying the upper fuselage decking and the cockpit canopy in a manner similar to the Yak-1 with improved visibility; a bulletproof windscreen and a rear bulletproof glass panel were installed and some other alterations introduced. To make the airframe as lightweight as possible, the fighter's armament was restricted to one 20-mm ShVAK cannon. Bearing in mind the low probability of a second firing pass against an aerial target at altitudes close to the practical ceiling, this armament's weight of fire was clearly inadequate, but a choice had to be made between the aircraft's high-altitude performance and the capabilities of its armament. The Yak-7PD's service ceiling reached 11,300 m (37,064 ft) and was superior to that of all Soviet production fighters at the time (in 1942 the MiG-3 was no longer in production). The flight performance of the Yak-7PD could have been much higher if it had been provided with automatic, not manual, control of the turbocouplings (ie, control of the supercharger's first stage speed).

The lack of automatic turbocoupling control made operation of the aircraft more complicated: the pilot was compelled to constantly make corrections in the speed of the supercharger's impeller, which distracted his attention from piloting the aircraft.

Besides, the pilot was physically unable to maintain the nominal value of the supercharging pressure in accordance with the change in the atmospheric pressure; as a result, the aircraft's performance inevitably suffered.

In October-November 1942 the Yak-7PD was still used for development work on a device for automatically controlling the turbocouplings, but positive results could not be obtained at the time. The work on the M-105PD engine was continued at a later stage.

Yak-7V two-seat conversion training fighter

At the end of 1941 Plant No. 153 completely switched to production of fighters, and soon the resulting replenishment of the Red Army's Air Force with first-class fighters had a noticeable effect on its combat capabilities. However, the output of fighter trainers was halted completely. It must be recalled that the Yak-7UTI was the only such type in series production since the beginning of the war. In the middle of 1942 the Yak-7UTIs, produced in small numbers, were already fairly worn out. Directorate of combat training of the Soviet Air Force repeatedly urged upon the People's Commissar of the Aircraft Industry the need for creating an aircraft that would serve for transition from the Polikarpov U-2 or the Yakovlev UT-2 to a real fighter.

The Yak-7V (*vyvoznoy*; this adjective was the Soviet term for familiarisation trainers at the time) filled this role. Development of this version was conducted at the end of 1941, making use of operational experience gained with the Yak-7UTI. As distinct from its predecessor, the undercarriage of the Yak-7V was non-retractable; this lessened the wear and tear on the undercarriage and precluded the possibility of the mainwheel legs collapsing because of malfunctions or the trainee's mistakes. Now, in contrast to the 'combat' Yak-7s, the mainwheel legs were mounted strictly vertically (when seen from the front, that is) and the wheel rotation planes were not canted outwards. This measure also simplified production of the machines. The Yak-7V was stripped of all armament, hence the upper decking of the engine cowling had no recesses for the machine-gun barrel. The Yak-7V proved to be a simple, reliable and rugged aircraft; it could perform nearly all aerobatic

Above and below: Two views of the Yak-7 M-82 prototype during manufacturer's flight tests. The bulky radial engine ruined the sleek lines of the fighter, giving it a rather tubby and overweight appearance.

The Yak-7 M-82 nearing completion at the Yakovlev OKB's experimental shop (plant No. 115).

manoeuvres. When the output of the Yak-7Vs reached 510 machines by the end of 1943, the command came to the conclusion that the needs of the Air Force had been fully met. Further production of machines of this type was stopped; however, shortly before the termination of hostilities 87 Yak-7Bs were converted into fighter trainers at the Air Force's repair shops.

The Yak-7 is gradually supplanted in service by the Yak-9

Work on perfecting the Yak-7B went on unabated in the middle of the war. This was all the more necessary since the Luftwaffe began re-equipping with the Bf 109G-2, 'G-4 and 'G-6 which offered improved performance. In the winter of 1942-1943 it proved possible to achieve a better quality standard of series-built machines. Tests of a Novosibirsk-built Yak-7B from the 25th batch revealed that its maximum speeds were 22 to 25 km/h (13.7 to 15.5 mph) higher than those of machines from the 22nd batch at all altitudes thanks to a considerable improvement in production methods achieved in December 1942. The vertical manoeuvrability of combat machines was also improved.

Outstanding results were achieved when the OKB, LII and NII VVS jointly undertook an improvement programme on Yak-7B c/n 3101. The following improvements were incorporated in this fighter: the radio antenna was stowed inside the fuselage and the aerial mast was deleted; the leading edges of the wings and tail surfaces were given a polish; ejector exhaust stubs were installed in accordance with TsAGI recommendations; all airframe joints were carefully sealed; wheel well doors and maintenance access panels were made more tightly fitting, and a fully retractable tailwheel was introduced.

Furthermore, numerous other measures were taken, each of which afforded a speed increment of one to two km/h (0.6 to 1.2 mph). As a result, the fighter attained 547 km/h (340 mph) at sea level and 615 km/h (382 mph) at 4,000 m (13,120 ft); no other Yak fighter had shown such high results before – or showed them later, with the exception of the Yak-3 versions. The Bf 109 and the Fw 190 showed lower speeds at low and medium altitudes.

The quality of Moscow-built fighters proved to be much worse. They were 25 to 30 km/h (15.5 to 18.6 mph) slower than the Novosibirsk-built machines, had high control stick forces and were more sluggish when performing different manoeuvres. When a Moscow-built Yak-7B (c/n 820936) had been tested by NII VVS, the test report stated: 'It is necessary to ask the People's Commissar of Aircraft Industry Comrade Shakhoorin to point out the inadmissibility of manufacturing aircraft with low performance characteristics and to demand that all the defects noted be eliminated within the shortest tome possible.'

In the meantime, improvement of the fighter's airframe continued – from the end of 1942 onwards the Yak-9 (the subject of the next chapter) was series-produced on a mass scale. However, production of the Yak-7B had to be continued due to the shortage of duralumin from which the wing spars of the Yak-9 were manufactured. In the meantime, some features characteristic of the Yak-9's external appearance were incorporated into the design of the Yak-7B. Thus, beginning with the 40th batch of Plant No. 153 and the 12th batch of Plant No. 82, the upper decking of the rear fuselage of the Yak-7B was cut down and a tear-drop canopy provided with an emergency jettisoning system was fitted.

When the 157th and the 728th IAPs had taken delivery of new Yak-7Bs (aircraft from batches 39 to 41 of Plant No. 153, in both 'razorback' and 'bubbletop' versions, to use the analogy with the Republic P-47 Thunderbolt), the pilots noticed considerable discrepancies in the maximum speeds of different machines. As it transpired, this was due to differences in the machines' production standard and to differences in the nominal power of their engines. Liberal oil spillage from breathers during flight at maximum speeds, uneven fuel consumption from the port and starboard groups of fuel tanks, insufficient range of radio communication and various

Above: The Yak-7 M-82 with virtually every panel open for inspection. Note that the cowling design is patterned on that of the Polikarpov I-185 and Lavochkin La-7, with a large one-piece cowling panel on each side rather than a two-piece folding panel as on the Polikarpov I-180 and La-5.

The Yak-7PD was a high-altitude interceptor version with a turbocharged engine. These examples were operated by one of the PVO units defending Moscow.

defects that hampered the maintenance of the fighters led to the conclusion: the results of the checkout tests were unsatisfactory.

In the late spring of 1943 dozens of Yak-7Bs were completely put out of action in the 7th Air Army which was operating at the Karelian Front. As it turned out, the large amount of water resulting from the melting of snow on the airfields and freezing again at night led to the emergence of a mixture of dirt, ice and water. This mixture clogged the Yaks' radiators, which led to overheating of the engines, with frequent forced belly landings as a result.

Even more disturbing were the cases when the skinning of Yak fighters was torn off in flight. Such facts had been noted earlier: four Yak-7Bs had crashed in the period between June and October 1942. In the spring of the following year the number of accidents and incidents sharply increased due to breaches of the prescribed techniques of bonding the wing structure and to the use of substitutes of various chemical substances. Hero of the Soviet Union F. Arkhipenko, who had shot down 30 German aircraft during the war, recalled:

'In April 1943 we were moved to the town of Novokuznetsk (Penza Region) where the 13th ZAP was deployed. Here replenishments were being trained for front-line units; squadrons equipped with Yak-7Bs (we dubbed them 'hunchbacks' for the characteristic outline of their rear upper decking) were formed and sent to the front.

The Yak-7Bs were delivered in crates from Novosibirsk to Novokuznetsk by rail, reassembled and test-flown. I tested approximately 20 Yaks, one of which caught fire in mid-air, but I managed to land on the airfield. Before that, in another regiment, one of the fighters burst into flames right after take-off and the pilot was killed'.

In spite of the frequently voiced complaints concerning the Yaks, they were well liked by pilots. There were many cases when these machines displayed high combat sur-

Above and below: The prototype of the Yak-7V conversion trainer (c/n 1570) on skis during winter trials. The trainer could be distinguished from the combat versions by the glazed rear cockpit and the non-retractable main gear struts with no doors.

Above: A production Yak-7V (c/n 0266) during checkout trials at NII VVS.
Below: A winter-camouflaged Yak-7UTI trainer with retractable landing gear at a frontline airstrip.

vivability. For example, during the Belgorod operation in July 1943 on one Yak-7B the spar of the starboard wing was pierced by a shell and a portion of the skin measuring one square metre (10.6 sq ft) was torn off. On another occasion a direct hit by two shells destroyed 70% of the front spar flanges in the most stressed part of the wing; on a third aircraft the fabric skin of the fuselage was torn off and the compressed air system was damaged. All three aircraft belonging to the same unit (the 483th IAP) returned to base and made safe landings.

As the battles at the Kursk Bulge began, the frontline aviation fighter element had exactly 400 Yak-7Bs out of the 2,809 red-starred fighters in its inventory. By comparison, it may be mentioned that by the beginning of the counteroffensive near Stalingrad 351 out of the 1,646 fighters available were of the Yak-7B type. At that time especially many machines of that type were assigned to the Reserve Air Corps of the Supreme Command – before the start of wide-scale production of the Yak-9 and the La-5, the Yak-7B was considered to be among the best fighters of the Red Army Air Force.

Plant No. 153 continued manufacturing Yak-7Bs till the end of 1943, and Plant No. 83 did so till July 1944. At the end of 1943, after having studied 13 machines produced in Novosibirsk, a team of test pilots and engineers from LII stated that the all-up weights of these machines were practically identical and were of the order of 3,000 kg (6,615 lb). Deviations of up to 15 kg (33 lb) from this figure were due to the presence or absence of bulletproof windscreens and to insignificant differences in production processes. The maximum speeds of the Yak-7Bs showed more marked differences, amounting sometimes to 20 km/h (12.4 mph); this was due primarily to differences in the rated altitudes of the engines installed. Efforts designed to bring the quality of Moscow-produced fighters to the required level proved unsuccessful – on average, Yaks from Plant No. 82 were 30 kg (66 lb) heavier and 15 km/h (9.3 mph) slower than sister aircraft manufactured by Plant No. 153.

In all, the four production factories (Nos. 21, 82, 153 and 301) delivered 6,399 Yak-7s of different versions to the Air Force; of these, 5,210 were Yak-7Bs powered by the more powerful M-105PF engines. Yak-7 production at Plant No. 82 ended with the 28th batch, while the 50th batch was the last at Plant No. 153. In the final batches of this type built in Novosibirsk, several dozen in every batch consisting of 100 machines were fitted with direction finders, landing lights and undercarriage position indicators; they were produced specially for service in the PVO units.

262 Yak-7Bs remained on strength in the 36th, 106th, 126th and other Air Divisions of the PVO system by the end of 1944; they continued to be operated fairly intensively. Thus, on 20th December PVO fighters of the Northern Front made 23 individual sorties to disrupt the work of German reconnaissance aircraft that were taking aerial pictures of important railroad stretches used for bringing supplies to the troops of the Baltic and Belorussian Fronts; 383th IAP pilots Gaznia and Rozhnenko intercepted a Ju 88 near Wysokie Mazowieckie and shot it down. On 7th January 1945 the Yaks of the 126th Air Division began redeployment to the cape of Khersones near Yalta on the Crimea Peninsula where preparations were made for the holding of a conference of leaders of the three powers of the anti-Hitler coalition – the USSR, the USA and Great Britain.

The role played by the Yak-7 in the frontline aviation at that time was somewhat more modest. According to reports from different Air Armies, by 1st January 1945 sixty-five fighters of this type were engaged in operations against the Luftwaffe (60 combat-ready machines at the Leningrad Front, 1st Baltic, 1st Belorussian and 1st Ukrainian Fronts) and 14 reconnaissance machines (all of them airworthy; of these, 13 at the 1st Baltic Front). By the beginning of 1945 combat losses amounted to 1,373 Yak-7s, about 1,500 machines were written off as damaged or worn out, while others continued their service in the units deployed in the rear and in training units.

Yak-7 propulsion testbeds with DM-4S boosters

One of the unusual tasks tackled by the Yakovlev OKB was the construction of a flying testbed intended for the flight development of the experimental DM-4S ramjet engines designed by I. A. Merkoolov. The DM-4S had a diameter of 500 mm (1 ft 7.7 in.), measured 2,300 mm (7 ft 6.5 in.) in length and weighed 45 kg (99 lb); two such engines were suspended under the fighter's wings, one under each outer wing panel. They ran on gasoline fed from the machine's standard fuel tanks.

The DM-4S engine was designed in 1941; this was the version that was flight-tested on the I-15*bis* and I-153 fighters before the war. After a period of bench tests two such engines manufactured at the beginning of 1942 were mounted under the wings of a UTI-26 operated by the 12th Guards IAP. In the spring of 1942 the frontlines rolled back some distance to the west from Moscow; this made it possible to perform test flights without the risk of being intercepted by the Messerschmitts.

The testing proved abortive: installation of the engines led to a significant forward shift of the CG, entailing the risk of the aircraft nosing over. Furthermore, no special measures were effected on the fighter trainer to prevent a fire onboard, and vibrations caused frequent leakage of fuel tanks. The flights had to be suspended for almost two years.

In the middle of the war information started coming in about experiments with auxiliary powerplants conducted both by our allies and our adversaries. For example, the British performed many experiments with shipborne aircraft, while the Germans made use of jettisonable solid-fuel rocket boosters to assist the take-off of overweight bombers from small field airstrips.

In early 1944 certain alterations were introduced into the design of the DM-4S engine with a view to enhancing its reliability. The engines were mounted under the wings of a production Yak-7B; a seat for the test engineer was fitted in the second cockpit. The tests were conducted at LII, starting on 24th March 1944; on 15th May project test pilot Sergey N. Anokhin switched on the ramjets in flight for the first time.

The boosters guzzled up to 18 to 20 kg (44 lb) of gasoline per minute; therefore, the auxiliary powerplant could be put into operation only for shorts spells of time, for example, to break off an engagement or to chase the adversary. The flights revealed that the increase of maximum speed when the ramjets were switched off amounted to 53 km/h (32.9 mph) versus 22 and 42 km/h (13.6 and 26.0 mph) in the case of the I-15*bis* and I-153

Above: A summer-camouflaged Yak-7V on a snow-covered airfield. The aircraft was probably operated by a reserve regiment or flying school far away from the frontlines.

The cockpits of a Yak-7V or Yak-7UTI trainer.

This Yak-7B was used as a testbed for the DM-4S ramjets (it is often called Yak-7PVRD).

A four-view drawing of a Yak-7B fighter

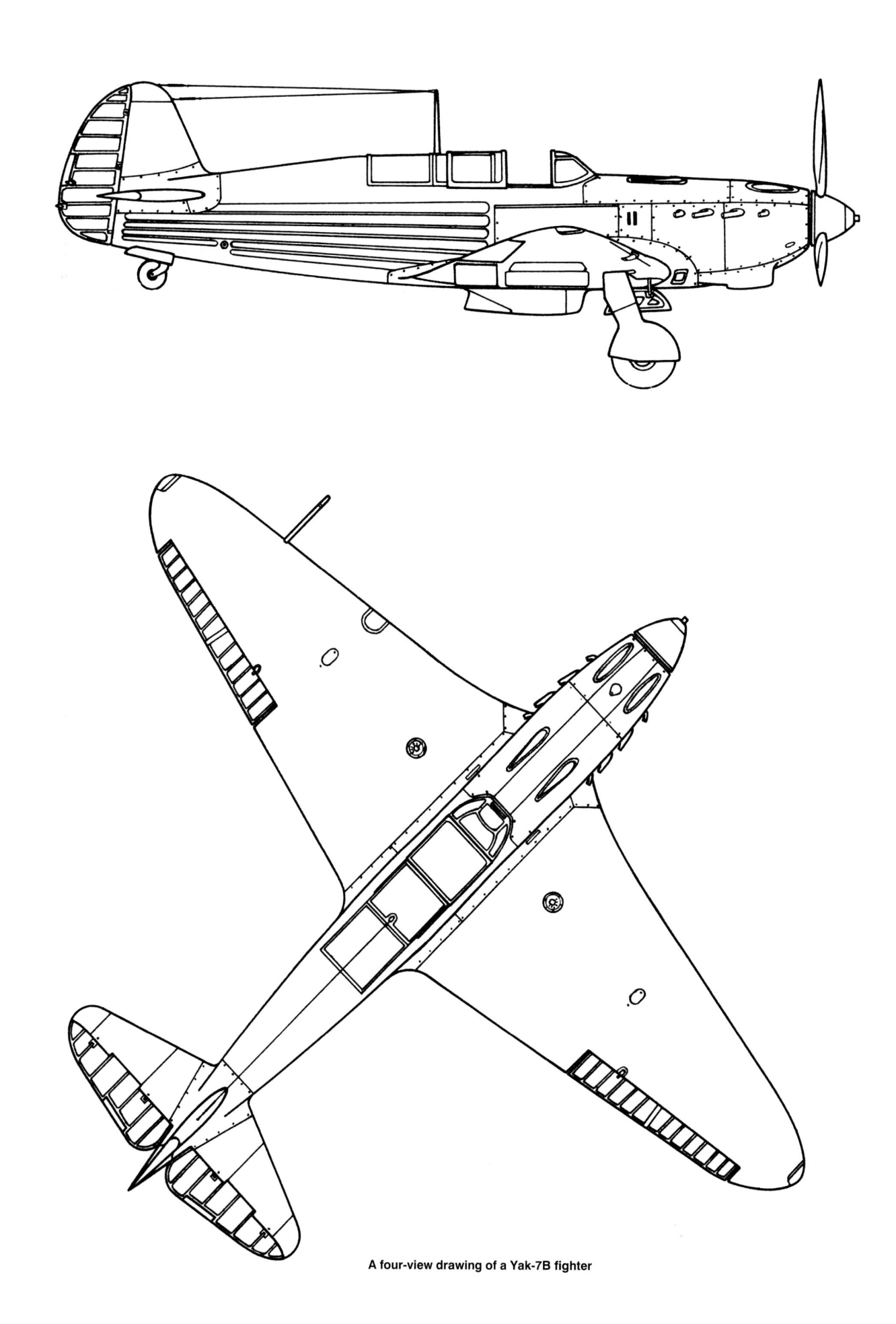

59

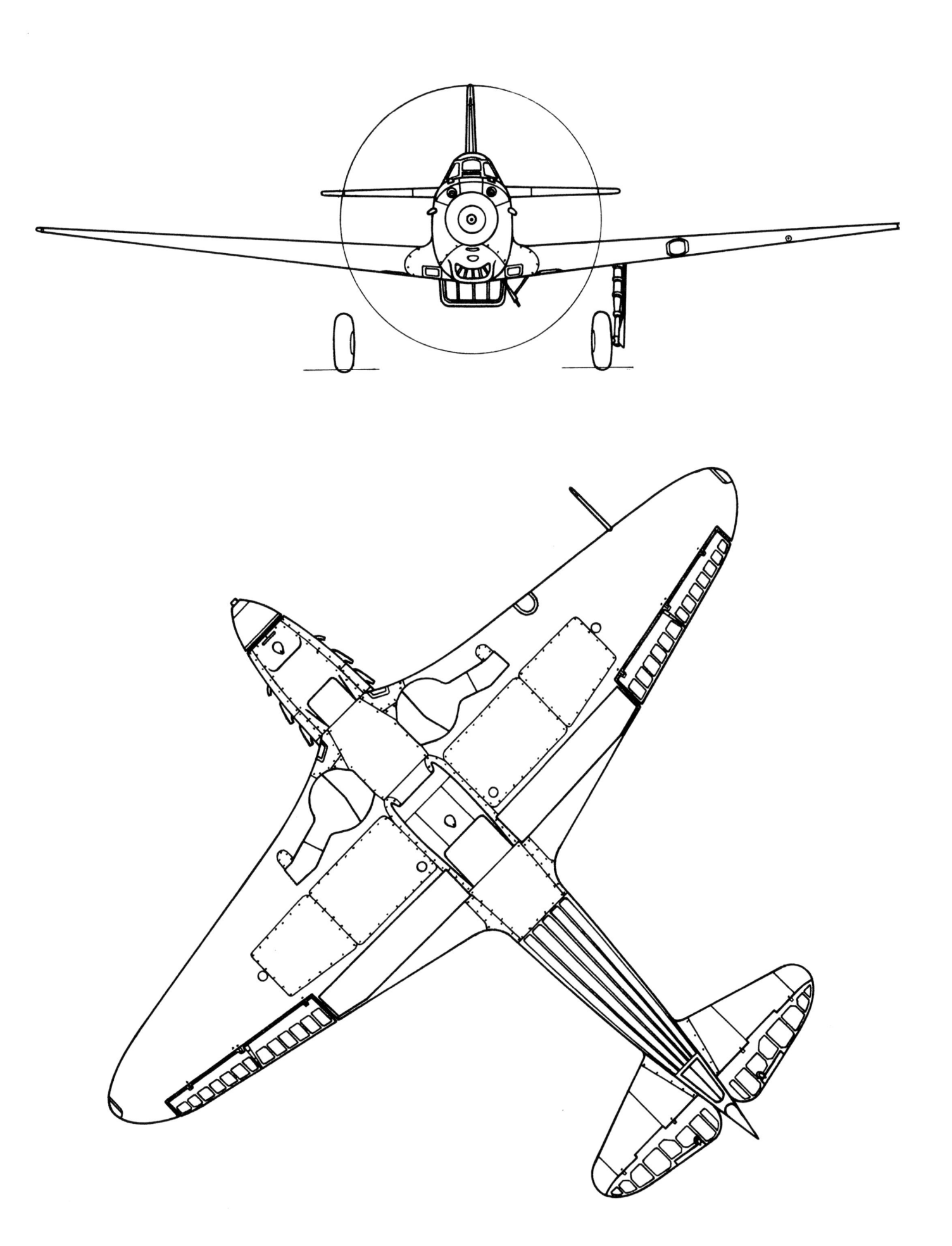

**Above: A Yak-7B development aircraft with a pressurised cockpit; note the non-standard sliding canopy.
Below: Another Yak-7 equipped with a pressurised cockpit of a different design. Judging by the black-outlined insignia, this was an earlier version (compare with the white-outlined stars on the other Yak).**

respectively. However, owing to the considerable additional drag of the wings and the massive hollow cylinders attached to them the net speed increase was only 19 km/h (11.8 mph).

These results were found to be disappointing. The work went on until the end of 1944. It encompassed the development of boosted modes of ramjet operation, installation of the ramjets in an aerodynamically refined airframe, making the booster engines easily detachable etc. Calculations showed that a maximum speed increase could be as high as 100 km/h (62 mph) in the course of 10 seconds, but it proved impossible to corroborate these estimates by real test results.

Nevertheless, several interceptor projects were evolved at the end of the war. One of them, designated Yak-7R (*reaktivnyy* – jet-powered) envisaged an aircraft featuring a combined powerplant which comprised two Merkoolov DM-4S ramjets and one D-1A liquid-fuel rocket motor designed by L. S. Dooshkin.

The DM-4S boosters were placed under the wings in the same way as on the previous model, and the D-1A was accommodated in the aft fuselage. The latter installation was intended for brief use at take-off and for imparting the maximum acceleration. The liquid-fuel rocket engine used petrol as a fuel and nitric acid as an oxidiser; this necessitated radical changes in the fuel system. Three additional tanks (two for petrol and one for the acid) were accommodated behind the cockpit. The project had a special feature – it dispensed with the installation of a piston engine.

Design work on the Yak-7R was completed on 27th August 1942. Many designers, including Yakovlev, were aware of the potential advantages of the ramjets and liquid-fuel rocket engines, but the enemy had forced its way to Stalingrad and the main effort was concentrated on series production. Besides, the flights of the rocket-powered BI fighter designed under V. Bolkhovitinov's direction (accompanied by several major accidents) showed that no reliable jet or rocket engines suitable for immediate installation in an aircraft were available in the USSR at the time. The experienced gained in designing the Yak-7R was used later for developing the Yak-3RD.

Subsequently the Yak-7 was probably used more extensively than any other Yakovlev fighters for numerous factory and field modifications. The former are exemplified by the development of the Yak-7L fighter with a laminar-flow wing which afforded a maximum speed increase of 15 to 20 km/h (9.3 to 12.4 mph) thanks to the use of low-drag airfoil sections, and of the Yak-7GK (*ghermeticheskaya kabina* – air-tight cockpit) with a bag-type pressurised cockpit.

Among the latter versions was the Yak-7P (***pushechnyy*** – cannon-armed) featuring heavier armament which was installed in the workshops of the 1st Air Army in July 1943 and comprised two ShVAK synchronised cannon in the manner of the La-5 instead of the two UBS machine-guns; another version of the fighter was fitted with a special hook for towing assault gliders.

The Yak-7L development aircraft with laminar-flow wings, seen here in front of one of LII's hangars.

Chapter 3

The Yak-9

The Private of the Skies

The Yak-9 aircraft that followed the Yak-1 and Yak-7 was the third basic type of the Yakovlev fighter family associated with the period of the Great Patriotic War. Structurally it was a further development of the Yak-7. Outwardly the Yak-9 differed little from its predecessor, yet it featured a host of improvements. This was natural because the design of this aircraft embodied the great experience of manufacture and combat operation of the Yak-7 and was backed up by the possibility of a wider use of duralumin which no longer was so scarce in the Soviet Union as had been the case at the beginning of the war. The use of metal made it possible to reduce the airframe weight substantially. This weight saving was used for increasing the fuel capacity; alternatively, it could be used for installing heavier armament or for fitting various items of equipment.

Of all fighter types operated by the Red Army Air Force, the Yak-9 was built in the greatest numbers. In mid-1944 the aggregate number of Yak-9s, Yak-9Ts and Yak-9Ds surpassed the number of fighters of other types in the inventory of front-line units, and they largely supplanted the Yak-1, Yak-7B and LaGG-3, to say nothing of the MiG-3s (which had been manufactured in 1941) and the Polikarpov fighters built before the war.

The main special feature of the Yak-9 was its ability to be modified into a great variety of aircraft types intended for different duties and operational uses. These included a front-line fighter with normal and heavy armament; a long-range escort fighter; a fighter-bomber; a photo-reconnaissance fighter; a high-altitude interceptor; a two-seat unarmed passenger aircraft for special duties; and a two-seat conversion training and familiarisation fighter.

This basic type had 22 (!) main variants, including 15 production versions. The Yak-9 featured the installation of five different new engines or engine versions; six variants with regard to the number and capacity of fuel tanks; seven variants of armament and two variants of special equipment.

The Yak-9 was series-produced at three major aircraft factories – Plant No. 82 in Moscow (only the M-107A-powered version), Plant No. 166 in Omsk and Plant No. 153 in Novosibirsk. The production tempo at the latter enterprise reached 17 machines per day in mid-1944. In all, no fewer than 16,769 machines were built, including the 14,579 manufactured before the end of the war.

Yak-7D and Yak-7DI prototype fighters

The Yak-9's predecessor was the Yak-7D. In the late spring of 1942 A. S. Yakovlev tasked engineer N. K. Skrzhinskiy with developing a Yak-7 version intended for use as a long-range reconnaissance aircraft to suit the needs of the Air Force's fighter element. Built in May 1942, the aircraft made use of the fuselage of a production Yak-7V conversion trainer combined with elements of the Yak-7B. A novel feature of the design was the experimental wings which differed greatly from all the wing types built earlier. The wings' framework was formed by two continuous full-span duralumin spars joined together by six duralumin ribs and two wooden ribs (the latter were placed at wingtips). The framework was covered with skinning made of properly shaped bakelite plywood and veneer which was bonded to the structure. While retaining the same area of 17.15 sq m (184.6 sq ft), the wings had a shorter span – 9.74 m (31 ft 11.46 in) instead of 10.0 m (32 ft 9.7 in) – and more angular tips introduced with a view to eventually fitting leading-edge slats at a later stage. Eight fuel tanks with a total capacity of 833

Above: The Yak-7D, the first step towards the Yak-9. It is seen here in single-seat configuration.

The same aircraft in two-seat configuration.

61

Above and below: The Yak-7Di featuring a cut-back rear fuselage decking and a bubble canopy was, in effect, the prototype of the Yak-9.

litres (183.26 Imp gal) were neatly 'squeezed' into the wings; a further 92 litres (20.24 Imp gal) of fuel were housed in the fuselage. The Yak-7D was unequalled in range and endurance, covering a distance of 2,285 km (1,420 miles) in the course of six and a half hours.

In mid-June 1942, when Yak-7D development work was in full swing, A. S. Yakovlev issued directions requiring the machine to be reworked into a long-range fighter. The result was the Yak-7DI (*dahl'niy istrebitel'* – long-range fighter). In fact, it was the fuselage of a production M-105PF-powered Yak-7B mated to the experimental wings of the Yak-7D. But this time the wing housed only four self-sealing tanks with a total capacity of 673 litres (148 Imp gal), or 500 kg (1,102 lb).

The Yak-7DI had its upper rear decking cut down and the cockpit canopy was given a tear-drop shape. The starboard UBS machine-gun was deleted for the sake of further reducing airframe weight. This subsequently became a 'trademark' recognition feature of the 'nine' – the starboard heavy machine-gun was not installed on any of the Yak-9 versions powered by the M-105PF engine.

An important novel feature employed on the Yak-7D consisted in all four fuel tanks being connected with a single service tank via check valves; this ensured uniform and complete consumption of fuel from the port and starboard groups of tanks – something which had not been possible on the Yak-1 and Yak-7.

The designers envisaged the possibility of the Yak-7DI being operated in two basic versions – the standard and the lightened one. In the latter case a 200-kg (441-lb) weight saving was achieved by reducing the amount of fuel and oil carried. In standard configuration the all-up weight reached 3,035 kg (6,692 lb) and the Yak-7DI possessed basic performance characteristics similar to those of the production Yak-7B manufactured in the summer and autumn of 1942, except that the range was appreciably greater. In this version the aircraft turned into a long-range fighter capable of lengthy patrolling, escorting bombers to the full stretch of their combat radius and fulfilling other missions that required the machine to stay airborne for a long time. In the lightened version the all-up weight was only 2,835 kg (6,251 lb), and the Yak-7DI became easy and tractable in handling, displaying very good manoeuvrability at low and medium altitudes. In mock combat with the Bf 109F conducted close to the ground the Yak-7DI gained an extra 250 m (820 ft) of altitude in a combat turn as compared to its opponent, fastening itself on the Messerschmitt's tail after three to four full-circle banking turns.

After a short stage of development work at the factory the Yak-7DI successfully passed State trials in August 1942. Leading engineer A. Stepanets wrote in his report that *'...thanks to the possibility of being operated in various versions and its excellent performance the Yak-7DI arguably ranks first among our country's production fighters'*. It was recommended that the Yak-7DI be put into series production as quickly as possible. The aircraft industry implemented this recommendation without delay. In production the fighter was allocated the designation Yak-9.

Yak-9 production fighter

Initially Plant No. 153 in Novosibirsk built the fighter in the lightened Yak-7DI version, deleting the two extra fuel tanks in the wing. The all-up weight rose by 35 to 40 kg (77.2 to 88.2 lb) compared to the prototype, which was due to the usually lower quality standard characteristic for mass production, but production machines suffered no deterioration in performance. The tests of the first production Yak-9s showed that the fighter had retained its excellent agility which enabled it to outmanoeuvre any adversary.

Plant No. 153 began manufacturing the Yak-9 from October 1942, when the workers assembled the first 16 machines (together with 290 Yak-7Bs). Production was getting under way successfully – the military representatives at the Plant accepted 15 Yak-9s. Subsequently, however, serious difficulties were encountered in the manufacture of the wings: of the 44 Yak-9s built in the course of the two following months, only four machines could be sent to the front-line units before the end of the year.

Three new production fighters were delivered to the 434th IAP in the middle of November 1942. The Yak-9s were committed to combat actions for the first time during the Soviet counteroffensive near Stalingrad in the second half of December 1942. Approximately at the same time a flight of Yak-9s was assigned to the 1st Air Army of the Western Front, but inclement weather prevented the machines from being actively used before the end of the year.

One machine (c/n 0118, ie, Batch 1, 18th aircraft in the batch) was transferred to NII VVS. The Yak-9 successfully passed tests there during February and March 1943. At the weight of 2,870 kg the fighter attained the speed of 520 km/h (323 mph) at sea level and

599 km/h (372 mph) at the second rated altitude of 4,300 m (14,104 ft). Only 5.1 minutes were needed to climb to 5,000 m (16,400 ft). Other important performance characteristics of the machine were equally impressive: it had a service ceiling of 11,100 m (36,408 ft); a full-circle banking turn at 1,000 m (3,280 ft) took 16 to 17 seconds and the aircraft gained 1,120 m (3,674 ft) of altitude in a combat turn. For the first time a Soviet production fighter was virtually equal to the contemporary Messerschmitts in vertical manoeuvrability while being superior to them in ease of handling and horizontal manoeuvrability. Importantly, the improvement of performance was achieved without resorting to such radical measures as installation of a new engine.

Interestingly, the testing of Yak-9 c/n 0118 was not confined to determining its basic performance characteristics. Along with that, tests were made to determine the airfield performance, the range at different engine operation modes, the gliding characteristics and even the engine's acceleration time in accordance with procedures adopted in the USSR. It was revealed that Yakovlev's new machine took more time to accelerate from cruising speed to a speed close to the maximum compared to the Yak-1 and the Bf 109G-2; on the other hand, it could be decelerated more quickly.

At the beginning of 1943 assembly of the Yak-9 was initiated at Plant No. 166 in Omsk which had halted its work on the Tu-2 bomber. The fighters of the first batch had a number of production defects, but already from the second batch onwards the Plant's personnel, assisted by engineers from the Yakovlev OKB, achieved considerable success in improving the manufacturing quality. During tests conducted at LII NKAP (Flight Research Institute of the People's Commissariat of the Aircraft Industry) and completed in April 1943, Yak-9 c/n 1102014 (Product 11, Batch 2, 14th aircraft in the batch), weighing 2,840 kg (5,822 lb), attained a speed of 539 km/h at sea level and 577 km/h at 3,810 m (12,497 ft); it climbed to 5,000 m (16,400 m) within five minutes flat. Consequently, in most parameters this machine was on a par with similar machines built in Novosibirsk.

In January and February 1943 Plant No. 166 turned out 61 Yak-9s. A total of 135 such machines were built in the first quarter of that year, and the number of those accepted by the military representatives was even higher (140). Most of the 'nines' went to reserve regiments and training centres where these machines were assigned primarily to air formations of the Supreme Command's Reserve. Despite all the advantages of the Yak-9, series production of this type in its original form did not last long. This was due to the emergence of three versions developed by

Above and below: The fourth production Yak-9 (c/n 0104) during manufacturer's flight tests.

the Yakovlev OKB at the end of 1942; two of them subsequently became the mainstay versions. They supplanted the Yak-9 (without a suffix letter, also known as 'the Yak-9 with two fuel tanks and standard armament'), which by that time had been built in numbers nearing 500.

At the beginning of 1943 the Yak-9, like other Yakovlev-designed fighters, was plagued by numerous cases of the wing skin warping or even breaking away in flight, which frequently led to tragic results. This was mainly due to such reasons as breaches of bonding techniques in the wing manufacture, the use of substitutes of various chemical substances (this refers primarily to the production of Plant No. 153) and considerable fluctuations in the ambient temperature and humidity within twenty-four hours. The skinning was successfully reinforced on most of the fighters by July of that year.

M-106-powered Yak-9 prototype
Along with machines intended for large-scale production, the Yakovlev OKB built some experimental fighters based on the Yak-9.

One of the first such versions was the M-106-powered Yak-9 (Yak-9 M-106). Installation of the M-106 engine with a single-speed supercharger was effected in the same way as on the similarly powered version of the Yak-1. The machine was built as a *dooblyor* (literally, 'understudy', or second prototype, in the Soviet terminology of the time) of the Yak-7DI by mid-November 1942; shortly thereafter Pavel Fedrovi performed the maiden flight. Prior to the installation of the new engine the Yak-9 M-106 had passed operational tests, performing more that 1,000 different aerobatic figures and making 500 landings. Yet no signs of permanent deformation were noted on the fighter.

Tests of this aircraft at NII VVS showed that a speed of 602 km/h (374 mph) was attained at 3,250 m (10,662 ft), accompanied by an improvement in rate of climb and take-off performance compared to the standard Yak-9. The Yak-9 M-106 demonstrated its ascendancy in mock combat with the Bf 109G-2/R6, an example of which had been captured near Stalingrad. Test pilots noted that the Yak fighter was much more respon-

Above and below: Yak-9 c/n 0118 at NII VVS during State acceptance trials. Note the new three-tone grey camouflage, a departure from the dark green/black scheme used hitherto.

A Yak-9 fitted experimentally with an M-106-1sk engine. This one appears to have the dark green/black camouflage scheme.

sive to the controls compared to the overweight Messerschmitt; in consequence, a well-trained pilot on the Yak-9 had a better chance of imposing his will on the adversary in combat. The cockpit of the Soviet fighter afforded a considerably better view, especially in the rear hemisphere. At the same time the Yak-9 was clearly inferior to its opponent in firepower and performance at high altitudes.

The Government demanded that the Yak-9 M-106 be urgently put into large-scale production. One of the telegrams sent to Novosibirsk and addressed to director Lisitsyn stated: *'You are supposed to regard switching completely to the production of the M-106P-powered Yak-9 fighters as your most important task for the first quarter of 1943 and to ensure the completion of 176 such machines.'* Huge resources were committed for the implementation of this task. Still, the immaturity of the M-106 engine prevented this machine from being put into series production in Novosibirsk, just like the Saratov factory had failed to master production of the Yak-1 M-106.

Yak-9T production fighter

It was the Yak-9T (*tahnkovyy*, tank-busting) that became the first mass-produced version of the Yak-9. It differed from the prototype and the initial production Yak-9 in having the 20-mm (0.78-in.) ShVAK cannon replaced by the 37-mm (1.45-in.) 11P-37 cannon developed by the OKB-16 design bureau (subsequently it was redesignated NS-37). Design work on this weapon was conducted in 1941-1942 by a group of engineers under the direction of A. Nudel'man and A. Sooranov. They continued the work on the development of a large-calibre aircraft cannon initiated by Yakov Taubin and M. Baboorin. By the time when it attracted A. Yakovlev's attention the 11P-37 cannon had successfully passed bench tests and a trial installation on the LaGG-3 fighter. In similar fashion to the LaGG-3, it was mounted between the cylinder banks with the barrel passing through the propeller hub; the cannon was attached at two points: to the engine and to the airframe. The barrel protruded 160 mm (6.29 in) from the propeller spinner, which led to an increase of the fighter's length from 8.50 m (27 ft 11 in) to 8.66 m (28 ft 5 in).

The installation of a big and heavy 37-mm cannon weighing 150 kg (331 lb) necessitated the introduction of a number of substantial changes into the design of the Yak-9. The fuselage structure was reinforced. To provide space for the cannon breach and to keep the CG within acceptable limits the cockpit was moved 400 mm (1 ft 3.74 in) aft. This led to a marginal improvement in rearward visibility and made the fighter more manoeuvrable.

The potent 37-mm cannon made it imperative for the staff of the Novosibirsk plant to raise the fighter's production standard. This was a matter of prime concern because the N-37's considerable recoil force (about 5,500 kg/12,127 lb) caused piping joints to leak and some elements of the airframe structure to develop fatigue cracks and fail.

The Yakovlev OKB built the Yak-9T prototype in January 1943; the aircraft passed special tests at the Aviation Armament Firing Range in February 1943 (L. Los' was the leading engineer) and flight testing at NII VVS in March of that year, with A. Stepanets as leading engineer. With an all-up weight of 3,025 kg (6,670 lb) the Yak-9T attained a speed of 533 km/h (331 mph) at sea level and 597 km/h at 3,930 m. Manoeuvrability remained good, a full-circle turn being performed within 18 to 19 seconds and 1,100 m (3,608 ft) of altitude being gained during a combat turn. Immediately, in the same month of March, the Yak-9T was put into series production. The Government demanded that a fighter regiment be fully equipped with the Yak-9T fighters by the middle of March. In actual fact, three aircraft were built by the end of March; another 75 machines with the heavy cannon rolled off the assembly line in April. Shortly thereupon the monthly output reached approximately one hundred Yak-9Ts.

34 Yak-9Ts were used in combat evaluation tests conducted at the Central Front in the 16th Air Army in the period between 5th July and 6th August 1943 during the battle of Kursk. According to official Soviet information, almost a half of the 110 enemy aircraft destroyed there were shot down by Yak-9Ts (the rest was accounted for by Yak-1s, Yak-7Bs and Yak-9s). Own losses amounted to 12 Yak-9Ts, or a third of all the Yak fighters lost. On average, only 31 rounds of the NS-37 cannon were needed for the destruction of one enemy aircraft, while the corresponding figure for the 20-mm ShVAK cannon was 147 rounds.

The appearance of the Yak-9T at the front had a strong psychological effect on enemy aircrews. Until then, for example, the highly survivable and heavily armed Fw 190A had willingly undertaken head-on attacks against Soviet fighters. When the Yak-9T came into wide-spread use, the Fw 190As began to avoid head-on attacks.

The installation of the 37-mm cannon made it possible to substantially increase the distance at which fire could be opened. This proved very important because thereby the probability of the pilot being hit by return fire from the enemy bomber or reconnaissance aircraft was reduced. The fighter pilots could effectively use this weapon against twin-engined aircraft at a distance of 500 to 600 m (1,640 to 1,968 ft); in the case of enemy fight-

Above: The experimental Yak-9-37 armed with a 37-mm cannon firing through the propeller hub.
Below: As this side view shows, the 37-mm cannon required the cockpit to be moved aft for CG reasons. These pictures were taken during the aircraft's State acceptance trials.

Above and below: The prototype of the Yak-9T production-standard 'tank killer' version (c/n 0108) during State acceptance trials.

Above and below: The open upper cowling of the Yak-9T, showing the ammunition boxes and belt feed mechanisms of the NS-37 and 20-mm ShVAK cannons.

ers being the target this distance did not exceed 400 m (1,308 ft). But if the purpose was to disrupt the enemy bombers' formation, it was possible to open fire at a distance of 1,000 to 1,200 m (3,208 to 3,936 ft), providing the ammunition included fragmentation shells with distance fuses. Effective use of the Yak-9's heavy armament was severely hampered by the imperfect design of gunsights and the limited ammunition supply.

A pilot flying the Yak-9T was expected to fire his weapon only after aiming it carefully, and then only in short bursts of one or two rounds, three at the most. Firing long bursts meant spending ammunition to no avail (the fighter had only 30 to 32 37-mm rounds on board) because the strong recoil of the cannon caused the fighter to drop its nose and lose alignment with the target after a few shots, and the pilot had to take aim anew.

Of course the stability of flight when firing the N-37 depended on the speed of flight and on the length of the burst: the greater the speed and the shorter the burst, the less was the influence of the cannon on the direction of flight. Lieutenant-Colonel Shinkarenko, Commander of the 42nd IAP of the 240th Air Division, noted that the Yak-9T was appreciably more stable during firing than the LaGG-3-37 which had been flown by his unit earlier.

As deliveries to front-line units increased, the Yak-9T came to be widely used and earned high praise from the flying personnel. As of 1st July 1943, only 14 machines out of the 153 Yak-9s in the front-line aviation had the 37-mm cannon, but shortly thereafter the 'tank-busting fighter' became one of the main types in the fighter element of the Soviet aviation – in all, 2,748 Yak-9T aircraft were built before the end of the war. Expeditious mastering of this machine in production and operational use played an important part in helping Soviet airmen win air superiority.

For example, in the autumn of 1943 the Yak-9T was widely used during battles at the Smolensk direction. Massed actions of German aviation seriously hampered the efforts of the Red Army striving to mount an offensive at this direction; it was necessary to find a method of resolutely counteracting the enemy's big formations. The Soviet commanders were of the opinion that the Yak-9Ts were best suited for this purpose: their powerful armament could be put in action from big distances, and the fighters themselves, thanks to their performance, needed no protection against Messerschmitt and Focke-Wulf fighters.

When tackling this task, Soviet commanders and airmen encountered many difficulties. The only radar station available in the area often malfunctioned and could not ensure a timely warning of approaching large formations of enemy aircraft. Since German fighters were constantly patrolling the air, seeking targets of opportunity, it was necessary to chart the flight route in broken lines, so as to avoid being attacked by German 'hunters' and to be able themselves to deal a sudden blow.

Thus, on 4th September four Yak-9Ts from the 42nd IAP were conducting a search for enemy aircraft in the area of Smolensk where they discovered a group of up to 20 He 111s heading for Dookhovshchina. Earlier, Soviet airmen had closely watched the routines of the enemy aviation (aircraft from several airfields taking off, gathering into a joint formation and heading for the target). The group's leader, Lieutenant S. Brazhnets, made a surprise attack and downed one Heinkel, dispersing the rest of the formation. A bombing attack against Soviet troops was thereby frustrated.

When dealing with the events of 4th September, German sources paid the main attention to the success of one of the best aces of the Luftwaffe – *Kapitän* Walther Nowotny who shot down a Yak near Dookhovshchina (this was his 189th victory). For this success the commander of I/JG54 was awarded the *Eichenlaub* (oak leaves, a supplement to the Iron Cross). As for the engagement between the Soviet fighters and Heinkels, according to the reports of German crews, the II/KG4 group was attacked by Soviet anti-aircraft artillery. 37-mm shells tore large holes in the fuselage and wings of He 111H-16 WNr. 161284; the radio operator and the flight engineer were killed and the bomb-aimer was seriously wounded. The pilot managed to cross the front-line and make a crash-landing in German-held territory. After examining the wrecked machine the Germans could not imagine that the aircraft had been destroyed by shells from an aircraft cannon, not by anti-aircraft fire.

Yak-9D long-range fighter

Even more widespread was the Yak-9D (**dahl'***niy* – long-range) – another version of the production Yak-9 intended for large-scale production. This fighter featured as standard the fuel system borrowed from the prototype Yak-7DI. The installation of four fuel tanks holding a total of 650 litres (143 Imp gal)/480 kg(1,058 lb) instead of 440 litres (96.8 Imp gal)/320 kg (705 lb) on previous Yak-9 versions necessitated an increase in the amount of engine oil to 48 kg (109 lb).

The need for such a fighter arose in 1943 when Soviet ground troops began to undertake deep penetration of enemy defences. The rapid advance of the Red Army formations and the absence of prepared airfields ahead of them created the danger of the Soviet aviation losing contact with ground troops; the latter complained about not getting sufficient air cover.

The Yakovlev OKB built the Yak-9D prototype in January 1943; by the end of February 1943 the machine had passed State trials at NII VVS (pilot V. Golofastov, leading engineer I. Rabkin). The tests showed that the Yak-9D had the same maximum speed as the other Yak-9s. However, the increase in all-up weight to 3,117 kg (6,873 lb) resulted in poorer manoeuvrability: the fighter needed 19 to 20 seconds to perform a banking turn and 6.1 minutes to climb to 5,000 m (16,400 ft); it gained 950 m (3,116 ft) in altitude during a combat turn.

Like the Yak-9T, this aircraft was immediately placed into large-scale production. As had often been the case previously, the decision to build the first one hundred long-range fighters was taken before the State trials had even begun. All 100 Yak-9Ds were assembled before the end of the spring of 1943, whereupon the industry increased the output of such machines. It should be noted that, in its directive dated 18th February, the State Defence Committee had demanded that all fighters manufactured at Plant 153 be fitted forthwith with four fuel tanks.

The first Yak-9Ds were assigned to the 20th and 18th Guards Fighter Air Regiments. Both units joined battle actively on 12th July, after the beginning of the counteroffensive of Soviet troops against the German troops concentration near Oryol (during the air battles over the Kursk Bulge). Low clouds and long spells of heavy rain hampered the operational activities of aviation. When the clouds lifted somewhat, the Yaks mainly participated in providing cover for attack aircraft. The fighters flew at altitudes

The prototype of the Yak-9-23 fighter armed with an engine-mounted 23-mm cannon. The aircraft type is painted on the tail in lieu of the construction number.

Above and below: Two Yak-9Ds pictured during checkout trials at NII VVS. Judging by the style of the national insignia, the aircraft on the upper photo is a later example.

of 200 to 400 m (656 to 1,308 ft), and the pilots often returned to base on machines riddled with bullets and shell fragments.

For example, in the period between 12th and 27th July pilots of the 18th Guards IAP commanded by Hero of the Soviet Union Lieutenant-Colonel A. Golubov made 503 sorties (425 of them for the purpose of escorting Soviet attack aircraft) and waged 52 air battles in which only four Yak-9Ds were lost. The Soviet airmen claimed the destruction of 30 enemy aircraft; they got to know the strengths and weaknesses of the new Yaks very well. Therefore the command took a decision to conduct service tests for the operational use of the Yak-9D in this unit.

During operations over the Western Front in August-September 1943 the regiment had, apart from three Yak-9Ds, 12 'regular' Yak-9s on strength. All types of aircraft were uniformly distributed among the three squadrons and flew roughly the same type of combat missions. Many a sortie was made by the airmen of the 18th Guards IAP together with the 'Normandie-Niémen' squadron which was deployed close at hand and also made up part of the 303rd IAD. At the end of August the French unit operated six Yak-9Ds, three Yak-9s (with two fuel tanks) and 11 Yak-9Ts. The pilots of the 'Normandie-Niémen' squadron disapproved of having 'excess' fuel on board; at their own initiative they blanked off the fillers of outer wing fuel tanks, making it impossible to fill them with fuel, and made use only of the inboard fuel tanks.

In the course of service trials conducted in the 18th Guards IAP, 58 flights were performed on the three Yak-9Ds (each of them with an average duration of an hour and a quarter); the regiment's pilots conducted seven dogfights, claiming two Ju 87s, two Fw 190s and one He 111 shot down. Of the three own machines one was shot down by the enemy, another one was damaged and sent for repairs. On 30th August 1943, Yak-9D c/n 0415317 (ie, Batch 4, Plant No. 153, 17th aircraft in the batch) received the following damage in the course of a combat engagement with an Fw 190: a wing-root fuel tank was pierced by a cannon shell, the engine reduction gearbox casing was pierced by bullets and the fuselage was damaged in several places. Nevertheless, the pilot succeeded in bringing the machine back to base and landing safely, which testified to the high survivability of the 'nine' in its 'four-fuel-tank' version.

Combat experience showed that it was inexpedient to use Yak-9Ds jointly with 'regular' Yak-9s for fulfilling the same missions in fighter regiments where the vast majority of aircraft had the standard two fuel tanks and was unable of staying airborne for several hours due to the limited amount of fuel. For instance, in the 303rd IAD the Yak-9Ds used up an average 270 litres (59,4 Imp gal) of fuel, or about 40% of the available amount, in each sortie. The remaining fuel merely increased the weight of the aircraft and made it more vulnerable compared to other Yaks.

On one occasion, when the service trials had been completed, 18th Guards IAP CO Lieutenant-Colonel A. Golubov came under anti-aircraft fire during a reconnaissance sortie on a Yak-9D. Enemy shells hit the outer wing fuel tank, and the aircraft burst into flames. Seconds after the pilot bailed out at low altitude, the burning fighter exploded. The seriously wounded commander ended up in hospital.

Experience gained during service trials led to the conclusion that the Yak-9D would best be used for fulfilling special duties which could not be tackled by fighters carrying a limited amount of fuel (the Yak-1, Yak-7B and La-5).

Yak-9Ds were widely used for escorting bombers on missions deep into the enemy's rear areas; they provided cover for the actions of tank and mechanised infantry groups making incursions into the enemy's rear. They were also used for patrol flights of long duration. They proved useful in the cases of an abrupt change in weather conditions when returning to one's own airfield proved difficult and it was necessary to cover a considerable distance in order to reach an alternate airfield which, for example, was not blanked off by low clouds. Undoubtedly the Yak-9D would have been more useful, had it not been for the absence of navigation equipment (in particular, the artificial horizon and the direction finder) which limited the possibility of operations in adverse weather conditions. The full use of the machine's potential was also hampered by the discrepancy between the aircraft's range in high-speed flight mode (905 km/562 miles) and the range of two-way radio communication with the ground (about 60 km/37.3 miles); in the course of virtually the entire flight the pilot could not receive assistance from a ground air control station.

In combat with the German Fw 190A-4 and Bf 109G-6 fighters the Yak-9D had an advantage in horizontal manoeuvrability at altitudes up to 3,500 m (11,480 ft), especially when some amount of fuel had been used up. However, the Soviet fighter was inferior to the enemy machines in speed, even at low altitude.

Large-scale production of the Yak-9D began in the summer of 1943. While the workers of Plant No. 153 conducted the assembly of 'four-tank' Yak-9Ds on one continuous flow line, the workers of another line built the two-fuel-tank Yak-9T. By the end of 1943 the Novosibirsk plant had built 706 long-range machines. In Omsk, 463 'four-tank' machines were built at Plant No.166; the plant started providing the fighters with extended fuel capacity from September of that year on.

A production Yak-9 taxies out from an unpaved airfield in the second half of the war, kicking up a local dust storm.

M-105PF-powered Yak-9 at the fronts in 1944

At the end of 1943 the first machines of the 9th batches of the Yak-9D and Yak-9T respectively were tested at LII NKAP. As might be expected, the former type proved to be somewhat heavier when fully equipped, the all-up weight being 3,070 kg (6,769 lb) and 3,025 kg (6,670 lb) respectively; the Yak-9D was a little slower, the speed at sea level being 526 km/h (327 mph) and 532 km/h (331 mph) respectively, and the speed at the second rated altitude being 577 and 591 km/h (359 and 367 mph) respectively. The rate of climb was virtually identical, the fighters climbing to 5,000 m (16,400 ft) in 5.6 and 5.5 minutes respectively. On the whole, that kind of performance could not satisfy the Red Army command on the eve of major offensive operations.

In consequence, a modified Yak-9D (c/n 08-05) was submitted to NII VVS for tests; it had an all-up weight of 3,117 kg (6,873 lb) and featured improved aerodynamics in accordance with recommendations from TsAGI. The tests were conducted under the supervi-

A happy Soviet Air Force pilot wearing fur-lined boots - a necessity in the harsh climate of the northern regions - poses for the camera on the wing of his Yak-9D.

Above and below: The prototype of the Yak-9TD which combined the Yak-9T's engine-mounted 37-mm cannon (and hence the aft location of the cockpit) with the increased fuel tankage of the Yak-9D. It is seen here during manufacturer's flight tests.

sion of leading engineer I. Rabkin. Flights performed by pilot V. Golofastov in January and February 1944 showed that the fighter had become 20km/h (12.4 mph) faster thanks to the sealing of fuselage and engine cowling joints, the generally improved finish of the wing surface and some other measures. The speed rose to 535 km/h (332 mph) at sea level and to 591 km/h (367 mph) at 3,650 m (11,972 ft), while other performance characteristics remained virtually unchanged: time to 5,000 (16,400 ft) was 6.1 minutes, a banking turn was performed within 19 to 20 seconds, the aircraft had a practical ceiling of 9,100 m (29,848 ft) and a landing speed of 141 km/h (87.6 mph).

In early 1944 the Soviet command gave up the practice of sending front-line units to the rear for reorganisation; therefore, the majority of the Yak-9s of different models were sent to replenish the losses of other Yaks directly in front-line conditions 'piecemeal', as it was usually termed. Thus, by 29th March 1944, the inventory of the 427th IAP was reduced to 19 Yak-1s after combat activities in the south of the Ukraine; at the beginning of April the regiment received 13 Yak-9Ds as attrition replacements. The pilots had barely taken delivery of these aircraft at the airfield of Bel'tsy when, as a result of a raid performed by a group of Focke-Wulf fighters, four machines were put out of action, including two Yak-9Ds (c/ns 0454 and 0972) that burned down. The remaining fighters participated actively in combat in the Yassy (Iasi) area where in the late spring of 1944 the German command undertook one of its last major counteroffensives supported by substantial Luftwaffe forces.

In the course of May 1944 combat loses amounted to six Yak-9s, one of which (c/n 0981), piloted by Lieutenant Shokoorov, was attacked and seriously damaged by a Soviet Air Force Bell P-39 Airacobra in a 'friendly fire' incident. Combat attrition in these fierce battles averaged one aircraft lost per 16 individual sorties. In its analysis of the air battle in the Yassy area the Soviet command did not criticise the performance characteristics of the aircraft, but admitted the low average level of training of the flying personnel and poor coordination of actions of aircraft groups in the course of a battle.

On the eve of the Soviet summer offensive in Belorussia (Operation *Bagration*, named after a famous Russian general who played a major part in defeating Napoleon Bonaparte in 1812) the Yak-9 fighters were assigned by way of replenishment not only to regiments and divisions, but also to Air Corps. For example, two Fighter Air Corps from the reserve of the Supreme Command were transferred to the 1st Air Army. By 20th June 1944 the 2nd IAK had 252 fighters in its inventory, including 81 Yak-9s; in the 3rd IAK the Yak-9s made up 116 of the total of 253 aircraft. From the first days of the operation these formations played an important role in ensuring complete air superiority for the Red Army Air Force.

The combat activities of Soviet airmen over Belorussia were conducted mainly in small groups; in contrast to that, during the L'vov offensive operation that started on 13th July 1944 the Soviet Air Force resorted to massed air strikes. The German opposition there appeared to be stronger, and a number of Yak-9-equipped air units and formations were waging continuous battles. The intensity of the fighting can be illustrated by examples of the activities of the 611th IAP which was part of the 8th ShAK (*shtoormovoy aviatsionnyy korpoos* – Attack Air Corps). On 16th July Lieutenant Yu. Panin was seriously wounded in a dogfight with a Bf 109 while escorting a group of attack aircraft. His comrades aided the profusely bleeding pilot in bringing the aircraft to the Ol'khovets airfield and making a landing. Having lost much blood, Panin could not even climb out of the cockpit – he lost consciousness, dying in hospital a few days later.

On 18th July Lieutenant P. Mordovskiy from the same unit made a landing on what might be termed the remnants of a Yak fighter: the fuselage framework was laid bare, large holes gaped in the stabilizer, and the port elevator had been stripped of its fabric skin. Additionally, a shell fragment punctured the compressed air piping to the flap actuators and wheel brakes; as a result, the Yak-9 made a landing run of some 850 m (2,788 ft) and overran the airstrip, stopping in a field of sunflowers. On the same day Lieutenant (Junior Grade) I. Mamaikin attempted to bring his damaged machine to base, but the fighter went out of control not far from the Ol'khovets airfield and crashed, killing the pilot.

In the period from 15th to 18th July 1944 the formations of the 2nd Air Army lost 16 of their own fighters in combat with enemy fighters in the area of L'vov; six fighters were lost to flak and 39 failed to return to base for unknown reasons . However, bearing in mind the high intensity of the fighting and the great number of combat engagements, on average it was one irretrievable loss per approximately 100 individual sorties, which was a pretty good result. 19 of the 61 fighters lost were Yak-9s.

In the second half of 1944 increasingly more often the Yak pilots had to deal not with the late-model Messerschmitts to which they had become accustomed, but with Focke-Wulfs which were also used by the Germans in the attack and fighter-bomber roles. Tests of the Fw 190A conducted in the Soviet Union seemed to support the view that this fighter was not a dangerous adversary for Yakovlev and Lavochkin fighters in air combat because of its overweight airframe. However, numerous encounters with the type showed that Soviet airmen could not get on the Fw 190's tail in a dogfight; nor had the red-starred machines an advantage in speed because the Focke-Wulf was equipped with a water/methanol injection system. On the other hand, it was believed that the Fw 190 had considerably better diving characteristics and gained speed quicker in a steep descent; yet, if the Yak-9 managed to chase the opponent, the latter was considerably less efficient in levelling off and the Soviet pilot had a good chance of shooting the enemy down.

Unfortunately, at times Soviet airmen fought not only against the Germans and their allies, but also against the British and American aviation as well. Such 'friendly fire' incidents occurred during the final stage of the war due to cases of poor co-ordination of actions. Thus, on 7th November 1944 a dozen Lockheed P-38 Lightnings mistakenly strafed the troops of the Soviet 37th Army in northern Yugoslavia; the casualties included General G. Kotov, commander of a Cavalry Corps. A group of Yak-9s from the 866th IAP was sent on an intercept mission; it was led by Captain A. Koldoonov on a Yak-3.

The American pilots mistook the Yaks for Bf 109Gs and engaged them. Before the melee could be stopped, two Yak-9s and three P-38s had been shot down; one more American machine and one more Soviet machine were hit by anti-aircraft artillery, but both pilots parachuted to safety. Investigating the incident, Commander of the 866th IAP Lieutenant-Colonel S. Koozin noted that, despite their bigger dimensions and substantial wing loading, the Lightnings had better horizontal manoeuvrability thanks to good high-lift devices and could easily get on the tail of the Yak-9s, while the latter enjoyed superiority in vertical manoeuvring.

Numerous statistical reports dating back to 1944 make it possible to cite a few figures characterising the service rendered by different versions of M-105PF-powered Yak-9 fighters. Of the 6,289 machines of this type

Above and below: The Yak-9M featured an aft-positioned cockpit la Yak-9T, even though it did not have the big cannon. This feature was introduced to ensure commonality between aircraft with different armament fits and simplify production at the Novosibirsk factory.

Another Yak-9 with an aft-positioned cockpit pictured during checkout tests at NII VVS.

manufactured in that year, nearly 5,000 were sent to active Air Force units. During the same time 1,754 Yak-9s were written off for various reasons. 141 Yak-9s were shot down in air-to-air combat, 94 fell prey to anti-aircraft fire, 787 failed to return from a combat sortie, 12 were destroyed on the ground, 454 were lost in

71

Another view of the same Yak-9M as shown on the preceding page.

fatal and non-fatal crashes and 266 were worn out completely. Thus, combat attrition of the Yak-9 amounted to 1,034 machines (the total combat losses of Yaks of all basic types being 3,571 aircraft). It can be noted that relative attrition of the Yak-9s was approximately one loss per 150 individual combat sorties, which was lower than that of the more refined Yak-3s or La-7s – that was due to the latter two types being used at those sectors of the front where the fighting was of greater intensity.

In the course of 1944 a number of substantial design changes were incorporated into the Yak-9 fighter on the production line. As an example, here are the upgrades effected on the Yak-9T:

• from the 11th batch (February 1944) onwards all machines were built with four tanks holding a total of 480 litres (105,6 Imp gal). When the 37-mm Nudel'man/Sooranov cannon was installed, the model was designated Yak-9TD;

• from the 13th batch (the end of March) onwards a two-way radio was fitted to all fighters, not to every second one as before;

• from the 14th batch (April) onwards a push-button control was introduced for the radio transmitter. The switch was located on the throttle lever, enabling the pilot to easily maintain two-way communication in the air while keeping his attention on flying the aircraft (who said the HOTAS [hands on throttle and stick] concept was new?);

• from the second half of the 14th batch (May) onwards a weight installed in the aft fuselage was deleted (it had been introduced at an early stage for CG reasons) and the wing design of the Yak-9D and the Yak-9T was standardised;

• from the 15th batch (June) onwards an emergency canopy jettisoning feature was introduced and dust filters were installed on the carburettor air intakes to ensure trouble-free operation from unpaved airfields;

• from the 16th batch (June) onwards the wire braces in the fuselage framework were altered, the wingtips were reshaped and the design of the identification lights was changed;

• provision was made on several machines of the 17th batch (end of July) for the installation of the RPK-10 direction finder (*rahdiopolukompas*), for which purpose a hatch with a plywood cover was made in the upper fuselage decking;

• from the 19th batch (September) onwards a pneumatic engine starting system based on recommendations from LII NKAP was introduced;

• from the 20th batch (October) onwards the Hucks starter dog intended for starting the engine by a truck-mounted starter was deleted and the spinner was give a more streamlined shape.

Yak-9M production fighter

The Yak-9 powered by the VK-105PF engine (as the M-105 was redesignated in the spring of 1944) was subjected to the most significant alterations during the manufacture of the 25th batch. The new fighter emerged as an upgrade of the Yak-9D, from which it differed mainly in having a fuselage patterned on the Yak-9T, ie, the cockpit was moved 400 mm (1 ft 4 in.) aft. This version designated Yak-9M (*modernizeerovannyy* – updated) was convenient in production, making it possible to standardise the design of the fuselages and use them for manufacturing either the Yak-9T or the Yak-9D, depending on the need.

Besides, on the Yak-9M the designers effected major changes and improvements intended to enhance combat efficiency and make the fighter easier to operate. In this version they succeeded in eliminating almost all the design and manufacturing defects which had been noted in various documents of the People's Commissariat of Aircraft Industry and the Air Force stating the nature of complaints, shortcomings, defects etc.

On this model a radical solution of the wing strength problem was achieved. The wings were strengthened by increasing the skin thickness, using bakelite plywood, increasing the area of bonding between the skin and the wing framework etc. As a result, the strength of the wings and fuselage was brought up to the specified level. Additionally, an automatic device for regulating the coolant temperature was introduced and all machines with even construction numbers were fitted with direction finders.

As regards fuel amount and armament, the Yak-9M differed little from the Yak-9D, whereas the location of the cockpit was identical to that of the Yak-9T. Moving the cockpit aft by 400 mm in comparison with the Yak-9D had practically no adverse effect on forward visibility; at the same time it was very useful in lessening the tendency to nose over. The Yak-9M did not differ from the Yak-9D and the Yak-9T with regard to piloting techniques and basic performance characteristics. It may be mentioned that this modification was effected directly at Plant No. 153 which was producing the Yak-9D and Yak-9T. The designation Yak-9M was allocated to all Yak-9 aircraft from the 25th batch onwards.

The ground personnel had their fair share of problems. Engineer N. Alimov from the 288th Fighter Air Division recalled: *'Our regiments were equipped with the Yak-1, Yak-1B, Yak-7B and various versions of the Yak-9. These machines were basically similar and the differences between them were of no special significance for the pilots. As for the technical personnel, the presence of different types in the same unit seriously hampered the preparation of fighters for combat sorties.'* After all, interchangeability of the most essential units and parts could not be ensured even on machines manufactured at the same factory. Now, with the advent of the Yak-9M, a certain degree of unification with other machines was achieved.

The first production Yak-9M underwent State trials at NII VVS in December 1944, with V. Ivanov as project test pilot and engineer G. Sedov in charge of the testing. At a weight of 3,095 kg (6,824 lb) the fighter attained a speed of only 528 km/h (285.4 mph) at sea level and 573 km/h (356 mph) at 3,750 m (12,300 ft). The rate of climb and manoeuvrability characteristics proved to be similar to those of other Yak-9s with the same all-up weight. Such performance could not be considered satisfactory for the end of 1944. Suffice it to say that the Yak-9M was some

50 km/h (31 mph) slower than a production Yak-3; it was also inferior to contemporary Focke-Wulf and Messerschmitt fighters.

The Yak-9M was built in series at Plant No. 153 from May 1944 until June 1945, up to the moment when production of the Yak-9U powered by the VK-107A engine got under way there. The production run totalled 4,239 aircraft. In October 1944, when VK-105PF-2 engines (the -2 stands for 'boosted for the second time') with a take-off rating of 1,290 hp became available to Plant No. 153, Yak-9Ms began rolling off the production line with this more powerful engine. Until then, the entire output of the VK-105PF-2 had been reserved for installation on the Yak-3.

To get an idea of how the various Yak-9 versions, above all the Yak-9M, performed in actual service, one can cite the example of the 8th IAK (Fighter Air Corps) commanded by General A. Osipenko. The fighter corps included the 323rd Fighter Air Division, all the three regiments of which (the 149th, 269th and 484th IAPs) fought only on the Yak-9s. In the course of the first four months of 1945 the abovesaid units performed 5,537 individual sorties, providing close air support to ground troops and escorting attack aircraft and bombers to targets near Gdynia, Danzig (Gdansk) and Stettin (Szczecin). On average, the Yak-9s stayed airborne for 55 minutes, spending less than half the available amount of fuel. Combat attrition averaged one Yak-9 lost per every 131 individual sorties; 42 fighters and 25 pilots were lost as a result of enemy opposition.

Yak-9P and Yak-9TK fighter prototypes

The next area on which the Yakovlev OKB concentrated was the Yak-9's armament which needed to be reinforced. On one aircraft the designers installed a synchronised Shpital'nyy/Vladimirov ShVAK-20 (SP-20) cannon with 175 rounds instead of the standard synchronised 12.7-mm UBS machine-gun with 200 rounds. This did not entail any major modifications.

The performance of the new fighter designated Yak-9P (*pushechnyy* – cannon-armed) remained unchanged, while the weight of fire increased by 25% as compared to the Yak-9. The aircraft was regarded favourably by the specialists of NII VVS. Firing the synchronised cannon, as well as the synchronised machine-gun, through the propeller disk was quite safe and the armament functioned reliably in all flight modes, regardless of the aircraft's attitude. Initially the Government envisaged building 100 Yak-9Ps. In fact, however, this model never entered production because of the decision to reinforce the armament of the Yak-9 by using cannons of even greater calibre (for example, 37 and 45 mm).

These efforts resulted in the emergence of the Yak-9TK. It was intended specially for trial installation of different hub-mounted cannons. For the first time the possibility was provided to install alternative cannon types, depending on the demands of the Air Force: the 20-mm (0.78-in.) ShVAK, the 23-mm (0.9-in.) Volkov/Yartsev VYa, the 37-mm (1.45-in.) Nudel'man/Sooranov NS-37 or the 45-mm (1.78-in.) NS-45. The weight of fire in these cases was 1.997, 2.71, 3.74 and 4.07 kg (4.4, 5.97, 8.25 and 8.97 lb) respectively. To mount an alternative armament version, it was necessary merely to replace the attachment fittings and ammunition feed devices suited to other types of rounds. Importantly, replacement of the weapon could be effected in field conditions by the front-line units' personnel.

Pilot V. Khomiakov and armament engineer A. Aronov who conducted the flight testing of the Yak-9TK in October 1943 came to the conclusion that the all-up weight, CG position, piloting techniques and performance depended wholly on the type of cannon armament installed.

When the ShVAK and VYa cannons were fired, their recoil had virtually no effect on the machine's behaviour, even at low speed. Firing the NS-37 had a more noticeable influence on piloting. At indicated airspeeds of 300 to 350 km/h (186 to 218 mph) the Yak-9TK rocked violently and accurate sighting was possible only during the first shot. Finally, firing the NS-45 cannon proved possible only in single shots at speeds close to the maximum.

Yak-9K production fighter

Versatile installations of cannon armament found employment on the Yak-9 at a later stage when the Yak-9U powered by the M-107A (VK-107A) engine was launched into

The Yak-9TK development aircraft which incorporated provisions for installing engine-mounted cannons of various calibres. Here it is seen with a 20-mm cannon; this configuration was also known as the Yak-9T-20, hence the designation on the tail.

Above and below: Yak-9T c/n 0121 was converted into the prototype of the Yak-9K armed with a 45-mm NS-45 engine-mounted cannon. The large muzzle brake of the cannon was the chief recognition feature of this version.

The Nudel'man/Sooranov NS-45 was a potent weapon, allowing the Yak-9K to be used effectively against enemy tanks.

mass production. Nevertheless, at the end of the war the NS-45 cannon attracted the attention of test pilots and engineers impressed by its exceptional capabilities. The work on the installation of this cannon on a fighter was continued on a machine which received the designation Yak-9K (*kroopnokalibernyy* – large-calibre). In this machine the designers took into account the main peculiarity of the NS-45 cannon installation – the thin walls of its barrel and the very small radial gap between the cannon barrel and the hollow shaft of the engine gearbox, the shaft's bore measuring merely 55 mm (2.16 in).

The recoil power of the 45-mm cannon exceeded that of the 37-mm cannon by 40%; to reduce it, the barrel was fitted for the first time with a big muzzle brake which absorbed 85% of the recoil energy. The muzzle brake protruded noticeably from the propeller spinner, due to which the overall length of the Yak-9K was 8.87 m (29 ft 1.21 in) as compared to 8.66 m (28 ft 4.94 in) of the Yak-9T and 8.50 m (27 ft 10.64 in) of the usual Yak-9.

The NS-45 had a continuous belt feed, like that of the NS-37. It had an ammunition supply of 29 rounds, a counter in the pilot's cockpit showing the number of the remaining rounds. As regards the salvo weight, the Yak-9K was superior to all Soviet fighters and the majority of foreign fighters. Only such 'flying artillery batteries' as the Fw 190A-6/R1 or the Bf 109G-6/R6 boasted heavier armament. But these two fighters had two or even four cannons mounted under the wings, which led to a substantial deterioration of performance and handling, while the Yak-9K was little different from basic versions of the Yak-9: its all-up weight was only 3,028 kg (6,677 lb).

The Yak-9K was completed by the Yakovlev OKB at the end of 1943; from the beginning of the following year it underwent State trials at NII VVS. Building on the results of these tests, a batch of 53 machines was manufactured for the Air Force. Almost all of them were assigned to the 3rd Fighter Air Corps commanded by Lieutenant-General Yevgeniy Ya. Savitskiy. These powerful fighters went into action for the first time in mid-August 1944, when German bombers (against which the Yak-9Ks were primarily intended to be pitted) had virtually ceased their activities on the Eastern front, their role being taken over by fighter-bombers – Fw 190s and, less frequently, Bf 109s.

In consequence, a considerable percentage of the Yak-9K sorties was accounted for by ground attack missions. One well-aimed 45-mm shell was usually enough to set a truck, a wooden house, an enemy locomotive and other similar targets ablaze. Major A. Nikashin from the 812th IAP, a participant of service trials, defined the tactics of combatting enemy aircraft on the Yak-9K in the following way:

'Yak-9 fighters should be used in cooperation with Yak-3 lightweight fighters (they will be described in the next chapter – author's note) *making up a cover group. Tangling with fighters is undesirable for the Yak-9Ks because they are heavy and, owing to the insufficient engine power, have poor vertical component* (ie, poor vertical manoeuvrability – author). *When bombers are encountered, the Yak-9K fighters should make a surprise attack from behind the clouds or out of the sun, trying to disrupt their formation. It is expedient to make the first attack from above at a distance of 400 to 600 m (1,308 to 1,968 ft). If any part of a bomber is hit by one or two shells, this is enough for the bomber to be destroyed.'*

Pilots reported that the Yak's airframe could withstand a lot of punishment. One of the Yak-9Ks was hit by numerous shells from a 20-mm Oerlikon cannon; in addition, it lost a piece of skinning measuring nearly a square metre (some ten sq inches). Despite this serious damage, the Yak-9K covered a distance of more than 100 km (62 miles) and safely landed at its unit's airfield.

Alongside with the merits, some shortcomings of the Yak-9K were also noted. The powerful recoil of the NS-45 cannon seriously affected the aircraft's structure and caused leakage of water and oil through various seals and cracks in piping, radiators etc. The insufficient reliability of the cannon prevented the Yak-9K from entering large-scale production. Subsequently this work was continued with the improved Nudel'man-designed N-45 cannon – its development was carried out on the Yak-9U.

Yak-9B fighter-bomber

Limited production was undertaken of a version designated Yak-9B (*bombardirovshchik* – bomber). Bearing the factory designation Yak-9L, it was a modified production Yak-9D. The modification consisted in fitting four bomb bays behind the cockpit (in the space previously occupied by the rear cockpit on the Yak-7). The four bomb bays were arranged in two pairs, one after the other, and could house either four 100-kg (220-lb) FAB-100 bombs or four cassettes with small PTAB-2.5-1.5 anti-armour bomblets weighing about 2 kg (4,4 lb) each. The cannon and machine-gun armament was identical to that of the Yak-9D.

The addition of bomb bays made it possible to considerably extend the range of combat missions performed by the 'nine'. Without bombs the Yak-9B could be used as a tactical fighter; with bombs it became a high-speed fighter-bomber intended for pinpoint attacks against well-protected targets.

For CG reasons and out of concern for the longitudinal static stability the bomb load had to be restricted to 200 kg (441 lb). In this configuration the all-up weight reached 3,356 kg (7,400 lb), and the aircraft could be flown by pilots possessing satisfactory piloting skills. A bomb load of 300 to 400 kg (661 to 882 lb) was considered to be an overload configuration. Only highly-skilled pilots were permitted to fly the Yak-9B with such a bomb load, and then only in special circumstances.

The Yakovlev OKB managed to convert the tactical fighter into a fighter-bomber fairly quickly – by March 1944 the Yak-9B was prepared for flight testing and subsequent thorough evaluation. State trials were conducted in four stages and lasted throughout the summer of 1944. The aircraft's stability and handling characteristics were determined and spinning trials were conducted during this period.

Above and below: A production Yak-9K. Note the badge of the 3rd IAP which operated this particular aircraft (a winged sword piercing a swastika).

One of the prototypes of the Yak-9L fighter-bomber pictured during manufacturer's flight tests.

After that, Plant No. 153 manufactured a batch of 109 Yak-9Bs. The aircraft were delivered primarily to the 130th IAD commanded by Colonel F. Shinkarenko in the autumn of 1944. Two of its regiments (the 168th and 909th IAPs) were equipped with Yak-9Bs, while the newly formed 409th IAP received Yak-9D and Yak-9M fighters. Already in the course of preparations for combat activities several serious incidents occurred in the units, the aircraft catching fire in mid-air. It turned out that production defects in the manufacture of engine valve cotter pins led to the their failure due to engine vibration, the failure

75

Above: A Yak-9L at NII VVS during State acceptance trials.

Above: Another Yak-9L (c/n 0975), also photographed at NII VVS.

A production Yak-9B. Outwardly the fighter-bomber version differed from the Yak-9D in having a lengthened and reshaped rear canopy section associated with the provision of a bomb bay aft of the pilot's seat.

resulting in a fire. At that time workforce at aircraft factories consisted largely of women and teenagers who did not always observe the stringent technical requirements.

The type was committed to action for the first time on 22nd October 1944 when 53 Yak-9Bs provided escort for attack aircraft of the 311th ShAP (*shtoormovoy aviatseeonnyy polk* – Attack Air Regiment) in the area of Gumbinnen and themselves attacked the targets that were discovered. At the end of December in the course of one sortie 120 Yaks from the 130th IAD took off on a mission; they encountered no visible opposition, yet two machines were downed and three were damaged (including the aircraft piloted by Il'ya Shinkarenko, the Commander's brother). Later it transpired that the small PTAB bombs loaded into the bomb bays had collided in the air after being dropped, exploding under the aircraft. In the course of combat activities up to 20th February 1945 the Yaks performed nearly 2,500 individual sorties on attack and bombing missions. According to information from Soviet sources, they succeeded in destroying 29 tanks, 11 armoured personnel carriers, more than 1,000 soft-skinned vehicles and many enemy depots and trains.

Despite these impressive results, the Yak-9B was adjudged as unsatisfactory on the basis of the service tests. The absence of a special sight for precision bombing prevented the Red Army Air Force from getting an efficient fighter-bomber, and many pilots noted that the bombed-up Yak-9B was difficult to fly. Much vexation was caused by the bombs refusing to leave the bomb bays when

Top and above: A 100-kg (220-lb) FAB-100 HE bomb leaves the bomb bay of a Yak-9B. The open bomb bay doors aft of the radiator bath are clearly visible. Curiously, the tailwheel is extended in the lower photo.

Right: Despite the relatively small size of the Yak-9B's airframe, the capacity of its bomb bay was surprisingly large, as shown by this photo. Here the aircraft disgorges a load of 2-kg (4.4-lb) PTAB shaped-charge armour-piercing bomblets. In Soviet Air Force slang these munitions were dubbed *kapoostka* (little cabbage) because the smoke puffs created by them resembles a head of cabbage when seen from the air.

Top and above: A highly decorated example of the Yak-9B undergoing evaluation with the 130th Bomber Division. The aircraft wears the Guards badge on the nose and a red lightning bolt along the rudder trailing edge; the white fuselage band is highly unusual.

Left: Loading the bombs into the Yak-9B was rather tricky; the rear canopy section had to be detached and the bombs hoisted into the sloping guide tubes by means of a hand-driven winch.

Top: Self-inflicted injuries. This Yak-9B was extensively damaged on the ground when its bomb load detonated spontaneously, tearing open the rear fuselage.

Above: The 45-mm cannon of the Yak-9K was a deadly weapon. This photo shows the wreckage of a German aircraft with a hole torn in the fuselage side by a 45-mm shell.

Right: The Yak-9B's bomb bay seen from above, with two of the four FAB-100 bombs that could be carried by the aircraft peeping through holes in the upper stiffener of the bomb bay. Note the cables controlling the bomb release mechanisms

Above and below: Yak-9 c/n 0989 was effectively the prototype of the Yak-9DD long-range escort fighter. It is seen here at NII VVS during State acceptance trials.

A production Yak-9DD undergoing State acceptance trials. The taller aerial mast aft of the cockpit and the additional short aerial mast atop the fin were the main identification features of this version.

dropped in a shallow dive, as well as by difficulties in loading the bombs on board the aircraft. Besides, fighter pilots lacked precision bombing skills, since they were not specially trained for bombing missions.

Marshal A. Novikov, commander of the Red Army's Air Force, considered it necessary to write when approving the report on the service tests: 'The Yak-9B aircraft is suitable only for very limited combat use; it is inexpedient to issue it to front-line units. The flying personnel flies this type of aircraft very reluctantly. It is necessary to ask the designer to improve the aircraft.' After this appraisal further work on the machine was abandoned.

Yak-9DD long-range escort fighter

Yet another version of the Yak-9 was the Yak-9DD (DD stands for *dahl'nevo deystviya* – long-range, the factory designation being Yak-9Yu). It embodied the concept initiated by the Yak-7D – creating a fighter with still greater range. The work was undertaken in response to a requirement for a fighter with a range exceeding 2,000 km (1,243 miles) issued in 1944. The special feature of the Yak-9DD was the wings which incorporated eight metal fuel tanks and featured strengthened ribs. The fuel amount totalling 845 litres (186 Imp gal)/630 kg (1,390 lb) enabled the fighter to cover a distance of 1,325 km (768 miles) in high-speed flight mode and attain a range of 2,285 km (1,420 miles) in economic cruise.

The armament of the fighter was reduced to a single 20-mm ShVAK cannon. The Yakovlev OKB paid much attention to special equipment: the aircraft was fitted with a gyro horizon, the RPK-10 direction finder, an American SCR-274N radio set and oxygen bottles of increased capacity. The new radio equipment ensured reliable two-way communication at a distance of up to 150 km (93 miles) with the aircraft flying at 1,000 m (3,280 ft) and a reception range of 300 km (186 miles) at an altitude of 7,000 m (22,960 ft).

Despite its higher all-up weight of 3,387 kg (7,468 lb) accompanied by heavier handling and some deterioration of manoeuvrability, the Yak-9DD could still be operated from unprepared airfields. The long range and endurance enabled the Yak-9DD to be used as escort fighter, as well as for performing independently special duties in the enemy's rear.

The Yak-9DD passed State trials and was built in series from May 1944 onwards; a total of 399 machines was delivered. Production Yak-9DDs differed from the prototype mainly in navigation equipment which had to be simplified, imported equipment items being replaced by locally-produced ones.

The first forty production Yak-9DDs underwent service tests in the 386th IAP (commanded by Major M. Zhoolin) in the course of operations aimed at liquidating enemy troop concentrations in East Prussia. The Yak-9DDs were used mainly for escorting Petlyakov Pe-2 and Tupolev Tu-2 bombers. Providing cover to the latter proved to be a fairly difficult task because the fast Tu-2s could rival the Yak-9DDs in speed.

The high all-up weight, the considerable spanwise distribution of the weight and the inadequate engine output for this type of aircraft were the main causes for the deterioration of the machine's performance, handling and manoeuvrability characteristics. Therefore the pilots were very reserved in their appraisal of the Yak-9DD, dubbing it, rather unkindly, a 'flying cistern'.

Maintenance of the overweight machine proved fairly troublesome: there were such nuisances as the short service life of wheel tyres and frequent failures of the tailwheel fork. Uneven consumption of fuel caused air ingestion in the carburettor, and there were instances of the engines cutting in flight.

On the other hand, the Yak-9DD proved its worth as a long-range fighter in August 1944, when a group of 12 aircraft of this type commanded by Major I. Ovcharenko flew non-stop from Bel'tsy in Moldavia to Bari, Italy, in order to render assistance to the People's Liberation Army of Yugoslavia, covering a distance of 1,300 km (808 miles) without external tanks. Accompanying the group as a 'pathfinder' aircraft was a Douglas A-20G Boston bomber with a crew captained by M. A. Nyukhtikov, an experienced NII VVS test pilot. This successful long-distance flight and the subsequent missions associated with escorting Douglas C-47 transports to Yugoslav territory liberated by partisans demonstrated the high operational and flying qualities of the Yak-9DD. During the whole period of their stay in Bari there was not a single case of technical failures or malfunctions, despite the fact that in the course of each sortie (they numbered 155 in all) the aircraft had to cross the Adriatic Sea twice, covering a distance of 400 to 600 km (249 to 373 miles) over water, and make landings at small airstrips high up in the mountains with strong side or even tail winds.

Yak-9PD high-altitude fighter

The Yak-9PD signified the continuation of work on a high-altitude fighter initiated by the Yakovlev OKB with the I-28 and Yak-7PD. The OKB embarked on this work in November 1942, but, owing to delays with the delivery of M-105PD engines, the prototypes were not completed before April 1943. Structurally these were normal production Yak-9s with minor changes effected by the OKB and with the armament restricted to one 20-mm ShVAK cannon.

All five Yak-9PDs that had been built

Above and below: Another production Yak-9DD undergoing pre-delivery flight tests at the factory.

'29 White' was one of the five Yak-9PD interceptors powered by M-105PD engines.

underwent operational evaluation in the 12th Guards IAP commanded by Major K. Marenkov which made part of the fighter element of Moscow's PVO system. By 25th June the high-altitude fighters had made 69 sorties; in 39 of them the machines climbed to altitudes in excess of 10,000 m (32,800 ft). The tests showed that the design was still immature. In particular, a continuous climb in optimum climb rate mode proved impossible: at 7,000 m (22,960 ft) the temperatures of water and oil exceeded the maximum values permissible for this engine. In order to continue flight it was necessary to level off from time to time, allowing the engine to cool down. This greatly reduced the fighter's real rate of climb.

81

Left and below: Two more views of Yak-9PD '29 White', showing to advantage the non-standard enlarged oil cooler and enlarged water radiator changing the aircraft's appearance completely. These features were brought about by the installation of the supercharged engine which was prone to overheating. The propeller spinner is not cropped - the tip is simply painted white, as are the wingtips and fin cap. Note also the moulded windscreen and the non-standard presentation of the national insignia (the outline is red instead of red and white).

Bottom: this previously unpublished photo shows Yak-9 c/n 0401 during manufacturer's flight tests.

The report stated that that the Yak-9PD's operational evaluation results were unsatisfactory. This was due to powerplant deficiencies, the insufficient service ceiling for this class of aircraft (only 11,650m/38,220 ft) and inadequate firepower.

It was high-altitude reconnaissance aircraft, primarily the Junkers Ju 88R-1 equipped with superchargers and a pressurised cockpit, that were the main opponents of Soviet fighters engaged in the air defence of Moscow in the summer of 1943. These aircraft repeatedly put in an appearance over the city. For example, on 2nd June 1943 Lieutenant-Colonel L. Sholokhov, an Air Corps piloting skills inspector, scrambled from the capital's Central airfield (Khodynka) to intercept an unidentified aircraft. The Soviet pilot quickly caught up with the adversary, while being some 1,000 to 1,500 m (3,280 to 4,920 ft) below the latter's altitude. He saw the yellow outer wing panels and the dimly visible Balkenkreuze painted on the wings of the Junkers machine. Sholokhov was on the point of opening fire when the oil pressure dropped all of a sudden and the cockpit windshield iced up. Having lost sight of the enemy, the Soviet pilot gave up the chase and headed for home. Other attempts to intercept the Ju 88R-1 also proved abortive. On 23rd August G. Gromadin, commander of Air Defence troops of the Western Front, reported to the Air Force command that no practical solution had yet been found in the question of creating a high-altitude fighter.

However, the Yakovlev OKB continued its quest for the stratosphere, working in concert with LII NKAP. One modified example of the fighter was fitted with an experimental M-105PD engine in which the gear ratio of the engine-driven centrifugal supercharger was increased from 8.48 to 9.72. Also, measures were effected for raising the altitude efficiency of coolant, oil and fuel systems. The prototype Yak was provided with wings of greater area, the span being increased by one metre (3.28 ft). This, coupled with an all-up weight reduced to 2,845 kg (5,479 lb), created favourable prerequisites for raising the aircraft's service ceiling.

The aircraft attained an altitude of 12,500 m (41,000 ft); still, many of the preceding model's defects had not been rectified. Then the designers re-engined the machine with the prototype M-106PV (PV stands for *povyshennaya vysotnost'* – enhanced high-altitude performance) which had the rated altitude increased from 8,500 to 9,500 m (27,880 to 31,160 ft). On 16th October 1943 a Yak-9 fitted with this engine reached an altitude of 13,100 m (42,968 ft).

In 1944 the Yakovlev OKB tried once more to develop a high-altitude interceptor, this attempt being the most successful so far. As

Above and below: This Yak-9PD was fitted experimentally with am M-106PV engine optimised for high-altitude flight. Apart from the new powerplant, the aircraft had new wings of increased span and area.

before, the main means of raising the aircraft's practical ceiling consisted in improving the powerplant's functioning at great altitudes, as well as a further lightening of the aircraft's.

The new updated version of the fighter was powered by the M-106PV engine which was fitted with a device for reducing the temperature of the air that had passed through the supercharger; this was achieved by injecting a cooling mixture (50% alcohol and 50% water). An additional pump in the fuel system ensured normal fuel feed at high altitude. Numerous weight saving measures brought the airframe weight down to 2,500 kg (5,512 lb), which was an unprecedentedly low figure for the Yak-9.

The cooling systems ensured the possibility of a continuous climb up to the service ceiling of 13,500 m (45,280 ft) without intermediate levelling off. The success of this work made it possible to start manufacturing a series batch of 30 Yak-9 M-106PVs. However, there was no opportunity to check their operational qualities because no overflights of Moscow by German aircraft were noted in the summer of 1944.

All high-altitude versions of the Yak-9 had one drawback in common – it was the absence of a pressurised cockpit. An experimental pressurised cockpit designed by A. Shcherbakov was not ready for installation in a fighter until May 1944, and even that proved to be faulty, as revealed by subsequent testing.

Yak-9R tactical reconnaissance aircraft

The Yak-9 served as a basis for the development of the Yak-9R reconnaissance fighter (R = *razvedchik*). This version was produced both in the short range configuration based on the 'two-tank' Yak-9 and in the long-range configuration based on the Yak-9D. In the latter case the machine-gun and its ammunition supply were often deleted to reduce the all-up weight. The photographic equipment comprised AFA-IM or AFA-3S/50 cameras installed behind the cockpit.

The fighters were often converted into photographic reconnaissance machines under field conditions, reflecting the need for relatively high-speed and manoeuvrable aircraft for fulfilling such missions in the enemy's rear areas adjoining the front-line. Besides, 35 Yak-9Rs were built at Plant No. 166 in Omsk in the summer of 1943. Some of them were delivered to the 48th Guards Long-Range Reconnaissance Air Regiment of the Supreme Command (led by Lieutenant-Colonel Sadov) for operational evaluation.

Above and below: The Yak 9S prototype during State acceptance trials at NII VVS. This was one of the last attempts to reinforce the fighter's armament without radical changes to the airframe and powerplant.

The prototype of the two-seat Yak-9V at NII VVS. The aircraft had no aerial mast fitted at this stage.

developed a special air defence version intended for operations at altitudes of 10,000 m (32,800 ft); it featured a more substantial equipment fit, including a direction finder for navigation. This work drew on the experience gained in developing the Yak-1 and Yak-7B. This version was also built in series.

Yak-9S

The Yak-9S emerged as one of the last versions developed in the process of updating the armament of the M-105-powered Yak-9. Along with installing the VK-105PF-2 engine with additional boost and introducing the new VISh-105SV-01 propeller the blades of which featured airfoil section at the root, Yakovlev continued to develop promising new weapon installations. The Yak-9S was armed with an engine-mounted 23-mm NS-23 cannon and two synchronised B-20S cannons in the front upper decking.

This armament variant was considered to be promising and met the Air Force requirements for 1945. Two examples of the aircraft were completed literally on the eve of victory over Nazi Germany; manufacturer's tests and State trials conducted in the summer of 1945 confirmed the soundness of the Chief Designer's concept. The weight of fire, as measured during the tests, was 4.23 kg (9,3 lb), which enabled the fighter to engage effectively both aerial targets and soft-skinned ground targets. Yet, since the basic flying characteristics of the Yak-9S were appreciably inferior to those of the Yak-3 and La-7 fighters, it was not put into series production. Yakovlev continued experimenting with this armament layout on fighters powered by the VK-107A engine.

Yak-9V two-seat conversion (familiarisation) trainer

The work on the development of a two-seat conversion (familiarisation) trainer initiated before the war on the UTI-26 was continued on the Yak-9. In contrast to its predecessor, the Yak-9V (thus designated by analogy with the Yak-7V) had a retractable undercarriage and the armament consisted of an engine-mounted ShVAK-20 cannon. The new Yak featured a more substantial complement of equipment, which was important for the training of future pilots.

As distinct from the Yak-7V, the Yak-9V was provided with an intercom, a two-way radio which could be operated by the trainee and the instructor alike, an updated artificial horizon and some other instruments. True, the range of equipment was sufficient only for performing flights in daytime at altitudes up to 4,500 m (14,760 ft) because there was no provision for oxygen equipment. As regards the basic flight performance, the Yak-9 was little different from the Yak-9M, which was a distinct advantage for the training of flying per-

On the whole, the results of the service trials were positive, but they showed that the Yak-9Rs, despite their high speed and manoeuvrability, could not supplant the Petlyakov Pe-2R aircraft in the reconnaissance air units; they could only supplement them when the enemy opposition in the air was particularly strong. After all, one airman whose attention was occupied by flying the aircraft could not make as many observations as a well-trained crew comprising three persons.

In addition to the versions described above, at the end of the war the Yakovlev OKB

sonnel. The Yak trainer entered production after the end of the war. In all, 456 such machines were built at Plant No. 153 and a further 337 were converted from Yak-9Ms.

Yak-9 'Courier' liaison aircraft

This aircraft was intended for the transportation of one passenger over a considerable distance under the conditions of a possible enemy fighter opposition. Structurally it was a Yak-9V fuselage mated to the wings of the Yak-9DD; it was a prototype VIP transport aircraft derived from production Yak-9 fighters.

Yakovlev appointed N. Avtsyn as leading engineer for this aircraft. Under his direction a certain amount of reworking was effected by July 1944; it was restricted primarily to ensuring a certain level of comfort for the pilot and the passenger during flights of long duration. Thus, the 'Courier' aircraft had comfortable seats, both cockpits were provided with urinals. The passenger's cockpit was stripped of its second set of controls and the instrument panel; instead, it was provided with cloth upholstery, a false floor and pockets for maps on the side walls. In other words, measures were taken to ensure that the crew would feel very comfortable in this case, as distinct from the generally spartan style of crew accommodation in Soviet military aircraft.

The aircraft was not built in series and no documents were found testifying to its operational use.

Yak-9U production fighter

The Yakovlev OKB was well aware of the fact that the Yak-9's performance, despite all its merits, was falling short of the demands that

Above: A production Yak-9V undergoing checkout tests; note the aerial mast installed on the starboard side.

Above and below: Reminiscent of 'war weary' North American P-51Ds converted into squadron hacks, the Yak-9 'Courier' was a custom-built high-speed VIP transport with comfortable cockpits. Note the stripes on the propeller blades, as applied to the I-26 prototypes before the war.

Above and below: 40 White was a stock Yak-9D converted into a trainer by a service unit. The rudder is painted yellow.

Above and below: The Yak-9U VK-105PF-2 prototype. The lack of the chin-mounted oil cooler (the oil coolers are housed in the wing roots) and the aft position of the water radiator gave the fighter a much more 'racy' appearance.

should be met by a fighter at the end of the war. From the outset of series production the Chief Designer endeavoured, as far as possible, to improve the design without introducing basic changes into production techniques in the manufacture of the Yak-9. It was with these thoughts in their minds that the designers embarked on the development of a new production model for the following year in November 1943.

This version of the Yak-9 marking the peak of its development received the 'U' suffix signifying '*ooloochshennyy*' (improved). It embodied, first and foremost, the rich experience in the perfecting of aerodynamic design that had been accumulated by the design staff. Furthermore, the effort was directed at reducing the all-up weight, making the aircraft more reliable in operation and improving the pilot's working conditions. Many of the novel features were borrowed from the successful Yak-1M which is described later.

The following main differences from the production Yak-9 can be noted. The wing centre section was altered to house an oil cooler in the same fashion as on the Yak-1M. The fabric skinning of the fuselage was replaced by 2-mm (0.07-in) plywood; the sealing of the fuselage was improved and the aircraft was made more easily controllable while on the ground;

The pilot's armoured seat back was cut down, a bulletproof windshield and an aft bulletproof glass panel were installed, plus an armoured headrest and armrest; all this provided excellent protection for the pilot in combat. The engine's output at low altitudes was increased by raising the boost pressure from 1,050 to 1,100 mm Hg. A further speed increase was obtained thanks to installing a propeller with blades featuring airfoil section at the root.

New, capacious water and oil radiators were installed on the Yak-9U; the carburettor air intake design was changed in accordance with recommendations from TsAGI. The self-sealing coating of the fuel tanks was made variable in thickness so as to cater for both survivability and weight saving.

In A. S. Yakovlev's opinion, the optimum armament complement should include an engine-mounted 23-mm cannon and two large-calibre 12.7-mm UBS machine-guns. The only 23-mm cannon available in November 1943 was the VYa-23; accordingly, it was installed between the cylinder banks. Installation of another cannon of the same calibre – the lighter and quicker-firing NS-23 – was effected by the OKB later on the Yak-9S fighter. Regrettably, this weapon came too late to be fired in anger on the Yaks.

However, the VYa-23 was also a potent and reliable weapon which had proved its worth on the Il-2 attack aircraft. The high muzzle velocity of its shells, coupled with their high destructive power, permitted the cannon to be used not only in air combat but against ground targets as well. The shells of the VYa pierced 25-mm (0.98-in.) armour at up to 400 m (1,308 ft). Yet, despite all its merits, the Red Army's Air Force found the VYa cannon to be too heavy and insufficiently rapid-firing to be used on fighter aircraft, and production was restricted to a trials batch.

The designers paid much attention to making the pilot's work as convenient as possible. Thus, control of the radio set was effected by push-buttons mounted on the throttle lever. The placement of the equipment was carefully chosen and came close to the contemporary standard. Outwardly the Yak-9U differed from the Yak-1M only in having shorter main undercarriage legs with one-piece gear doors.

Pilot V. Khomiakov who test-flew the aircraft in January 1944 noted that, as regards the piloting techniques, the Yak-9U did not differ from production machines, retaining good stability, light controls and pleasant handling. The fighter's performance was appreciably enhanced thanks to improved aerodynamics and greater engine power. Speed rose to 558 km/h (347 mph) at sea level and 620 km/h (385 mph) at 3,850 m (12,628 ft). The weight was reduced to 2,900 kg, which afforded an improvement in vertical manoeuvrability – a climb to 5,000 m (16,400 ft) took only 4.8 minutes, ie, less than it took the opposing Messerschmitt fighters. In a climbing turn the Yak-9U gained 1,190 m (3,903 ft) versus 1,200 m (3,936 ft) for the best of the Bf 109's versions, the G-10, which testifies to the machines being roughly equal in this respect.

The protocol on the results of the State trials contained a recommendation to introduce in production all the changes associated with improving the fighter's aerodynamics and lightening its structure (as described above). Whereas the Yak-9U powered by the VK-105PF-2 embodied an evolutionary line of development, a 'revolutionary' trend was associated with a sharp increase in the power output of a liquid-cooled engine. Such an engine existed in V. Klimov's OKB – it was the VK-107A. As early as at the end of 1942 this engine had passed 50-hour bench running tests, albeit with great difficulties.

The work on the VK-107 was arduous: a number of new technological breakthroughs had to be scored, and that was difficult to achieve during the war years. The first flight-cleared engine was installed in a Yak-7 in December 1942. At the beginning of January the machine received new wings with metal spars and was renamed Yak-9. Manufacturer's trials of the Yak-9 M-107 were conducted by P. Fedrovi. On 23rd February 1943 the

This page: Another Yak-9U VK-105PF-2 prototype. This aircraft had a non-standard sharply raked windshield fitted to reduce drag.

Above and below: The ill-starred Yak-9U VK-107A prototype. The aircraft was damaged beyond repair in a forced landing on 23rd February 1943 when the engine caught fire in a test flight.

Yak-9U c/n 0312 illustrates the dorsal air intake just aft of the spinner, the one-piece moulded windscreen and the seven exhaust stubs on each side characteristic of the VK-107A engine. The aircraft is seen here during checkout tests at NII VVS.

well-known test pilot P. M. Stefanovskiy performed the last flight at Chkalovskaya airfield before handing the machine over for State trials. That flight ended in an accident.

'Having climbed to a thousand metres [3,280 ft], I levelled off and flew some distance in level flight over the airfield in the direction of Shcholkovo to determine the maximum speed, – Stefanovskiy was to recall later. – *The machine was surging forward at an increasing speed. Glancing at the engine cowling I noticed that smoke was pouring out of slits between the cowling panels. Then a sheet of flame burst out. The engine was on fire…'*

Attempting to land the burning machine, the pilot was knocked unconscious by the impact. As for the aircraft, the damage sustained in the crash-landing was so heavy that the fighter had to be written off.

Despite this setback, P. Fedrovi wrote to People's Commissar of Aircraft Industry A. Shakhoorin that the M-107A-powered Yak-9 was one of the best fighters at the moment and that it could be compared only to Polikarpov's I-185 prototype. The latter had roughly the same speeds but possessed heavier handling and poorer manoeuvrability due to greater airframe weight. P. Fedrovi asked the People's Commissar to issue an order requiring M-107A engines to be installed on 10 to 15 production Yak-9 fighters for operational evaluation purposes. But the abovementioned accident and difficulties encountered in ironing out the bugs of the powerplant delayed the work by at least seven months.

In April 1943 eight Yak-9D airframes were fitted with M-107 engines; attempts to eradicate the engine troubles at the experimental Plant proved unsuccessful, and four machines were transferred to LII NKAP for development work. Test flights were resumed in early August, leading to the conclusion that the main reason for the unsatisfactory operation of the engine lay in the poor functioning of its ignition system. Between 4th August and 21st October LII test pilots performed a total of 64 flights and the technicians had to dismantle five engines out of seven because of serious defects. Engine No. 317-2 on one of the Yaks burst into flames after only 28 hours of running.

As noted earlier, many Soviet fighters were ordered into series production even before the commencement of serious testing. This was exactly the case with the M-107A-powered Yak-9. The Government demanded that L. Sokolov, Director of Plant No. 166, should organise the manufacture of the new machine from June 1943 onwards and deliver 25 Yak-9 M-107As to the military by August.

It was no accident that the Omsk Plant was chosen to fulfil this complicated and important task. In the opinion of Aleksandr Yakovlev, it was easier to get production underway in small workshops, provided that production routines were put under control and prescribed techniques strictly adhered to, coupled with seconding experienced engineers from the OKB to the Plant. It would be easier to perfect the new machine under the conditions of limited production. However, this did not remove all the problems.

In the meantime, a new prototype was built in December 1943. Originally it was to be completed as a duplicate (*dooblyor*, or literally, 'understudy') of the Yak-9U VK-105PF-2 that had been transferred to NII VVS for testing. Yakovlev decided to make use of the experience gained with the new engine, albeit a negative one, and of the positive results shown by the latest machine. The fighter featured a modified engine mount, increased area of the radiator cooling surfaces, and fuel and oil tanks of greater capacity. As distinct from the first Yak-9U prototype, the fighter was armed with the standard engine-mounted ShVAK-20 cannon. The all-up weight increased due mainly to the massive engine, reaching 3,150 kg (6,946 lb).

In the course of State trials which the fighter passed in January-April 1944 (with A. Stepanets as the leading engineer and A. Proshakov as the test pilot) the aircraft attained a speed of 600 km/h (373 mph) at sea level and 700 km/h at 5,500 m (18,040 ft). The report of the NII VVS on the results of

Above and below: Yak-9U c/n 25166021 was the first VK-107A-powered example built by factory No. 166 in Omsk. It is seen here during State acceptance trials.

A standard production Yak-9U VK-107A pictured during checkout trials at NII VVS.

the State trials said: '*The Yak-9U powered by the VK-107A engine* (that was the name allocated to the engine in March 1944 in honour of its designer Vladimir Klimov) *is the best among the known Soviet and foreign fighters as regards basic performance characteristics in the range of altitudes from sea level to 6,000 m [19,680 ft]*'. However, it was also noted that it would be impossible to operate the fighter in the Air Force units unless the basic defects of the powerplant were rectified.

With regard to piloting techniques, the Yak-9 VK-107A remained just as simple to fly

89

Above: One of the first production Yak-9U VK-107As. This aircraft is unusual in having the old-model angular windshield and lacking the protruding dorsal air intake.

Above: A crew chief waves out a pair of Yak-9Us about to depart on a combat sortie. The nearest aircraft is equipped with a gun camera in front of the windshield.

A rare air-to-air shot of a pair of Yak-9Us equipped with gun cameras. Note the white fuselage band and the numeral 5 on the rudder of the example serialled 9 Yellow.

and easy to master for pilots of medium skill as the VK-105PF-powered Yaks.

Series production of the machine was started at three factories already in April 1944. Plant No. 166, which by then had become one of the most advanced enterprises, was working at full capacity. It was there that the first production Yak-9U was built. It was not quite so refined aerodynamically as the prototype. At an all-up weight of 3,914 kg (8,630 lb) and at maximum engine speed (3,200 rpm) the fighter reached 562 km/h (349 mph) at sea level and 654 km/h (406 mph) at 5,150 m (16,892 ft). A climb to 5,000 m (16,400 ft) took 5.2 minutes. Thus, the characteristics proved to be sufficiently high, even though they fell short of the expectations.

However, production machines were plagued by the new engine's shortcomings of to an even greater extent than the prototype. The main bugs of the VK-107A were the oil spill from the breather and the front sealing of the hollow gearbox shaft, oil pressure dropping below permissible values as the altitude increased, vibration at low rpm etc.

The main defect of the powerplant at that time undoubtedly consisted in the water and oil temperature exceeding the specified limits. This occurred with the engine running in combat contingency mode (3,200 rpm) and, during hot summer months, also at nominal revs (3,000 rpm).

During level flight at maximum speed the oil temperature exceeded admissible values even with the radiator shutters fully opened. When gaining altitude in the optimum climb rate mode, the pilot had to level off repeatedly in order to bring the water and oil temperature down. Airmen in service units discovered that the operation of the aircraft was beset with great difficulties. It was far from always that the aircraft could demonstrate its performance to advantage.

The 42nd Guards IAP commanded by Major Ya. Aleksandrovich was among the first to receive the Yak-9U VK-107A. Re-equipment of the unit proved to be a protracted affair which lasted till 25th August 1944. This was due in part to the fact that the Yak-9Us were powered by engines from the first batches manufactured at the end of 1943 and the beginning of 1944 – their cylinder banks often malfunctioned due to gases bursting through the seals. To boost the airmen's confidence in the new materiel and provide a visual comparison of the manoeuvrability characteristics of the Yak-9U and the Bf 109G-4, the command arranged a kind of a contest. Captain L. M. Koovshinov, a test pilot from NII VVS, arrived by air to a front-line airfield. It was he who piloted the captured German machine.

Despite all Koovshinov's skill, his opponents in a mock combat – I. Gorboonov and G. Pavlov (both Heroes of the Soviet Union) from the 42nd Guards IAP – emerged victorious from the single combat in vertical and horizontal manoeuvring. The Yak-9U gained 1,250 to 1,300 m (4,100 to 4,264 ft) of altitude in a combat turn and always proved to be positioned somewhat higher up than the Bf 109G. These demonstration flights imbued the airmen of the entire regiment with confidence in the merits of the new aircraft.

The new fighters came to be used on a relatively wide scale in the late summer of 1944. The enemy's command took note of these air-

This page: An Omsk-built Yak-9UT (c/n 40166022) seen during manufacturer's flight tests. The aircraft looked like a cross between the Yak-9U and the tank-busting Yak-9K. The muzzle brake of the 37-mm engine-mounted cannon is well visible, as is the dorsal carburettor air intake moved aft to a position about halfway between the spinner and the windscreen. Because of the Yak-9UT's strike role a bulletproof windshield was a must.

Above: Another Yak-9UT undergoing tests at NII VVS. Curiously, this example has a moulded windshield lacking the bulletproof windscreen.

Centre and above: The Yak-9UV prototype built by plant No. 82 (c/n 0000) seen during State acceptance trials. Like the Yak-9 'Courier', it is grey overall with a red stripe running the full length of the fuselage.

craft and their high operational qualities. On the other hand, maintenance of the Yak-9U in field conditions presented great difficulties. Continuous efforts were needed to overcome them and to do that at the least possible detriment to the fighter's performance.

Thus, it was recommended that the use of the combat contingency rating be relinquished and flights intended to reach maximum speed be performed at not more than 3,000 rpm. This entailed a marginal decrease of speed and rate of climb but helped reduce the number of engine failures.

In October 1944 the command of the Red Army's Air Force considered it possible to conduct a service evaluation of the Yak-9U. All 32 machines were taken from the assembly line of Plant No. 84 in Moscow which had embarked on the production of modern fighters shortly before that. The airframes and engines, though, were subjected to the necessary improvements before the beginning of the trials, the leading specialists from the Yakovlev OKB lending a hand.

The important task of conducting the service trials was entrusted to the airmen of the 163rd IAP in the 3rd Air Army (the regiment was commanded by Lieutenant-Colonel V. Ukhanov). The Yaks were opposed in air combat chiefly by Fw 190As, 'Fs and 'Gs which tried to prevent the Red Army from destroying the German troops concentrations in the Baltic area. In the course of the trials which lasted nearly till the end of 1944, 398 individual Yak-9U sorties were put on record in documents; they were accompanied by 299 dogfights. According to the regiment's documents, the Soviet airmen scored 28 victories for the loss of two aircraft (it should be noted, though, that the big losses mentioned found no confirmation in Luftwaffe documents). As for the two Yak-9Us lost, in one of the cases the pilot managed to fly back over the front line in his damaged machine before bailing out.

The Yak-9U demonstrated its complete ascendancy in dogfights with various versions of the Fw 190, especially during combat in the vertical plane. Lieutenant Petrov gained a special distinction, scoring five 'kills'. Lieutenant Kapustin fought alone against two Fw 190s and shot down both of them.

Commanders, pilots and ground crews of the 163rd IAP spoke highly of both performance and serviceability of the Yak-9U. They noted that the aircraft could fairly easily be mastered by young pilots and average-skilled technicians. Maintenance of the aircraft proved simple: preparation for a combat sortie did not exceed thirty minutes.

On the down side, Major Mankevich, navigator of the 163rd IAP who had taken part in the service evaluation, noted: *'The spark plugs of the VK-107A engine fail after every 10 to 12 hours of operation. After 10 to 15 hours of operation the engines begin to emit smoke. There are frequent cases of the throttle seizing. The throttle lever either goes into the absolute minimum position, requiring the ignition to be switched off, or gets stuck in a middle position, which is even more dangerous at take-off.'*

The enemy, too, became painfully aware of the Yak-9Us capabilities. The pilot of a Fieseler Fi 156C Storch liaison aircraft who lost his bearings and landed on a Soviet airfield at Sedy in north-western Lithuania by mistake said during interrogation: 'Our command issued an order to avoid combat with Yak fighters having no antenna mast!'.

Walter Wolfrum, a German ace who had flown the Bf 109G and scored 137 victories by the end of the war (which says a lot for his flying experience), noted: *'The best fighters that I have encountered in combat were the American P-51 Mustang and the Russian Yak-9U. Both of these types were clearly superior in their performance to all versions of the Bf 109, including the 'K. The Mustangs had unrivalled altitude performance, while the Yak-9U was a record-holder in rate of climb and manoeuvrability'.*

In addition to the abovementioned 42nd GvIAP and 163rd IAP, a number of new units joined the fighting on the Yak-9U. Among these were the 761st, 431st, 269th, 139th Guards IAPs and other units. Thus, in October 1944 forty-two brand-new fighters were delivered to the 149th IAP. Most of them had improved VK-105 engines on which a number of defects had been eradicated. However, new problems cropped up, such as leakage of petrol from the fuel injector nozzles, loosening of the engine's attachment to the engine mount, leakage from fuel tanks at spot-welded joints, jamming of pressure reduction valves etc.

It was the 4th Air Army that had accumulated the most comprehensive operational experience with the Yak-9U . On 6 th February 1945 I. Osipenko, the Air Army's chief engineer, submitted a report detailing both the merits and the shortcomings of the new fighters. Among the former he mentioned the ascendancy in performance over all Bf 109 and Fw 190 versions at low and medium altitudes, and a large speed envelope enabling the pilot to perform vertical aerobatic manoeuvres with ease. As for the latter, he cited numerous cases of generator failures and breakage of the UBS machine-gun attachment brackets. Airmen of the Air Army managed to keep the temperature of oil and water in the VK-107A engine within prescribed limits, but numerous cases were noted of the engines being overcooled in winter.

In the spring of 1945 the Red Army Air Force command embarked on a programme of re-equipping the active units with Yak-9U aircraft. Up to that time the machines had been assembled primarily at Plant No. 301 in Khimki near Moscow. Now they were sent in kit form by rail to the west, and assembly workshops were established at Brest, Minsk, Kiev and L'vov. On the very eve of termination of hostilities in Europe assembly workshops were established in Insterburg, Bialostok, Poznan etc. They also served for distribution of the aircraft to the units and formations of the active army.

In all, nearly 2,500 VK-107A-powered fighters had rolled off assembly lines by the end of the first half of 1945. As of 10th May 1945, approximately 750 Yak-9U fighters were on strength (out of the total of 6,267 fighters in the air arms of all the Western Fronts).

Yak-9U versions with reinforced armament

Like many other basic subtypes of the Yaks, the Yak-9U served as a kind of proving ground for developing different armament options. In one machine provision was made for replacing the ShVAK-20 cannon in factory conditions by more potent cannons – an NS-23, an N-37 or even an N-45; in the latter case one of the two synchronised weapons in the front upper decking had to be deleted to lighten the machine. Synchronised machine-guns were replaced by new B-20 cannons (synchronised, of course).

The possibility of installing different engine-mounted cannons without any major redesign of the aircraft was a distinct advantage, making it possible to switch series production quickly to this or that type of armament, depending on the requirements of the Air Force. The NS-37 and its derivative, a 45-mm cannon, were experimental lightened weapons developed by OKB-16. A prototype fighter featuring this kind of armament (c/n 39166083, ie, Batch 39, Omsk aircraft factory No. 166, 83rd aircraft in the batch) was built under A. Yakovlev's direct guidance in February and allocated the designation Yak-9UT, the T denoting **tahn**kovyy (tank-busting).

Naturally, each armament version had its own all-up weight, CG position and flight performance. But the speeds were identical to those of the production Yak-9U. The handling qualities of the Yak-9UT were virtually the same as those of its predecessors, except for the control stick forces from the elevator: they proved to be too high, and that was the most serious shortcoming of the aircraft.

On the credit side was the weight of fire: with the installation comprising one NS-37 and two B-20s, it amounted to 6.0 kg/sec (13,2 lb/sec) as compared to the Yak-9U's 2.81 kg/sec (6.2 lb/sec). In the final stages of the war such sizeable figures commanded respect even from the Germans who also strove to increase the firepower as much as possible in order to fight the sturdy and highly survivable Boeing B-17 Flying Fortresses and Consolidated B-24 Liberators.

Tests of this aircraft were conducted by engineer G. A. Sedov and pilot A. Manucharov at NII VVS in March 1945. The Yak-9T proved to be considerably more stable under different manoeuvres compared to the Yak-9T and Yak-9K, owing primarily to lesser recoil of the cannon and greater speed envelope. The aircraft was recommended for series production, and Plant No. 166 delivered 282 machines with the engine-mounted NS-23 cannon and two synchronised B-20S cannon.

An important stage in the history of the VK-107A-powered fighters was the emergence of the 'etalon' (production standard-setter) for 1945. The main tasks facing the Yakovlev OKB were to eliminate the main defects of the Yak-9 VK-107A; to ensure a top speed of 600 km/h (373 mph) at sea level and 700 km/h (435 mph) at the second rated altitude with the engine at the maximum rating; to ensure a climb to 5,000 m (16,400 ft) within 4.1 minutes and a service ceiling of 11,000 m (36,080 ft); to achieve a cruising range of 900 km (559 miles) and a range of 1,200 km (746 miles) in optimum cruise mode.

The aircraft was built, using a production Omsk-built airframe (c/n 41166038). An important feature of the machine was its ability to accept alternative versions of armament in a manner similar to the Yak-9UT. The fighter was tested with three B-20s (two of them synchronised) and an all-up weight of 3,145 kg (6,935 lb). NII VVS specialists noted the advantages of the alternative armament options, the improved external finish and pointed out the need for using an antenna mast. At the same time they stated that only some of the Yak-9U's shortcomings had been eliminated. Thus, the installation of a bigger oil cooler with greater frontal area and introduction of an additional oil pump led to better engine running at nominal revs only at high altitudes. As before, considerable oil spill from the breather occurred at maximum power.

In the course of 45 flights performed by the fighter, four engine changes (!) had to be made. In the last engine (No.527-21), which was part of an 'improved batch', the crankshaft main bearings broke down during the 14th hour of engine running. An extremely disappointed Aleksandr Yakovlev ordered the aircraft with c/n 41-038 to be withdrawn from testing and returned to the OKB so that development work could be resumed. All subsequent improvements introduced into the design came after the end of the war.

Yak-9UV conversion (familiarisation) trainer

The VK-107A-powered Yak-9UV (*ulooch-shennyy vyvoznoy* – improved, familiarization) created by Plant No. 82 embodied the final stage of the work of the Yakovlev OKB on the development of a piston-engined fighter trainer. The armament of the Yak-9UV was restricted to one engine-mounted B-20M cannon, and the avionics and equipment fit ensured normal flights at altitudes up to 4,000 to 4,500 m (13,080 to 14,720 ft) in visual meteorological conditions for the trainee. In its handling the aircraft did not differ from production Yak-9Us.

To ensure more effective engine cooling the designers installed new radiators. Even so, the engine suffered overheating at nominal revs (3,000 rpm) due to the frequent take-offs and landings typical for the employment mode of familiarisation and training aircraft.

Above and below: The same Yak-9UT c/n 40166022 on a snow-covered airfield during State acceptance trials. Note that the carburettor air intake has now reverted to its original location immediately aft of the spinner.

Above and below: Yak-9UT c/n 40166074 is unusual in lacking the cannon muzzle brake.

Yak-9UT c/n 40166074 was probably the most heavily armed example of all; it was converted to the one-off Yak-9-57 armed with a 57-mm cannon. Remarkably, the cannon barrel did not protrude beyond the spinner, so this was something of a wolf in sheep's clothing.

These photos illustrate well the elegant lines of the Yak-9 VK-107A. Note the aft position of the carburettor air intake on this aircraft.

Yak-9 VK-107A c/n 52166082 was the 'etalon' (production standard-setter) for 1946 and, in fact, the prototype of the post-war all-metal Yak-9P. Note the enlarged oil cooler air outlet immediately ahead of the radiator bath and the aerial mast.

Therefore the permissible rpm were limited to 2,800; at this power rating the speeds decreased by 35 to 90 km/h (21.7 to 56 mph), depending on the altitude.

Shortly after the end of the war the Yak-9UV prototype (c/n 0000) was handed over for State trials, but it was clear that a different aircraft was needed. The Soviet Air Force started re-equipping with the first jet fighters; consequently, jet-powered conversion training machines were required. The Yak-9UV was not produced in quantity.

Yak-9P

The war with Nazi Germany was over; with the onset of peacetime the aircraft industry was faced with new tasks. Soviet aircraft of mixed construction which had achieved a fairly good record at the front when a combat machine usually did not survive more than several dozen flying hours in combat were not expected to remain in operation for several years. Emphasis was placed on ease of production and low cost. The war 'devoured' military materiel in hundreds and thousands of examples, and the aircraft had no chance of growing old.

In peacetime there was no longer any need to build aircraft in such large numbers. However, one could no longer put up with such deficiencies as a short service life, susceptibility to the influence of the elements and other adverse natural conditions, deterioration of aerodynamic qualities and, as a consequence, a drop in performance, especially maximum speed. Research showed that it was impossible to solve these tasks without resorting to new structural materials.

The aircraft industry, including Chief Designer A. S. Yakovlev, was faced with the task of gradually switching to the manufacture of aircraft of predominantly metal construction, to be followed by the creation of all-metal machines. Upgrading of the Yak-9 VK-107A fighter followed this pattern.

When construction of the Yak-9P (unofficially dubbed *poslevoyennyy* – post-war) was undertaken, the future aircraft had to meet fairly stringent demands concerning the quality of assembly work, production standards in the manufacture of airframe, powerplant and armament, and thoroughness of surface finish. They were laid down in a Government re-solution dated 17th June 1946. Also, the aircraft constructors were required to eliminate the main defects which had been noted in reports on the results of the Yak-9U's trials.

In 1946 most of the aircraft factories which had built Yakovlev fighters (including the Yak-9U) during the war were reoriented to other work. Thus, Plant No. 166 in Omsk switched to manufacturing Tu-2 bombers,

Plant No. 82 in Moscow was completing the work on converting Yak-9s into trainers and tooling up for production of trolley-buses; only the gigantic Plant No. 153 in Novosibirsk continued the work on perfecting the VK-107A-powered Yak-9. In the late spring of 1946 two initial production fighters featuring metal wings, c/ns 01-03 and 01-04, were built there; this was the beginning of a production batch bearing the P suffix.

After a brief period of adjustment work the two aircraft were handed over to NII VVS for State trials which they passed under the direction of leading engineer G. Sedov from 28th June till 23rd July 1946. Pilots Yuriy Antipov and V. Ivanov performed 108 flights on these machines, logging over 60 flying hours. The aircraft were evaluated with regard to their performance and maintenance qualities.

Switching to the metal wings was accompanied by a slight alteration of their planform – the wingtips became rounded instead of angular. The new version differed from the Yak-9U mainly in having increased compensation of ailerons, in featuring dust filters in the engine air intakes and additional locks for the flaps. Besides, the overall strength of the airframe was enhanced; thanks to this, the indicated airspeed in a dive could be increased from 650 to 720 km/h (404 to 447 mph), and the maximum G load in recovery from a dive was brought up to 8.0 instead of 6.5.

The LII test personnel also took a positive view of other alterations in the functioning of the engine and some units and equipment items. Nevertheless, some shortcomings were noted, including leakage of water through sealed joints, spark plug failures after a mere eight or ten hours of operation, high temperatures in the cockpit etc. To make a long story short, the military test pilots and engineers placed the Yak-9P somewhere between the Yak-9U and the postwar demands to aircraft. Air Marshal K. Vershinin, who replaced A. Novikov as Air Force Commander-in-Chief, acknowledged the results of the State trials as satisfactory and found it possible to start service tests.

These tests were prepared especially thoroughly, since they were the first such tests of 29 production machines in peacetime. From 4th October 1946 until 4th February 1947 hand-picked experienced pilots and engineers of the 246th Fighter Air Division led by General Ye. Toorenko not only flight-tested the aircraft at Tolmachovo airfield near Novosibirsk (now the city's airport) but also determined the time limits for inspection and overhauls, inspection procedures and some other issues which had not been on the agenda of service tests during the war.

This pristine Yak-9P (or 'all-metal Yak-9 VK-107A') is preserved at the Yakovlev OKB museum in Moscow.

Alas, the results of this work were far from encouraging. While recognising the merits of these machines – above all, their easy handling making them suitable even for pilots of less-than-average skill, – the military personnel noted a great number of defects precluding normal maintenance of the aircraft. They were also dissatisfied with the armament comprising one ShVAK-20 cannon and two UBS machine-guns (as on the Yak-9U) and the special equipment which was very austere by the standard of 1946.

Equally unsatisfactory was the fact that the Yak-9P could wage aerial combat only at altitudes up to 7,000 m (22,960 ft). Above that altitude the aircraft was plagued by frequent jamming of the armament and deterioration of handling qualities. Yakovlev's postwar fighters were assessed as unsatisfactory. For comparison purposes it may be noted that considerably fewer defects were noted during service trials of the postwar La-9 fighter which were conducted in mid-1947; the results of the Lavochkin fighter's testing were pronounced successful.

When the work on the service test batch had been completed, the engine speed was limited to 3,000 rpm so as to enhance the engine's reliability; a ban was imposed on the use of the 'combat' rating. Besides, it was stipulated that the industry should manufacture only all-metal aircraft featuring greater internal fuel tankage increased from 425 to 682 litres (93.5 to 150 Imp gal). The Novosibirsk plant met all these demands; after 29 Yak-9Ps with metal wings had rolled off the assembly line, all subsequent Yaks built by Plant No. 153 were of all-metal construction.

In December 1947 one production machine – Yak-9P c/n 03-92 manufactured in July – successfully passed a series of State tests conducted by engineer V. P. Belodedenko and pilot L. M. Koovshinov. In comparison with the Yak-9Ps c/ns 01-03 and 01-04, the new fighter possessed somewhat inferior performance. Maximum speed amounted to 590 km/h (367 mph) at sea level and 660 km/h (410 mph) at 5,000 m (16,400 ft) which was 12 to 13 km/h (7.4 to 8.0 mph) less than before. The aircraft needed 5.8 minutes to climb to 5,000 m (16,400 ft) versus 4.8 minutes required by its predecessor; this was due to the difference in the engine running mode and to the increase of weight from 3,227 to 3,550 kg (7,116 to 7,828 lb) caused by the extra fuel.

On the whole, the all-metal aircraft was virtually identical to its predecessor as

99

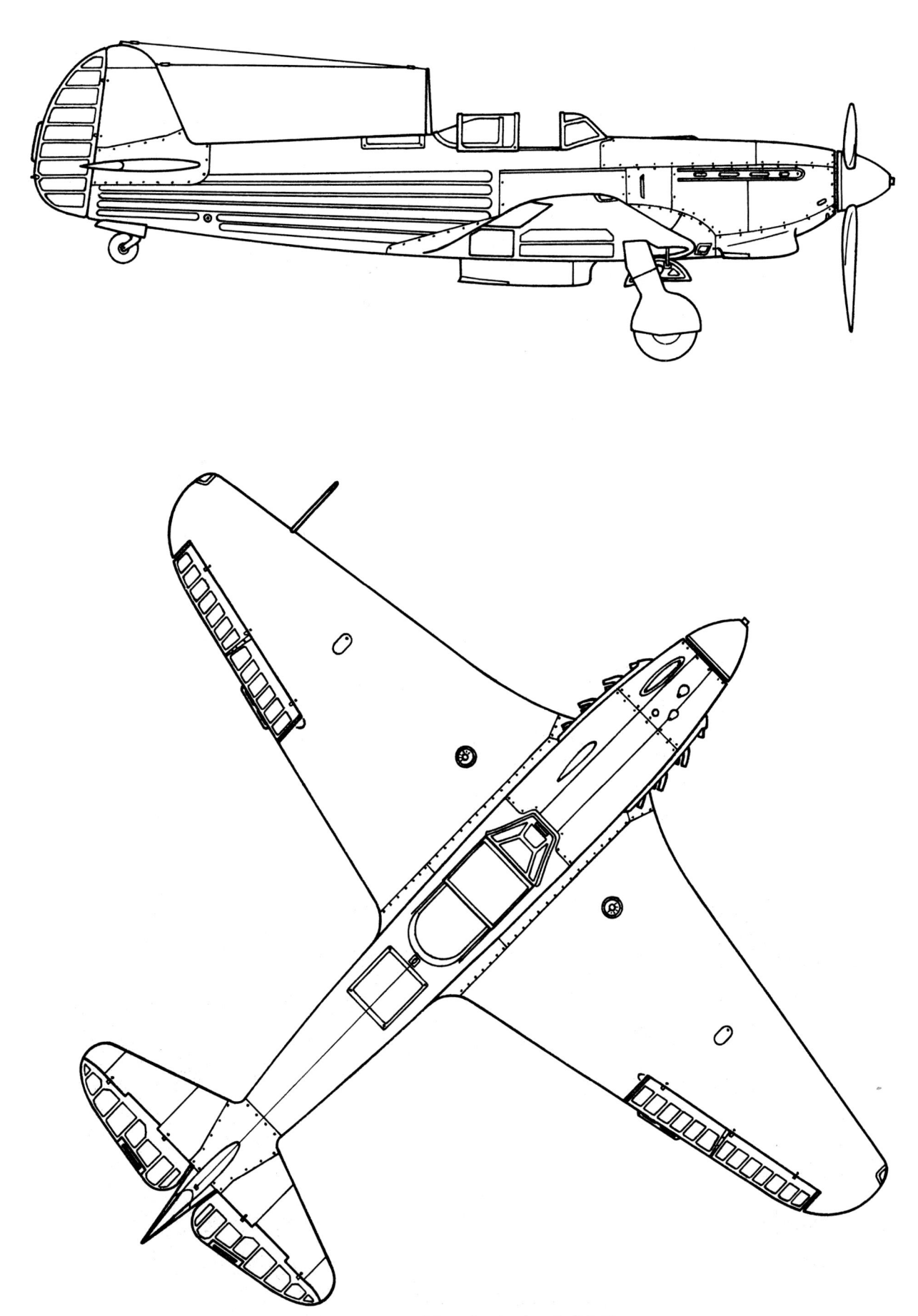

A four-view drawing of a Yak-9D

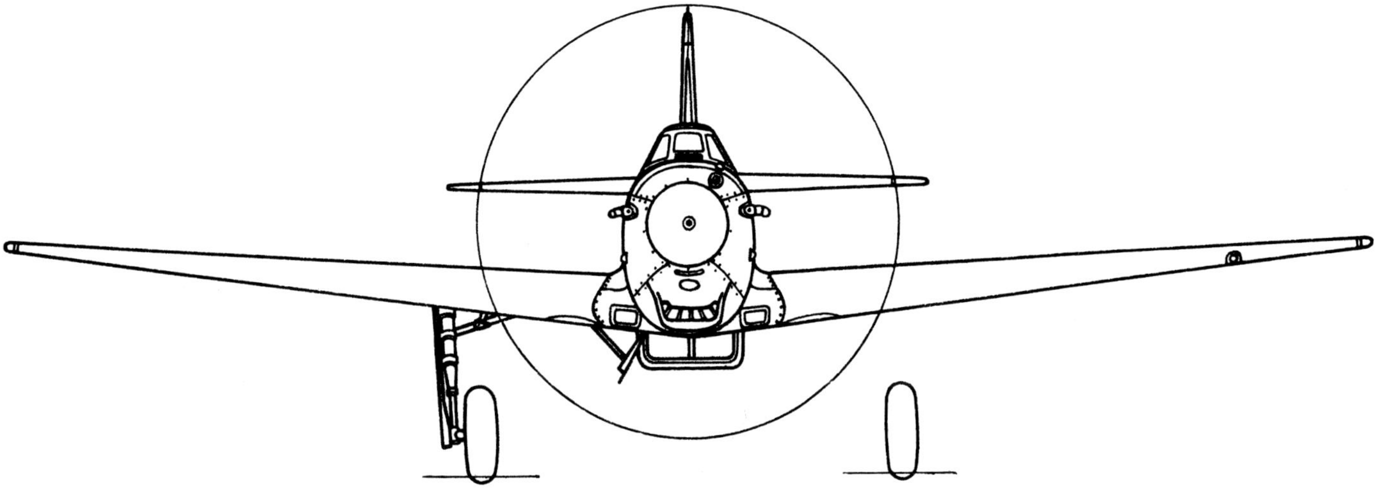

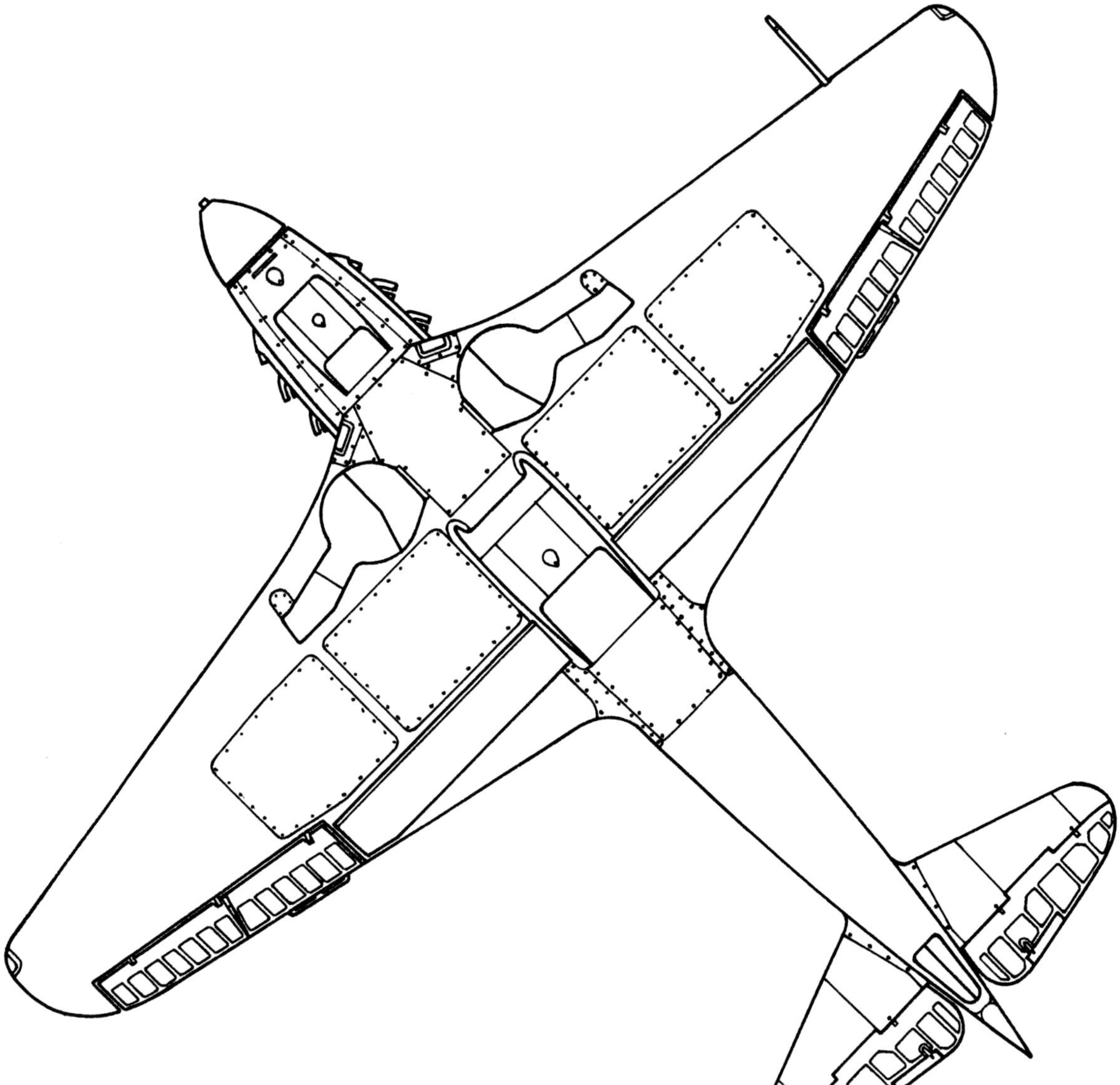

Left and below: An early-production Yak-9P undergoing State acceptance trials. The aircraft has an unusually dark finish (probably medium grey)

Bottom pair: This Yak-9P was equipped with a spin recovery parachute for the purpose of performing a spinning trials programme. Note the cutout in the fuselage spine closed by a Perspex panel, with the direction finder loop aerial visible underneath.

regards handling; it was provided with special equipment which suited the machine's mission as all-weather fighter more fully and included such additional items as the RPKO-10M DF, an identification friend-or-foe (IFF) transponder, ultra-violet lamps lighting the instrument panel, a gun camera etc. A better installation job and higher-quality electric bonding helped extend the range of radio communication to 118 km (73 miles) and the range of action of navigation instruments to 150 km (93 miles), which met the standards of the day. Unfortunately, like most of its predecessors, the production Yak was armed with one ShVAK cannon and two UBS-12.7 machine-guns.

In 1946-1948 much effort was expended on perfecting the contemporaneous armament, including Nudel'man's N-37 and N-45 cannons and Berezin's B-20s synchronised cannon. Besides, some of the Yaks were equipped with reversible-pitch propellers (to reduce the landing run), the ASP-1N automatic gunsight, the 'Anschütz' artificial horizon etc. Especially many flights on various Yak-9P examples were performed by Captain L. M. Koovshinov, in particular, for the purpose of perfecting methods of reducing the temperature in the cockpit and enhancing the aircraft's ease of handling.

In the meantime, the era of piston-engined fighters was coming to a close. Despite being beset by numerous teething troubles, the jet-powered machines of the late 1940s had a speed advantage of some 100 km/h (62 mph), enjoyed indisputable ascendancy in vertical manoeuvrability and carried more potent armament.

In late March 1948 the Soviet Government took the decision to terminate production of piston-engined Yak-9Ps at Plant No. 153 and to start manufacturing Yak-23 jet fighters instead. Production of the all-metal Yaks continued till the end of 1948; in all, 772 machines were delivered, supplemented by the 29 Yak-9Ps with metal wings. All of them remained in service until the mid-1950s.

Chapter 4

The Yak-3

The Last of the Line

The Yak-3 is the last and the most brilliant representative of Yakovlev's World War Two period fighter family. This fighter based on the experience of the first two years of the war was, in effect, a new aircraft type. It embodied the enormous work that had been conducted by the Yakovlev OKB, the production plants and scientific organisations of the USSR (first of all LII and TsAGI) with a view to improving the aerodynamic and structural design and enhancing the combat potential of fighters.

The aircraft incorporated all the best features that had been achieved in the Yak-1, Yak-7 and Yak-9. When it put in an appearance at the front for the first time in the summer of 1944, the Yak-3 powered by the VK-105PF-2 engine turned out to be the most lightweight and agile aircraft among the fighters of the USSR, the USA and Germany. Perhaps only the British Spitfire could rival this machine.

While possessing slightly lower performance than its stablemate – the VK-107A-powered Yak-9U, the Yak-3 powered by the VK-105PF-2 was superior to it as regards the maturity of the powerplant which made the Yak-3 more reliable in operation and, consequently, more combat-ready. A prototype Yak-3 powered by the VK-108 engine developed a speed of 745 km/h (463 mph); this was the highest speed attained by Soviet fighters which came close to the limit for fighters of the 'pre-jet propulsion era'.

Yak-1M ('*Moskit*') fighter prototype

The Yak-3's predecessor was the Yak-1M fighter, the prototype of which was also dubbed '*Moskit*' (Mosquito). The wings of the new fighter were structurally similar to those of the Yak-9, featuring metal spars, metal and wooden ribs and plywood skinning. However, wing area was reduced by 2.3 sq m (24.7 sq ft) in comparison with the preceding Yaks and made up 14.85 sq m (159.7 sq ft).

The fighter's wing span was reduced to 9.2 m (30 ft 2.2 in). A production break coinciding with the fuselage axis was introduced; this afforded the possibility of replacing the port or starboard wing panels in field conditions in case of damage. The control system, the fuselage and the undercarriage were all borrowed from the production Yak-1. As distinct from the latter, the fuel system com-

The Yak-1M (Yak-1 'Moskit') in the TsAGI wind tunnel.

prised three tanks: two main tanks in the wing outer panels and one service tank in the wing centre section. As for the armament, equipment and armour protection, the Yak-1M had much in common with the Yak-1 in the version featuring improvements in visibility, armour protection and armament.

The engine's cooling system featured a more efficient radiator buried more deeply in the fuselage. Two circular-shape oil coolers working in parallel were placed in the wing centre section under the cockpit floor. This made it possible to eliminate excrescences on the lower panel of the engine cowling and make it smooth, thus considerably improving its outward contours.

The Yak-1M had an all-up weight of 2,665 kg (5,876 lb), ie, some 245 kg (540 lb) less than that of a production Yak-1 manufactured in 1943. The wing loading rose marginally from 169 to 179 kg/sq m (34.70 to 36.75 lb/sq ft) while the power loading was noticeably reduced – from 2.40 to 2.19 kg/hp (5.30 to 4.83 lb/hp). The weight reduction was achieved mainly by reducing the wing area and substituting duralumin alloy spars for wooden ones; all this produced a weight saving of 150 kg (331 lb).

The prototype was completed in mid-February 1943. Throughout the spring months the aircraft was subjected to development work conducted under the direction of leading engineer M. Grigor'yev who had taken an active part in the design and construction of the Yak-1M. Pavel Ya. Fedrovi, chief test pilot of the Yakovlev OKB, made an uneventful first flight at the end of February 1943, after which the machine entered the factory tests phase.

Testing of the aircraft at NII VVS lasted throughout June 1943 (with A. Proshakov as project test pilot and A. Stepanets as leading engineer, both being the most experienced specialists of the Institute as regards Yakovlev's machines); the tests revealed the new fighter had excellent performance.

But the OKB held the opinion that the fighter's improvement potential had not yet been exhausted. At A. S. Yakovlev's insistence additional tests were conducted to determine the changes in the basic performance characteristics after the boost pressure of the M-105PF engine had been increased from 1,050 to 1,100 mm Hg.

Initially V. Ya. Klimov, Chief Designer of the engine, gave his consent to increasing the boost pressure only at the first supercharger speed. Additional tests showed that augmenting the engine's power by increasing the boost pressure produced a 6 to 7 km/h (3.7 to 4.35 mph) gain in maximum speed at low altitude, reducing the time to 5,000 m (16,400 ft) by 0.1 minutes and affording an extra 50 m (164 ft) in altitude gain during a combat turn. It also led to a marginal improvement of field performance

Above and below: The first prototype Yak-1M (Yak-1 'Moskit') during manufacturer's flight tests. Note the rather pointed and cropped spinner.

Two more views of the first prototype Yak-1 'Moskit'. At this stage the fighter was powered by an M-105PF engine (note the three dual exhaust stubs on each side).

Above and below: The Yak-1M during State acceptance trials at NII VVS which lasted from 27th June to 4th July 1943.

The Yak-1M differed from the late-production 'bubbletop' Yak-1 primarily in having new wings of reduced span and area, reduced fuel tankage and new oil coolers buried in the wing roots.

Above and below: The first prototype Yak-1M after re-engining with the M-107A (note the seven exhaust stubs). The photos show the fighter as originally flown with this powerplant.

and entailed virtually no change in the engine's water and oil temperature.

Later theoretical calculations showed the possibility of boosting the engine also at medium altitude. The boost pressure was also increased at the supercharger's second speed. While the M-105PF engine developed (without regard to the dynamic pressure) 1,180 hp at 2,700 m (8.856 ft), after boosting its output rose to 1,244 hp at 2,100 m (6,888 ft). With the boost pressure increased to 1,100 mm Hg the engine was designated M-105PF-2, and from the spring of 1944 onwards it bore the designation VK-105PF-2.

As regards performance, the Yak-1M was on a par with the best fighters of the final stage of the Second World War. Thus, in terms of maximum speed it surpassed production Yak-9s throughout the altitude range by at least 25 to 35 km/h (15.5 to 21.7 mph); it outperformed the Fw 190A-4 at altitudes up to 8,300 m (27,224 ft) and the Bf 109G-2 up 5,700 m (18,696 ft), judging by the results of tests at NII VVS. The Yak-1M enjoyed the greatest advantage at low altitude, whereas at high altitudes the German fighters were faster owing to the better high-altitude performance of the Daimler-Benz DB 605 and BMW 801 engines. For example, at the altitude of 7,000 m (22,960 ft) the Bf 109G-2 surpassed the Soviet fighter in speed by nearly 50 km/h.

With regard to the rate of climb up to 5,000 m (16,400), the Yak-1M was unrivalled among the contemporary fighters of the world. All known versions of the Bf 109, which was justly considered to be one of the best in performing upward vertical manoeuvres, were somewhat inferior to the Soviet fighter. The reduction of the wing area was accompanied by a reduction of the Yak-1M's all-up weight; as a result, it did not entail a deterioration of its field performance, spinning and diving characteristics. The handling of the prototype fighter, like that of the Yak-1, Yak-7 and Yak-9, was within the capabilities of wartime pilots possessing an average and even below-average skill level.

The test report noted: *'As regards the effectiveness and harmonious action of controls (from the point of view of stick forces from control surfaces) the Yak-1M, along with the Spitfire Mk VB (it was tested at NII VVS in June*

1943 – *Author*), is exemplary for all fighter aircraft, both indigenous and foreign.'

A few shortcoming of the prototype, typical for the Yaks (such as overheating of oil during climb at the optimum climb rate, poor functioning of the breather, oil leakage from various sealed joints, inadequate range of radio communication between airborne aircraft and with the ground etc.) could not spoil the favourable overall impression produced by the machine.

Yak-1M *'Dooblyor'* (second prototype)

While the first prototype Yak-1M was undergoing State trials, construction of the second prototype Yak-1M (dubbed *'dooblyor'*, in accordance with the practice of the time) was nearing completion under the direction of engineer M. Grigor'yev. It turned out to be still more refined and well-thought out in every respect.

Thus, the fuel tank bays were separated from the cockpit by sealed bulkheads; the fabric skinning of the fuselage was replaced by plywood skinning; the cockpit hood was provided with an emergency jettisoning system; some other improvements were introduced as well. The fighter was fitted with a new VISh-105SV-01 propeller which featured a lightened hub and blades with airfoil sections at the roots.

There were also changes in the armament. Instead of the ShVAK cannon the designers installed a prototype ShA-20M lightened cannon designed by Boris Shpital'nyy and reinstated the second UBS-12.7 heavy machine-gun after the pattern of the Yak-7B. At the same time the avionics suite was expanded. A feature that was bound to attract attention was the radio which could be remotely controlled by a push-button at the throttle lever. This was a novelty in the Soviet aircraft construction. The Yak-1M *'Dooblyor'* dispensed with the aerial mast, making use of a single-wire aerial.

As a result, the all-up weight remained virtually the same at 2,660 kg (5,865 lb). Construction of the aircraft was completed on 9th September 1943. At the beginning of October, after brief manufacturer's flight tests, the second Yak-1M was handed over to NII VVS for State trials which were successfully conducted by pilot A. Proshakov and engineer G. Sedov within ten days.

The tests showed an improvement of performance: the *'Dooblyor'* attained a speed of 570 km/h (354 mph) at sea level and 651 km/h (405 mph) at 4,300 m (14,104 ft); it gained 1,280 m (4,198 ft) of altitude in a combat turn and could perform a full-circle banking turn at low altitude within a mere 16 to 17 seconds. In addition, it was noted that the installation of more effective radiators, changes made to the ducting and the greater maximum opening of the radiator shutter had substantially improved the engine's temperature conditions. For the first time on an aircraft of the Yakovlev fighter family the possibility was ensured of performing prolonged horizontal flight at maximum speed and of gaining altitude in the maximum rate of climb mode with the engine at nominal revs (2,700 rpm).

Thanks to the thorough electric bonding and shielding of the basic metal elements of the structure, the range of reception of radio messages from the ground in the cockpit rose to 90 km (56 miles), and pilots could confidently maintain communication between themselves at a distance of 20 km (12.4 miles), which represented very good characteristics for the radio equipment of Soviet fighters at that time.

It is difficult to single out another Soviet aircraft that had received as many laudatory comments from test pilots, both those of the OKB and the military ones. For example, A. Koobyshkin considered it to be the best

The same aircraft after modifications as recommended by TsAGI. The pointed spinner and chin-mounted extra oil cooler gave a Fairey Firefly-like appearance to the fighter's front end.

Above and below: front and rear views of the modified first prototype Yak-1M.

among the known fighters of World War Two in overall performance. Test pilot V. Khomiakov who had flown the prototype fighter wrote in his report:

'The cockpit is comfortable. Forward visibility has been improved. The instruments and control levers are well placed and their arrangement almost fully conforms to the standard cockpit. Taxying is easy. [...] When airborne, the aircraft is stable and simple in handling. The machine has an excellent rate of climb and manoeuvrability, both in the vertical and in the horizontal plane. Performance has been improved in comparison with its predecessor, the [first prototype] Yak-1M.'

Bearing in mind these and other comments, the Government decision was not long in coming. Already in October 1943 the Yak-1M 'Dooblyor' was launched into production under the designation Yak-3, supplanting the 'straight' Yak-1. The designation Yak-3 had already been assigned to one of Yakovlev's fighters – that was the name intended for the production version of the I-30, but production of this fighter did not get under way in 1941 or at any later time. The destiny of the new machine proved to be much happier.

Production Yak-3 fighter

Preparations for series production of the Yak-3 started as far back as the summer of 1943. Initially it was envisaged that Plant No. 292 would start producing the new machines immediately upon completion of its restoration after the enemy bombardment. However, development of the prototype Yak-1M and the 'Dooblyor' dragged on well into the autumn; still, the war was at its height and it was necessary to turn out combat machines at an unabated rate while switching to the new model. Therefore in the winter of 1944 the Saratov plant tooled up for the new machine while continuing to manufacture an average of 250 Yak-1s every month.

The work was getting under way slowly, and the command was well aware of the fact that the delivery schedule of the most modern Soviet fighters (such as the Yak-3, Yak-9U and the La-7 – the latter designed by Semyon Lavochkin) to front-line units would not be kept. A. K. Repin, Chief Engineer of the Red Army's Air Force, even suggested in a letter to the Central Committee of the Communist (Bolshevik) Party that production plants be allowed to reduce the output of aircraft considered outdated by that time for the sake of speeding up the work on new types.

Although the Yak-3 had much in common with the Yak-1, the plant was making slow progress. What was the impediment, you may ask? The Yak-3 proved to be more labour-intensive than its predecessor because it required extreme care in the surface finish; initially the number of man-hours spent on manufacturing a single Yak-3 was 2.5 times greater than in the case of the Yak-1. The first production Yak-3 assembled at this factory was completed on 1st March 1944 and test-flown a week later. Only by the end of the following month were 22 fighters officially accepted by the military.

The production version of the Yak-3 differed from the 'Dooblyor' in having numerous changes which, however, were of minor importance. For example, the armament of early production machines was absolutely identical to that of their predecessor, the Yak-1 (the ShA-20M cannon never entered production). As for the production standards, a considerable number of defects was noted on the new Yaks, such as a slightly corrugated wing surface, a poor fit of the cowling panels, dents in inspection panels and so on.

Production Yak-3s suffered a deterioration of performance compared to the 'Dooblyor' on account of poorer production standards. Thus, the speed fell by 15 to 20 km/h (9.3 to 12.4 mph), while the time to 5,000 m (16,400 ft) rose by half a minute. High control forces caused a worsening of horizontal manoeuvrability. It was also noted that production machines had a shorter combat radius and radio communication range.

Service units started taking delivery of the new fighter in the late spring and early summer of 1944, when the Soviet command was making preparations for major offensive operations. Several of the first fighters were delivered to the 396th IAP, and combat evaluation of the Yak-3 was conducted in the 91st IAP (commanded by Lieutenant-Colonel A. Kovalyov) of the 2nd Air Army in June and July of 1944.

The regiment was assigned the task of keeping the air superiority in the course of the L'vov operation, and approximately a month before the beginning of the operation's active phase the unit received 41 brand-new Yak-3s. Nearly half of the flying personnel was taking part in combat for the first time, but all airmen had undergone a good conversion training course before being sent to the front. Also, for training purposes NII VVS arranged a session of mock combat between a Yak-3 and a captured Bf 109G-4, during which a considerable ascendancy of the Soviet fighter at altitudes from ground level to 7,000 m (22,960 ft) was witnessed and the most expedient methods of combat for the Red Army's Air Force pilots were determined.

Operational evaluation confirmed the conclusions that had been made in advance. The unit performed 431 combat sorties, including interception of enemy aircraft, supporting aircraft from other units on a mission, 'seek-and-destroy' missions and other duties. 20 enemy fighters and three Ju 87 dive bombers were shot down in aerial combat. Own losses included two Yak-3s shot down and three that were damaged by flak but managed to reach the area held by Soviet troops.

Combat experience demonstrated that the new Soviet fighter caught up with the enemy fighters both in horizontal flight and in upward vertical manoeuvres. Usually the Yak-3 could get on the tail of the Fw 190A at the second 360° turn, and of the Bf 109 at the third full circle. It was the Messerschmitts that remained the main opponents of the Soviet Yaks in the struggle for air superiority over the Western Ukraine.

The biggest air battle took place on 16th July 1944. Both sides called in reinforcements, and, when the skirmish was in full swing, 18 Yak-3s were opposed by 24 enemy fighters. According to the claims of the Soviet airmen, they succeeded in shooting down 15 German aircraft at the cost of one Yak-3 shot down and one damaged. It is worth noting that on the following day the Luftwaffe was appreciably less active at this sector of the front.

As a result of the operational evaluation it was determined that the Yak-3 would best be used for combatting the enemy's fighter aircraft. Its employment for providing cover to ground troops my means of patrolling, for escorting bombers or for other similar duties was less expedient because of the limited amount of fuel on board (the average duration of a combat sortie was about 40 minutes).

The Yak-3's special feature was its ability to accelerate very quickly – for example, in a shallow dive. As it were, the pilots had to 'hold the fighter back' because its good aerodynamic qualities made it easy to exceed the indicated airspeed of 650 km/h (404 mph), which was dangerous due to insufficient structural strength. One more peculiarity that had to be taken into account consisted in a marked compression of the undercarriage oleo legs during ground running of the engine; there was a danger of the aircraft nosing over during landing.

The service tests also revealed some obvious shortcomings of the early Yak-3s. There were cases of the undercarriage legs collapsing during landing runs and taxying; the main gear breaker struts and oleo leg attachment points sometimes failed. Generally, however, the maintenance of the Yak-3 was simple and the aircraft could be mastered by flying personnel and ground crews without any difficulties.

At the fronts and in the factory workshops

In the late summer of 1944 Yak-3 operations reached a fairly wide scale. The fighter's main opponent was the Bf 109G. The latter's mass-produced G-6 version, being heavier than its predecessors, lost its superiority in speed and vertical manoeuvre over the Soviet fighter for the first time since the beginning of the war. This fact had to be recognised, albeit painfully, by German pilots. They noted that the Messerschmitt was inferior in speed to the Yak-3 by 10 to 20 km/h (6.2 to 12.4 mph) at altitudes up to 4,000 m (13,120 ft) even when using the MW-50 methanol/water injection system for engine boost and when flying without underwing cannon pods, and that the German fighter was inferior in performing steep climb and combat turns. At the same time, in horizontal dogfighting the Yak-3's advantage proved insignificant. Still less favourable was the Yak-3's position in a manoeuvring combat against the Fw 190A.

Checkout tests conducted by NII VVS on Yak-3 c/n 11-12 (ie, 11th aircraft in Batch 12) in August 1944 showed that, with an all-up weight of 2,675 kg (5,898 lb), the fighter attained a speed of 555 km/h (345 mph) at sea level and 631 km/h at 4,200 m (13,776 ft), climbing to 5,000 m (16,400 ft) within 4.5 minutes. The military were also satisfied with other performance figures: a full-circle banking turn was performed in 21 seconds, the altitude gain in a combat turn amounted to 1,200 m (4,560 ft), the take-off run was a mere 280 m (918 ft) and the service ceiling was 10,400 m (34,112 ft).

Although the Yak-3s were not fitted with rocket launch rails or bomb racks, strafing ground targets was included into the range of their combat duties. Thus, shortly after converting to the new machines the airmen of the 515th IAP successfully attacked enemy vehicle convoys south of Warsaw. On 19th August, while on a reconnaissance mission, a pair of Yak-3s spotted two-way traffic on one of the roads and succeeded in setting three vehicles alight, making use of onboard weapons. However, the fuel amount carried by the Yak-3 was very limited and the 'hunters' had to return to base. The regiment commander decided that the vehicles would not have time to cover a big distance, so four Yaks were promptly refuelled and got airborne. They quickly spotted their targets and set three more vehicles on fire. Whereas the first attacks were made from low altitude, the fighters performing S-turns to avoid being hit by enemy AA fire, in the second pass the Yaks dived one by one towards the convoy out of the sun.

The pilots of this and of other units noted that the Yak-3 possessed a marginally better view from the cockpit to aft compared to the Yak-1 with 'improved visibility' because the latter's glazing was prone to misting up in the area of the bulletproof glass panels. The absence of the cockpit hood emergency jettisoning feature compelled Yak-1 pilots to fly

The second prototype Yak-1M seen during State acceptance trials.

Above and below: Two more views of the second prototype Yak-1M (*dooblyor*) during State acceptance trials. Note the rounded shape of the spinner.

The second prototype differed from the first aircraft in having an M-105PF-2 engine. This was, in effect, the prototype of the Yak-3.

Above and below: One of the first Saratov-built Yak-3s (c/n 0111) during State acceptance trials at NII VVS.

4 White, one of the Yak-3s operated by the 'Normandie-Niémen' regiment.

combat sorties with the cockpit hoods open; the windshield was often sprayed with oil, which obstructed the forward view. On the other hand, the Yak-3's moulded cockpit visor noticeably distorted the objects observed through it, hampering the use of the gunsight.

In mid-August 1944, when the 240th IAD was waging hard battles west and north-west of Kaunas, two Yak-3 fighters landed at Orany airfield. The command and the headquarters personnel of the formation knew about the new fighter: a short while earlier the *Pravda* (Truth) daily had published a photo of the machine, the caption stating that this was the best and the most lightweight fighter in the world. After landing one of the pilots who had ferried the aircraft handed his machine over Colonel G. Zimin (later Air Marshal) with the words: 'For your personal use. To the flying division commander from Marshal A. Novikov, commander of the Red Army Air Force'.

Shortly thereafter the command of this division was to play host to a delegation from the British allies. Commander Roberts, head of the delegation, immediately expressed the wish to see the Yak-3. A special aerobatics programme had been prepared for the guests; it was brilliantly performed by Major V. Skoopchenko, piloting skills inspector of the Division. Then the head of the British delegation was permitted to climb into the cockpit and examine it. Sure enough, far from all the questions posed by the British guests received an adequate answer. But, make no mistake, the machine strongly impressed the specialists – the delegation included several fighter pilots who had defended the skies of London shortly before that.

Another Division commander who personally made use of the Yak-3 in combat was General G. Zakharov. As soon as the new machines had been delivered to the 303rd Fighter Air Division, he performed up to 40 flights on Yak-3 c/n 310147 (ie, Tbilisi aircraft factory No. 31, Batch 1, 47th aircraft in the batch). His conclusion was: such a fighter had no equals. Zakharov wrote in his report: *'The Yak-3 is easy to maintain and poses no difficulties for ground crews. The aircraft is stable at take-off and landing and can easily be flown by any pilot – something that absolutely cannot be said about the La-5FN fighter.*

The pilots of the 18th Guards IAP and the 'Normandie-Niémen' regiment mastered the Yak-3 after logging 3 to 5 flying hours. The Yak-3 gains altitude very quickly and has a wide range of speeds (200 to 600 km/h) [124 to 373 mph]. *All aerobatic manoeuvres, both in the horizontal and in the vertical plane, are performed excellently. The fighter offers excellent visibility and has a comfortable, well-lit cockpit.'* The General expressed the wish that the Soviet Air Force be equipped with such fighters as quickly as possible.

Commanders of the Luftwaffe formations largely shared the high opinion of the Yak-3 that had been expressed by Soviet and British generals and senior officers. Appraising the characteristics of new Soviet fighters, Lieutenant-General Walter Schwabedissen wrote in his book *The Russian Air Force in the Eyes of German Commanders*:

'Whereas the German Bf 109G and Fw 190 models were equal to any of above Soviet models in all respects, this cannot be said of the Soviet Yak-3, which made its first appearance at the front in the late summer of 1944. This plane was faster, more manoeuvrable and had better climbing capabilities than the German Bf 109G and Fw 190, to which it was inferior only in point of armament.'

In waging combat against the Yak-3 German fighters relied heavily on the use of surprise attacks. That was the case on 17th September 1944 when Fw 190 fighter attack aircraft coming out of the sun bounced three Yak-3s from the 66th Guards IAP near Riga and shot down two of them. The regiment's pilots took their revenge on 23rd September when a group of Yakovlev fighters led by Major I. Vitkovskiy claimed seven Fw 190s destroyed in one dogfight alone.

On 29th October, in daytime, the units of the 4th Guards IAD successfully effected a simultaneous blocking of three German airfields in the Baltic area – Skrunda, Aizpute and Saldus. Patrolling in groups of six to eight which relieved one another, the Yak-3s prevented the Germans from using the airfields for combat activities for more than three hours. Fighters summoned by the enemy from other airfields were of little help. JG54 'Grünherz' lost one Fw 190 that was shot down; another one was damaged and yet another suffered an undercarriage failure after overrunning the runway. In contrast, not a single Yak-3 was shot down.

In the summer and autumn of 1944 a number of alterations was introduced into the design of the Yak-3 at Plant No. 292:

• from the 13th batch (August) onwards the second UBS-12.7 machine-gun was reinstated because this armament version was more in conformity with the needs of the front (about 500 production machines had been equipped with one cannon and one synchronised machine-gun);

• from the 16th batch (September) onwards the total fuel tankage was increased by approximately 20 litres (4.4 Imp gal);

• from the 17th batch (September) onwards the fighter was provided with modified radio equipment and dust filters which prevented excessive engine wear at the cost of a slight reduction in level speed;

• from the 19th batch (October) onwards the fabric skinning was replaced by plywood

Above and below: 96 White, a production Yak-3 M-105PF-2 (c/n 9626), during checkout tests at NII VVS

Collective farmer Ferapont Golovatyy hands over a Yak-3 to Maj. B. N. Yeryomin. The legend reads *The 2nd aircraft from Golovatyy - For the terminal rout of the enemy*. Note the red star on the spinner.

115

Three views of the first Yak-3 manufactured by the Tbilisi aircraft factory No. 31. Note the unusually small star on the fin.

skinning as on the second prototype (Yak-1M 'Dooblyor').

At the same time the Saratov plant built up a good production tempo: in the autumn of 1944 the monthly output averaged approximately 250 machines. A further 80 Yak-3s per month began rolling off the assembly lines of Plant No. 31 in Tbilisi which gradually switched its production from the LaGG-3 to Yakovlev's fighter. From the outset the Yak-3s manufactured in Tbilisi were armed with two large-calibre synchronised machine-guns in addition to the engine-mounted cannon; they differed externally mainly in the contours of the aft part of the radiator bath. Tbilisi-produced Yak-3s proved to be heavier by an average 25 kg (55 lb), which was due in part to additional armament and ammunition and greater tankage; their level speed was greater by some 15 km/h (9.3 mph) compared to Saratov-built machines.

Introduction of the Yak-3 into service units of the Red Army's Air Force was accompanied by its share of troubles. Numerous accidents and incidents took place in many regiments. The gravest accident occurred in the 402nd IAP of the 3rd IAK, when Captain P. Tarasov, one of the most proficient aerobatics performers in the corps, was killed in a crash. As it transpired, the wing skinning had loosened in the area of the wheel wells and, when subjected to high loads, broke away from the ribs along the lines of adhesive bonding, after which the spars and the wing as a whole disintegrated completely.

In all such incidents Saratov-produced fighters were involved. An investigation conducted by TsAGI confirmed that the wing strength had deteriorated because of breaches of the bonding procedures. After a sample checking of the condition of wing surfaces conducted by Chief Engineer of the Air Force and by subsequent special commissions 114 Yak-3s had to be grounded; 68 of them were in the 3rd IAK. The command was seriously concerned about the reduced combat efficiency of the air formation on the eve of the important Soviet offensive at the Wisla and Oder rivers.

Thanks to urgent measures and heroic efforts taken by ground crews of front-line units, factory repair teams and various scientific research institutions, it proved possible to eliminate the defect expeditiously and make the fighter safe to fly. A contributing factor was also the alternative variant of attaching the skin to the wing structure developed in the Yakovlev OKB specially for repairs and involving the use of pins. According to TsAGI conclusions, the fighter's structural strength came to meet the requirements of normal operation.

No less drastic measures were taken at Plant No. 292. Starting with the 28th batch, the casein glue was supplanted by the VIAM-B3 adhesive that had proved its worth, and from the following batch the area of contact between ribs and skinning was increased twofold and wheel well domes were strengthened in their uppermost part. By the beginning of the New Year of 1945 the number of unserviceable Yak-3s in active units had been brought down to 12.8%.

Initially, observance of the specified all-up weight was not enforced strictly enough, and some production machines weighed as much as 2,710 kg (5,976 lb). In the period from August 1944 to April 1945 the weight was anywhere between 2,629 and 2,692 kg (5,797 and 5,936 lb) which was found to be acceptable.

Acting in concert with LII, TsAGI and production plants, the Yakovlev OKB conducted serious work for the purpose of improving the fighters performance. As a result, from October 1944 onwards the performance was, in effect, improved enough to match the characteristics of the 'Dooblyor'.

This work was conducted in parallel with building up the output of production machines. Whereas in May 1944 the Yak-3 made up only 29% of the total production vol-

A production Yak-3 manufactured by the Saratov aircraft factory No. 292 undergoing tests.

ume at the Saratov Plant, it accounted for 52% in June, 84% in July, and in August the share rose to 100%. Importantly, switching to the new fighter type was effected practically without detriment to the overall output of aircraft.

Still more successful was the mastering of Yak-3 production by Plant 31 in Tbilisi. From the outset the Yak3 was built here in a version featuring better performance and heavier armament compared to machines produced in Saratov. And, most importantly, Tbilisi-produced fighters were not afflicted with the inadequate wing strength resulting from defective bonding of the skinning to the wing framework.

Until the end of 1944 combat losses of the Yak-3s amounted to only 56 machines (of which 42 were reported as missing after combat sorties); a further 34 fighters were written off for non-combat reasons. In all, by the beginning of 1945 the fighter element of the Soviet Air Force had 5,810 machines in its inventory, including 735 Yak-3s. Of these, 44% were on the strength of the 16th Air Army commanded by General S. Rudenko which joined in providing air cover for the troops at the Berlin direction from the second half of January.

As before, many sorties were flown not for the purpose of intercepting enemy aircraft (a mission to which the Yak-3 was best suited) but for other duties. Thus, the airmen of the 112th Guards IAP/10th Fighter Air Corps spent 98% of all the sorties flown between 12th January and 8th May 1945 for providing cover to bombers and attack aircraft. In the course of a battle conducted on 27th March a group of six Yaks repulsed all attacks against the Il-2s of the 224th Attack Air Division, scoring hits on three Bf 109Gs of JG77; one victory was claimed by Captain L. Dyoma, one of the Air Corps' best aces.

The 10th Fighter Air Corps operated in the skies of southern Poland, Austria and Czechoslovakia where the Luftwaffe was not

A production Yak-3 seen during special tests at LII.

The sleek lines of the Yak-3 are well illustrated by this example. Yakovlev was big on photographing his aircraft, leaving a lot of excellent pictures for posterity. Here the fighter is seen in standard configuration, but see the next page...

Three views of the same Yak-3 in identical aspects following installation of ejector fairings on the exhaust stubs. This measure increased top speed somewhat, even though it clearly did not make the fighter more aesthetically pleasing.

Above: CO of the 303rd Fighter Division Gen. Zakharov (second from left) with Soviet and French fighter pilots in front of a Yak-3 operated by the 'Normandie-Niémen' regiment.

Above: A fine air-to-air study of a Yak-3 belonging to the 'Normandie-Niémen' regiment.

Local residents examine a Soviet Air Force Yak-3 which has force-landed in a field.

very active. Still fewer air battles were fought by the new Yaks in the course of hostilities with Japan in August 1945. By that time the Soviet command had succeeded in redeploying 106 Yak-3s (78 of them combat-ready) to the Far East where they were integrated into the forces of the Transbaikal Front and the two Far East Fronts. Presumably the only Japanese fighter that could rival the performance of the Yak-3 at that time was the Nakajima Ki-84 Hayate, but Japanese airmen put up no active opposition in the air and there is no evidence of air combats between these aircraft. As for the Nakajima Ki-43 Hayabusa which was deployed in large numbers in the northern provinces of China, it had a disadvantage of more than 100 km/h (62 mph) in maximum speed compared to the Yak-3 and was also inferior to the Soviet fighter with regard to vertical manoeuvrability and armament.

One Yak-3 was preserved and exhibited in the Yakovlev OKB's museum until recently. This aircraft flown by Major Boris N. Yeryomin, Commander of the 31st Guards IAP, had been presented to him by Ferapont Golovatyy, a collective farmer from the Saratov region. Regrettably, this legendary machine is now in the USA.

A total of 4,848 fighters of this type were built; of these, 3,840 were manufactured by the main plant in Saratov. The production run in Saratov comprised 59 batches (50 of them completed before the end of the war), while eight batches were produced in Tbilisi (the sixth batch was completed shortly after VE-Day). Of the overall number, 737 machines were built after the war.

Yak-3P production fighter

After the war the two factories built primarily the Yak-3P (*pushechnyy* – cannon-armed). This version differed mainly in having revised armament. The ShVAK cannon and the UBS machine gun were replaced by new cannon designed by Berezin in two versions: the B-20M and the B-20S, the suffixes denoting *motornaya* (engine-mounted) and *sinkhronnaya* (synchronised) respectively. The three barrels together produced a weight of fire amounting to 3,52 kg (7.8 lb) per second versus 2,72 kg (6.0 lb) for the 'standard' Yak-3; the new installation had virtually no effect on the weight of the airframe.

The Yak-3P showed good stability when firing the B-20 cannon within the entire speed envelope and at all attitudes. The weapons' recoil affected the precision of sighting only to a negligible extent. The modified Yak-3P passed testing at NII VVS in March-April 1945 and was put into series production.

However, far more stringent demands concerning quality standards in aircraft manufacturing were introduced after the war. During tests conducted by NII VVS in October-November 1945 a production example of the Yak-3P (c/n 02-54) demonstrated speeds superior to those of the prototype: 572 km/h (355 mph) at sea level and 646 km/h (401 mph) at 3,900 m (12,792 ft), the time to 5,000 m (16,400 ft) being 4.8 minutes; nevertheless, the results of the tests were pronounced unsatisfactory. This was due, among other things, to persistent failures of the special brackets on which the B-20 cannon were attached.

In all, 596 Yak-3Ps were produced. None of them took part in combat.

Yak-3T fighter prototype

The Yak-3T (*tahnkovyy*, tank-busting) which was built in the OKB in January 1945 possessed even more potent armament. It retained the pair of synchronised cannons in the front upper decking, as on the Yak-3P, while the engine-mounted B-20 was replaced by a lightened 37-mm engine-mounted N-37 cannon designed by A. Nudel'man, with 25 rounds of ammunition.

Externally the Yak-3T differed from production machines in having a muzzle brake mounted on the barrel which protruded from the propeller spinner; it absorbed up to three-quarters of the cannon's recoil energy. Installation of the heavy cannon necessitated some changers in the design. Thus, the cockpit was moved aft 400 mm (1 ft 4 in) in a fashion similar to the Yak-9T; simultaneously, fuel capacity was reduced by 17 litres (3.74 Imp gal) and the self-sealing coating of the fuel tanks was deleted.

Despite the weight-saving measures, the weight rose to 2,756 kg (6,077 lb) and the performance deteriorated marginally: top speed was 560 km/h (348 mph) at sea level and 629 km/h (391 mph) at 4,000 m (13,120 ft), while the cruising range was a mere 559 km (347 miles). The designers succeeded in keeping the CG of the fully equipped Yak-3 at 25.7% of the mean aerodynamic chord, thanks to which good controllability was retained.

Tests revealed that the fighter remained as easy in handling as before. The armament fit of the Yak-3T ensured effective engagement of aerial targets and enabled the machine to be used for attacks against railway trains, trucks and armoured vehicles. There was virtually no loss of sighting when firing a burst of four rounds from the engine-mounted cannon. This made it possible to fire long bursts while retaining accurate sighting – something that could not be done on the Yak-9T.

However, major defects of the aircraft were also revealed. The combination of the engine with the new cannon was not yet trouble-free, the engine being plagued by overheating of water and oil. This precluded

Above: A beaming Soviet pilot from a Guards unit poses in the cockpit of his Yak-3 at a recently captured German airfield, with Deutsche Lufthansa DC-2 D-AIAS and Ju 86B-0 D-AQEA as a backdrop.

Above: As the legend on the fuselage reveals, this Yak-3 has been presented to fighter pilot Semyon Rogovoy by the Soviet Navy personnel serving on the Amur River in the Soviet Far East.

The prototype of the Yak-3P armed with three cannons seen during State acceptance trials.

The prototype of the Yak-3T 'tank killer' armed with a 37-mm engine-mounted cannon.

normal operation. The engine persistently malfunctioned; this included emission of smoke, vibration, spark plug failures, drops in fuel pressure and so on. All this prevented the Yak-3T from being ordered into production.

Yak-3PD fighter prototype

Using the airframe of the Yak-3 as a basis, the Yakovlev OKB created one of the most successful interceptor fighters. In September 1944 a production example of the fighter was fitted with the VK-105PD – one of the several high-altitude engine versions provided with a Dollezhal'-designed supercharger.

Testing of this aircraft at LII was conducted right before the end of the war. According to the test report, the aircraft possessed the following special features: the wing area was increased by half a square metre (5.4 sq ft); an experimental high-altitude propeller was installed; the engine's air inlet was moved from its original location to a place ahead of the radiator bath. The engine was provided with a device for injecting an alcohol/water mixture between the supercharger stages for the purpose of reducing the air temperature.

By restricting the armament to one NS-23 cannon the designers succeeded in reducing the all-up weight to 2,616 kg (5,768 lb). Pilot Sergey N. Anokhin reached an altitude of 11,500 m, but calculations showed that the service ceiling could be as high as 13,000 m (42,640 ft). A speed of 692 km/h (430 mph) was attained at 10,850 m (34,702 ft).

Certain imperfections of the engine caused the testing to be temporarily suspended. The aircraft was then re-engined with the VK-105PV that had been developed on the Yak-9. Before resuming the tests, some development work was effected by LII. At the suggestion of pilot-engineer I. Shooneyko who was conducting the flight testing, the aircraft was fitted with a device permitting a part of the airflow from the supercharger to be spilled into the atmosphere. This completely eliminated the instability in the supercharger's operation at high altitudes and enabled the machine to fly at altitudes in excess of 13,000 m (42,640 ft) with the engine running normally.

In the course of a flight performed on 26th June 1945 pilot I. Shooneyko attained a speed of 710 km/h at the altitude of 11,000 m (36,080 ft), and on 6th July he reached a practical ceiling of 13,300 m (43,624 ft). It was noted that flights to altitudes in excess of 13,000 m with the pilot provided only with an oxygen mask required special training of pilots for high-altitude flights – for example, in an altitude chamber.

The Yak-3PD was not built in series, but the work at LII continued. Materials from the research conducted there formed the basis for a report on the functioning of engine radiators in high-altitude conditions, issued in March 1947.

Yak-3RD experimental fighter

In December 1944 an experimental fighter featuring a mixed powerplant was created on the basis of the Yak-3. In addition to the production VK-105PF-2 engine, the machine was equipped with an RD-1KhZ (*khimicheskoye zazhigahniye* – chemical ignition) liquid-fuel rocket motor designed by D. Glooshko; it was intended to serve as a booster.

Yakovlev entrusted engineer B. Motorin with the design of the unorthodox machine. Motorin installed the RD-1KhZ rated at 300 kgp (661 lb st) in the aft fuselage under the vertical tail on a special mount and enclosed it with an easily detachable cowling faired into the fuselage contours.

In the course of manufacturer's trials test pilot Victor Rastorgooyev performed 21 flights on this aircraft designated Yak-3RD (RD stands for *raketnyy dvigatel'* – rocket motor). In eight of these flights he switched on the RD-1KhZ. On one occasion, on 11th May 1945, the aircraft attained a speed of 782km/h (486 mph) at the altitude of 7,800 m (25,584 ft), which was 182 km higher than the speed attained at this altitude by the Yak-3 without the rocket booster. However, the automatic devices of the rocket engine were faulty and there were several cases of the engine cutting unexpectedly in flight. Once an explosion occurred in which the engine nozzle was severely damaged.

The faults were rectified and repairs were made, whereupon preparations were started for the aircraft to take part in the air display on the occasion of the 1945 Air Fleet Day. However, two days before the event, on 16th August, while performing a regular flight, the aircraft suddenly entered a steep dive and crashed, killing V. Rastorgooyev. The cause of the accident was not established, but it is known with certainty that there was no explosion of the rocket booster; neither did the engine disintegrate in flight. Apparently, there was a failure in the control system linkage.

In connection with the emergence of turbojet engines in the post-war years the subject of fitting liquid-fuel rocket boosters to piston-engined aircraft became moot and the work was discontinued.

The prototype of the high-altitude Yak-3PD seen during manufacturer's flight tests.

VK-107A-powered Yak-3 fighter

An important direction of work on the Yak-3 in the Yakovlev OKB consisted in the installation of more powerful engines. This work was conducted by a group of designers under Yevgeniy G. Adler's direction. Installation of the VK-107A engine did not require any major modifications to the airframe, apart from moving the cockpit aft 400 mm (1 ft 4 in). The more powerful engine necessitated an increase of fuel capacity to 518 litres (114 Imp gal), and the armament was changed to comprise two B-20S synchronised cannons in the front upper decking.

Two prototypes of this version were completed in early 1944. The first was used for manufacturer's tests which lasted until November 1944; it was flown by Pavel Ya. Fedrovi. The other prototype, after a few development flights for the purpose of rectifying engine faults, was handed over for State trials. They were started in February 1944 by G. Sedov, leading engineer of NII VVS. Pilots Yu. Antipov and A. Proshakov had to interrupt the flights eight times; in one such case the flights were suspended for almost two months (from mid-May to mid-July) because serious defects of the powerplant had to be remedied. Up to late August 1944 the machine performed only 44 take-offs, logging nearly 26 flight hours.

On account of the heavier engine the all-up weight rose to 2,984 kg (6,580 lb). In spite of this, the VK-107A-powered Yak-3 remained a lightweight fighter with excellent specific characteristics: the wing loading was 201 kg/m2 (41.18 lb/sq ft), and power loading – 2.0 kg/hp (4.41 lb/hp). The handling qualities of the fighter enabled it to be flown by medium-skilled pilots, as had been the case with its predecessor, the VK-105PF-2-powered Yak-3. All this, coupled with the excellent aerodynamics, endowed the fighter with outstanding performance. The aircraft attained a maximum speed of 611 km/h (380 mph) at sea level and 720 km/h (447 mph) at 5,750 m (18,860 ft). Time to 5,000 m (16,400 ft) was 3,9 minutes and the altitude gain in a combat turn equalled 1,500 m (4920 ft). All these characteristics constituted record-breaking performance for the final stage of the war.

However, test pilots noted that the VK-107A engines failed to log their designated service life hours because the crankshaft's main bearings failed. Besides, the unreliable functioning of the throttle lever control system precluded flight at cruising speed, and oil spill spraying the entire windshield prevented the pilot from closing the cockpit hood and making use of the gun sight. At that time Soviet specialists did not yet have the experience with the VK-107A engine gained subsequently on the Yak-9U.

Work on the Yak-3 powered by the VK-107A continued after the end of the war.

Above: The Yak-3R mixed-power fighter. The rocket booster nozzle is closed by a conical fairing.
Below: The RD-1KhZ liquid-fuel rocket motor with the cowling removed.

Above and below: The prototype of the Yak-3 VK-107A seen during manufacturer's flight tests. Note the carburettor air intake immediately aft of the spinner.

Above and below: A production Yak-3 VK-107A manufactured by the Tbilisi aircraft factory; note the aft location of the carburettor intake. The fighter must be a test aircraft, hence the silver and red paint job.

Yak-3 VK-107A – production version

In the spring of 1945 the People's Commissariat of Aircraft Industry took a decision requiring the Tbilisi plant to continue work on the VK-107A-powered Yak-3. According to the plans, 75 all-metal fighters were to be assembled at Plant No.31, making use of the unfinished airframes stocked there. As noted earlier, the Yak-3s that had been built there during the war years had an edge in production quality standard compared to fighters of the same type assembled at Plant No. 292; therefore, it was presumed that the VK-107A-powered machines would have reasonably high chances of being a success.

Modifications were incorporated by a team of designers under K. Skrzhinskiy in a production machine (c/n 70-03). It was fitted with a VK-107A engine from the last batch featuring an additional oil pump; the designers replaced the plywood skin of the fuselage and the wings with duralumin, and the control surfaces received a skin of *elektron* magnesium alloy instead of the standard fabric covering. Besides, the new fighter had a slightly increased amount of fuel and oil which, however, was inferior to the fuel and oil tankage of the prototype Yak-3 VK-107A. As a result, the all-up weight made up 2,935 kg (6,472 lb).

Manufacturer's flight tests lasted less than a month; on 11th May 1945 the all-metal Yak-3 was handed over to I. Kolosov, leading engineer of NII VVS, for testing. The most skilled pilots of the institute noted that the Yak-3 had better controllability in comparison with the similarly-powered prototype, more effective mainwheel brakes, and its engine functioned better at medium and high altitudes.

The results obtained in 44 flights confirmed the machine's high speeds and good manoeuvrability, even though the use of the 'combat' mode of the VK-107A (3,200 rpm) had to be relinquished because of the engine's unreliability. His intention was to eliminate the main defects of the aircraft prior to launching series production. However, in actual fact development of this particular machine had to be continued concurrently with the assembly of other examples of the

A Saratov-built Yak-3 VK-107A undergoing checkout tests at NII VVS

fighter. Plant No. 31 assembled 40 all-metal Yak-3s in 1945 and a further eight in the following year. Work on weeding out various defects on these aircraft continued throughout the year of 1946, whereupon the Tbilisi plant switched to mastering production of the jet-powered Yak-15.

The next stage in the work the VK-107A-powered machines was marked by tooling up for building a batch of 30 fighters of his model at Plant 292 in the spring of 1946. They differed from the two prototypes in wing design and in having various changes in the powerplant. Whereas the prototype fighters had wings with metal spars and plywood skinning, just like the production Yak-3 and Yak-9, now the government demanded that all-metal wings incorporating new technology be installed. Besides, the fighters were fitted with the improved version of the VK-107A. Based on operational experience with the Yak-9U, it featured an air cooling system for the exhaust manifolds, more capacious radiators and dust filters in the carburettor air intakes.

Changes were introduced into the radio equipment and armament. The latter was restricted to two B-20S synchronised cannons on some of the fighters, while on others they were supplemented by an engine-mounted B-20M. Testing of the first three production machines (c/ns 01-01, 03-01 and 04-01) conducted in April and May 1946 showed that their performance, high though it was, fell somewhat short of the Government specifications for fighters of this type at the end of December 1944. Thus, maximum speed at sea level was within the specified 600 km/h (373 mph), whereas the speed at the altitudes of 5,400 to 5,900 m (17,712 to 19,352 ft) reached 695 to 697 km/h (431.9 to 433.2 mph) as against the specified 700 km/h (435 mph). Time to 5,000 m (16,400 m) was 4.2 to 4.5 minutes (the requirement called for a maximum of 3.9 minutes).

The testing was very thorough and comprehensive. Thus, test pilots A. Proshakov, Yu. Antipov and V. Khomiakov determined the spinning characteristics of the new Yaks and came to the conclusion that they were virtually identical to those of the production VK-105PF-2-powered Yak-3s. However, high stick forces from the ailerons and elevator made the VK-107A-powered Yak-3's handling unpleasant. This shortcoming fully came to the fore during mock combat sessions with a Spitfire Mk IX, especially when performing violent manoeuvres in the vertical plane.

Further, leading engineer A. Stepanets noted persistent powerplant troubles. The engines began vibrating when throttled back, and the oil pressure dropped below the admissible level at altitudes in excess of 4,000 m (13,120 ft). On one of the machines the engine suffered a complete breakdown;

Above and below: The prototype Yak-3 VK-108. Note the double rows of six exhaust stubs (dorsal and lateral), with heat-resistant steel panels aft of them, and the armoured seat back.

overheating of water and oil was occasionally noted on the others. The tests revealed also incomplete consumption of fuel from the fuel tanks – a defect characteristic of many Yaks.

Modifications applied to these aircraft at Yakovlev's experimental production facility and at LII failed to produce the desired result. The test report signed in June 1946 stated: *'Modified Yak-3 aircraft c/ns 01-01, 03-01 and 04-01 powered by VK-107A engines and featuring metal wings, produced at the Volga plant (Saratov plant – translator's note) have failed to pass the State trials due to numerous serious defects.'*

Besides, the mixed construction (metal wing and fuselage with plywood skinning) did not meet the demands of post-war aviation that had been formulated in the Soviet Union. In many respects (stick forces, controllability, survivability) the mixed-construction Yak-3s proved to be a step back as compared to the

This silver/red Yak-3 equipped with a gun camera was used by LII as a testbed of unknown purpose.

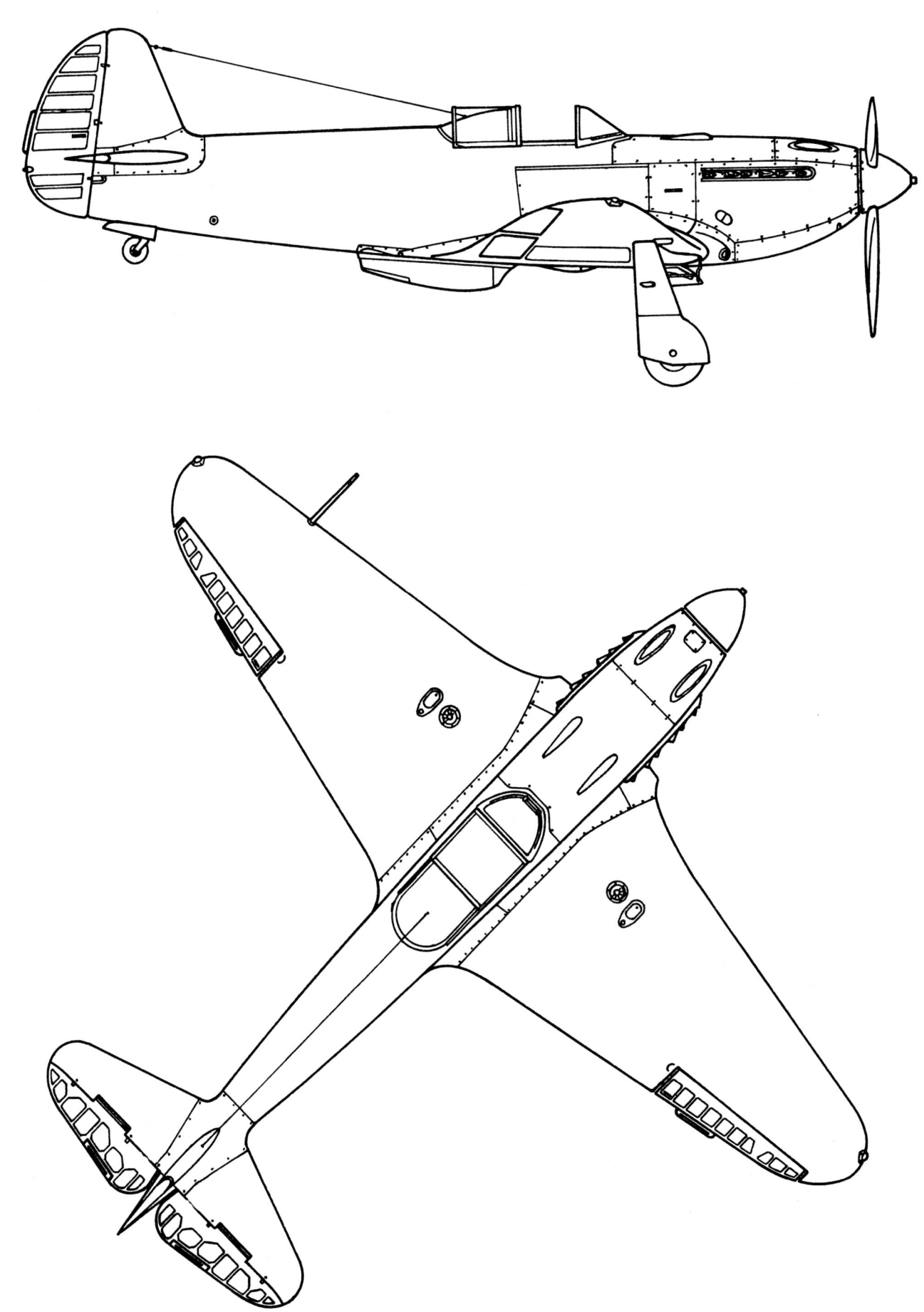

A four-view drawing of the Yak-3 powered by a VK-105PF-2 engine

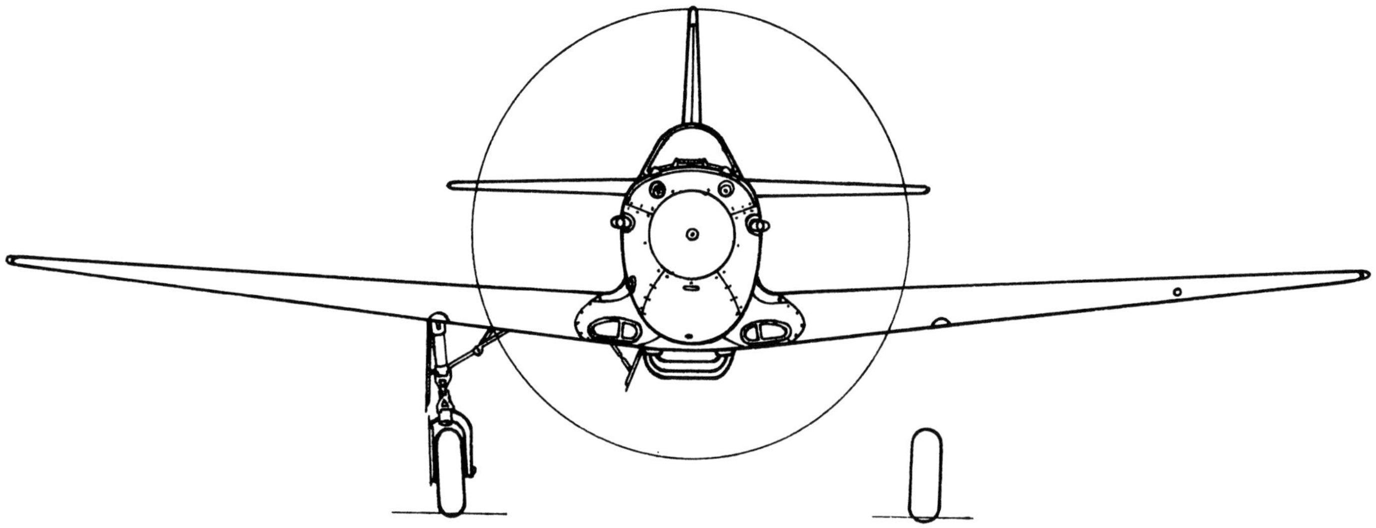

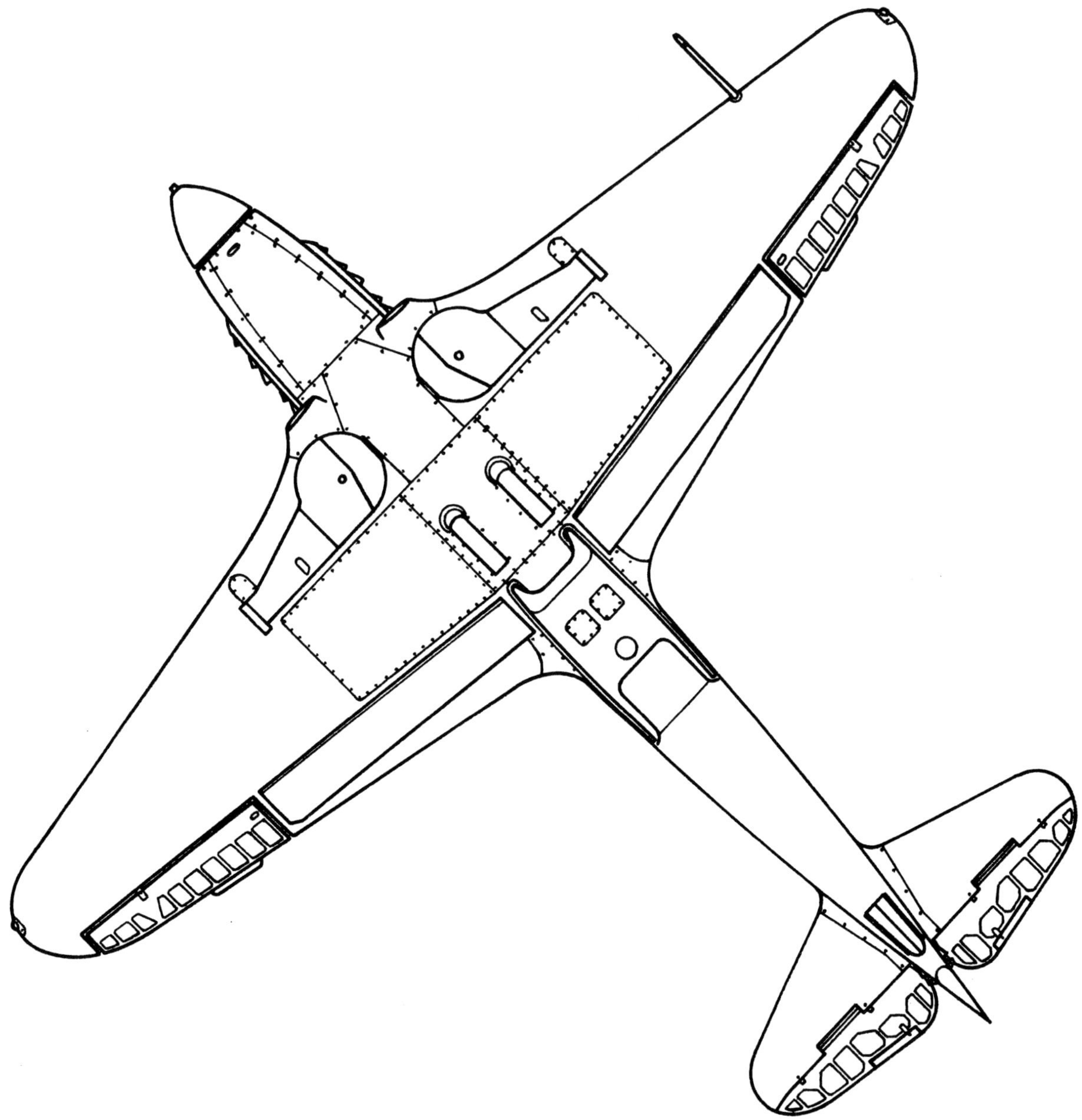

Three views of the Yak-3 M-82 development aircraft seen during manufacturer's flight tests.

all-metal machines built in Tbilisi. Therefore, the decision was taken to limit the production run to the three first machines already manufactured, and all unfinished airframes were scrapped.

The People's Commissariat of Aircraft Industry (renamed into the Ministry of Aircraft Industry by in late March 1946) considered that the stronger airframe of the Yak-9 was more suitable for comprehensive development of the VK-107A engine. Besides, the Yak-9 permitted the installation of potent 37-mm and 45-mm cannons between the cylinder banks and could be transformed into a long-range fighter – something that could not be effected on the Yak-3. These were the reasons for the Yak-9's longevity.

VK-108-powered Yak-3 prototype fighter

Installation of the VK-108 engine in the Yak-3 was, in effect, purely experimental. The VK-107A with a nominal rating of 1,500 hp was replaced by the VK-108 delivering 1,550 hp and operating in very adverse temperature conditions because the radiators were the same as on the Yak-9U. Owing to the special features of the engine design, the fighter's armament had to be restricted to one engine-mounted NS-23 cannon firing through the propeller hub.

The aircraft was constructed under the direction of engineer A. Kanookov; it was rolled out at the OKB's experimental production facility on 1st October 1944. Following a brief development period test pilot Victor Rastorgooyev performed the first flight, characterising the aircraft's performance as outstanding On 21st December 1944 the Yak-3 VK-108 (lightened to the utmost, with the armament deleted and a reduced amount of fuel in the tanks) developed a speed of 745 km/h (463 mph) at 6,290 m (20,631 ft). That was just 10 km/h (6.2 mph) less than the world speed record established in 1939 by a specially modified variant of the Bf 109. The Yak-3 climbed to 5,000 m (16,400 ft) within just three and a half minutes and literally pierced the skies, leaping into the air while still in a tail-down position (ie, without requiring the tail to be raised).

However, once again imperfect engine operation prevented the testing from being conducted at a normal pace. The flight schedule kept slipping because of vibrations, smoke emissions and numerous powerplant faults. Virtually every time the fighter covered a stretch in level flight, the oil temperature exceeded 110°C, which was the absolute limit for this engine. The work had to be discontinued on 8th March 1945 after one of the many flights plagued by failures.

Yak-3U fighter prototype

In the Yak-3U fighter the Yakovlev OKB made an attempt to combine its achievements in aerodynamic refinement with the merits of a Shvetsov-designed engine. In January 1945, when the aircraft was under construction, the ASh-82FN radial was a reliable and trouble-free engine, while the VK-107A (to say nothing of the VK-108) remained capricious and persistently malfunctioned.

The Yakovlev design team succeeded in creating a fighter that was very lightweight for a machine powered by the ASh-82FN – it had an all-up weight of only 2,792 kg (6,156 lb) versus 3,250kg (7,166 lb) in the case of the La-7. The maximum speed of the Yak-3U – 705 km/h (438 mph) at 6,100 m (20,998 ft) – was also superior to that of the La-7. The new machine proved to possess an excellent rate of climb. However, the forward shift of the wings, while improving stability, resulted in an inadmissible reduction of the aircraft's 'sit' angle increasing the risk of nosing-over; the aircraft became dangerous during landing and taxying.

In the course of development work the main defects of the aircraft were rectified; however, in the view of Aleksandr S. Yakovlev, this fighter was no longer needed in October 1945, and the work was discontinued.

Chapter 5

Yaks Abroad

The Frenchmen were the first among the Soviet Union's allies within the anti-Hitler coalition to have their air units equipped with Yaks for combat operations. Formation of the independent 'Normandie-Niémen' fighter squadron which initially comprised 14 volunteer pilots began in December 1942. The French pilots were offered a choice of several Soviet aircraft types; they opted for the Yak-1. In the opinion of *Capitaine* A. Litolff, one of France's most experienced pilots, this machine was similar to the well-known Morane Saulnier MS-406 in its piloting techniques but possessed a greater range of speeds.

Operational training of the squadron proceeded in several stages (this approach was subsequently practised with regard to other Allied pilots converting to the Yaks). The French pilots began their course in the training centre by examining the Yak-1 on the ground and studying the flight manual. Then they performed several training flights on the Yakovlev UT-2 *ab initio* trainer, followed by the Yak-7 conversion trainer and the Yak-1 fighter. Studying these machines posed no difficulties, and at the end of March *Commandant* J. Tulasne, the unit's Commander, reported that the squadron was ready to join the action at the Soviet-German front.

The unit did not stay long in the rear – the Yaks sporting French roundels on their sides (in addition to the Soviet Stars) actively joined battle at the central sector of the front in the ranks of the 303rd IAD, taking part, in particular, in the battle of the Kursk Bulge. According to official Soviet information, at the end of October 1943 the 'Normandie-Niémen' squadron was credited with the destruction of 75 enemy aircraft at the cost of some 30 Yak-1s and Yak-9s lost and 20 French pilots killed. Among those killed in action was the first commander of the French squadron.

By that time the squadron was reorganised into an air regiment which came to be commanded by Cdt P. Pouyade. An important landmark in the destiny of the unit was 13th August 1944 – the day when the 'Normandie-Niémen' regiment deployed at Alytus airfield in the Baltic area took delivery of Saratov-built Yak-3 fighters. One of the pilots, *Aspirant* F. de Geoffre, noted after examining the new machine:

Above and below: The Yak-3s donated to the 'Normandie-Niémen' regiment by the Soviet Government remained in service with for a few years. Here they are seen in post-war markings with French rudder flashes and the Lorraine Cross on the fins.

This Yak-3 is preserved in the *Musée de l'Aéronautique* in Paris in carefully restored wartime markings.

129

Above: This early Yak-1 was captured intact by the advancing German troops in the first days of the Great Patriotic War.
Below: Another captured Yak-1, this time in Luftwaffe markings showing it was evaluated by the Germans.

Above and below: Post-war pictures of polish Air Force Yak-9s operated by the 1. PLM 'Warszawa'.

'The Russian engineers under General Yakovlev changed the fuselage contours, appreciably improved the engine and enhanced the cockpit instrumentation. Cockpit visibility is marvellous, especially the forward view. The aircraft possesses excellent manoeuvrability. While performing a zoom climb, you get the impression that the aircraft is never going to stop. In a dive the aircraft develops high speeds. No sooner have you pushed the stick forward when the speed indicator already shows more than 600 km/h [385 mph]. This is undoubtedly an advantage, but you have to know how to make use of it. The only shortcoming is that the undercarriage extension on the first machines was not particularly reliable. But this cannot reduce our enthusiasm. We are gathering around the new machines, our eyes burning with admiration.'

Having mastered the Yak-3, the French pilots succeeded in considerably increasing the number of their victories. The most successful day in the history of the unit was 16th October 1944, when the combat results within the 24 hours amounted (according to the official information) to 29 enemy aircraft shot down without a single own aircraft lost. Asp. Roland de La Poype had the highest score of the day, having shot down two Ju 87 personally plus another three enemy aircraft as shared 'kills'.

Nevertheless, some of the air battles were extremely fierce. Thus, on 17th January 1945 an atrociously mutilated Yak-3 c/n 32-24 piloted by a wounded Cne René Challe, Commander of one of the regiment's squadrons, made a landing at Dolinen airfield in East Prussia. The pilot paid dearly for his sixth victory over a Fw 190: his aircraft had been hit by no fewer than four shells which blasted away the cockpit transparency; there were large holes in the fuselage and the wings. The machine seemed to be damaged beyond repair. However, three Soviet technicians (Youzefovich, Smirnov and Moorav'yov) repaired the fighter completely within twenty-four hours, having welded the fuselage framework, replaced the cockpit canopy glazing and patched up the wings.

Events of this kind imbued the French pilots with still greater confidence in the reliability and survivability of their combat machines. When Victory Day came, the unit had 273 'kills' to its credit at the cost of 55 own pilots put out of action (42 were lost in air combat and in crashes, nine were wounded, four were taken prisoner). By comparison, it can be noted that other air units of *la France Combattante* which had fought the Luftwaffe while flying British and American aircraft boasted a more modest record ('Lafayette' and 'Île de France' claimed 43 victories, having lost 74 own pilots for various reasons).

Many of the 'Normandie-Niémen' pilots considered that they owed their successes in no small part to Yakovlev's aircraft.

Ten months after the end of the war the British magazine *Aeroplane* published a comment made by one of the French pilots from the 'Normandie-Niémen' regiment:

'The main mission of the Yak-3 aircraft was co-operation with ground troops. They flew in support of ground formations during the offensive waged by the Red Army, attacking enemy aircraft and strafing its ground units in the vicinity of the frontline. Besides, ten minutes before the Pe-2s or Il-2s appeared over an enemy airfield, the Yak-3s flew over this area and destroyed enemy aircraft on the ground, shot them down in the air or prevented them from taking off. Then, after the arrival of the attack aircraft, the Yak-3s protected them from attack by enemy fighters coming from other airfields.

One more mission was the intercept. Pilots were to sit in their aircraft on quick-reaction alert, taking off every time they saw enemy aircraft or when they got information by radiotelephone about the appearance of enemy aircraft.

To tackle these duties, an aircraft exactly like the Yak-3 is required: a high-speed medium altitude interceptor with a high rate of climb. When attacking Fw 190s it never climbed to much more than 5,000 m [16,400 ft]. At this altitude the Yak-3 enjoys its best performance. Near the ground the Yak-3 was superior to the 'Hun' and many German pilots stalled and crashed while trying to chase it in a steep banking turn.'

It is a little known fact that one more French unit equipped with the Yak-3 fighters was being worked up for combat at Soviet airfields in the rear in the spring of 1945. It was the 3rd IAP 'Paris' staffed by French pilots and Soviet technicians and ground crews. The termination of hostilities prevented the 'Parisians' from joining battle, and the regiment was disbanded. As for 'Normandie-Niémen', the pilots of this unit returned to France on 40 Yak-3 fighters which they had received as a gift; some of them remained operational until late 1947.

Pilots of no other country that also had Soviet machines in its air force inventory could boast so impressive an experience of using the Yaks operationally. Among the first to get that experience were the Poles. In September 1943 the airmen of the 1st PLM 'Warszawa' (*pulk lotniczy mysliwski* – fighter regiment 'Warsaw') took delivery of their Yak-1s. They joined battle in July of the following year and performed an insignificant number of dogfights before the end of the war. The only victory on the Yak-1 achieved by a Polish pilot (over an Fw 189 reconnaissance aircraft) was scored by Captain Konieczny. Still, you have

Above: The crew chief of a Polish Yak-9 reports to the pilot that the aircraft is ready for the mission. The 55-gallon can beside the aircraft contains sand for fire-fighting.

Above: A technician performs maintenance on the engine of a Polish Air Force Yak-9M.
Below: A grey-painted Polish Air Force Yak-9P VK-107A

Civil-registered fighters are common nowadays (as warbirds, that is), but not in those days. This Hungarian Yak-9P VK-107A is registered HA-YEA or HA-YFA.

Above: A Yak-9M with pre-war Bulgarian roundels.
Below: This grey-painted Bulgarian Air Force VK-107A wears the post-war star-type insignia.

This ex-Yugoslav Yak-9D was operated by the RAF's 239 Wing. The initials 'JAS' below the cockpit denote the aircraft's pilot, Wg Cdr James A. Storrer.

to give him credit, for the Fw 189 was notoriously hard to kill, partly due to its tail gunner's station.

In January 1945 the 1. PLM began converting to the Yak-9 (in the D, T and M versions). On 19th April 1945 *podporucznik* (lieutenant) Kalinowski shot down an Fw 190 over the Oder river, downing one more on 25th April. According to official information, in the course of the war Kalinowski shot down 12 German aircraft, 10 of them while operating within the ranks of the Red Army Air Force.

The core of the flying personnel of the Polish air regiments was made up of Soviet airmen who were ethnic Poles. In addition to the 1. PLM, Yaks were also on strength with the 9th and 10th IAPs which had been formed on the basis of the Soviet 248th and 246th IAPs respectively. Initially these units were equipped with Yak-1s which, after a short while, were superseded by various Yak-9s powered by VK-105PF and VK-105PF-2 engines. The Polish Air Force also had a few Yak-7V and Yak-9V conversion trainers in its inventory.

Several Yaks were handed over to the Yugoslav Air Force; some of them were Yak-9DD ultra-long-range fighters from the 2nd production batch; they were in operation since April 1945. These machines took part in mock combat sessions with the British Hawker Typhoons, American Curtiss P-40N Warhawks and early versions of the North American P-51 Mustang. The Yaks carried a minimum amount of fuel, demonstrating excellent manoeuvrability at low altitude. The Yugoslavs sold one of the Yak-9Ds to the British. In 1945-1947 this machine was used as a 'personal hack' by Wg Cdr James A. Storrer of the RAF's 239 Wing.

Immediately after the end of the war about 60 Yak-9Us and 'Ps were delivered to Poland to replace the early versions which were progressively relegated to training duties. They were in intensive operation until the advent of Soviet-produced jet machines. Several VK-107A-powered Yak-9Ps found their way to Bulgaria. The Bulgarian Air Force had accumulated some experience of operating the Yak-9D, and their most experienced pilot was Hero of the Soviet Union Z. Zakhariyev. In response to the demands of Bulgarian airmen the fuel tanks in the outer wing panels of the Yak-9Ps were removed and two 12.7-mm UB machine-guns were fitted instead, thus increasing the fighter's firepower.

In September 1949 the Hungarian Air Force received its first batch of the Yak-9Ps numbering some fifty machines. They were delivered by rail to the town of Kécskemet In all, Hungary took delivery of up to 120 machines which were dubbed *Vércse* (Falcon) and remained on strength until the mid-1950s. Yugoslavia was one of the main recipients of the Yak-9P after the war. This country received early production machines; their operation was plagued by numerous failures and the aircraft were frequently grounded. Because of poor reliability and lack of spares the VK-107A engines on some machines were replaced by the VK-105PFs taken from the remaining Soviet Yak-1s.

In addition, Yak-9P fighters were delivered to Albania, China and North Korea which became Soviet allies in late 1940s. It is a known fact that the North Koreans were the last to use Yaks in combat. In all probability North Korea had some 40 to 50 VK-107A-powered machines (although some sources mention 100 Yak-9Ps) which had been delivered from bases in the Soviet Union and China. A pair of these fighters took part in the action on the very first day of the Korean War, 25th June 1950. As Robert Jackson described it in his book *Air War over Korea*, *'It was not long before the North Korean pilots demonstrated their aggressive ability. At 15.00 hrs on June 25th two Yak-9s raced low over Kimpo, spraying the field with cannon and machine-gun fire. Cannon shells shattered the control tower and found their mark in a fuel dump, which exploded in a tremendous mushroom of smoke and flame. An American Military Air Transport Service C-54 was also hit and damaged. While this attack was in progress four more Yaks strafed Seoul, damaging seven trainer aircraft* (North American AT-6 Texans and a Piper L-4 liaison aircraft – Auth.), *and at 19.00 hrs a second attack was made on Kimpo. This time the North Korean pilots concentrated on the C-54 damaged in the earlier raid, and this was sent up in flames.'* This was the first aircraft of the USAF lost in that war.

On 27th June the first air combat took place in the sky over Korea: five Yak-9s strafing Kimpo airfield (Robert Jackson claims they were Yak-7s) failed to notice the appearance of five USAF North American F-82 Twin Mustangs and the North Koreans lost three machines at once, but not before the Yaks had succeeded in destroying seven Texans on the airfield tarmac. In all, in the course of the first four days of hostilities the inventory of the Republic of Korea Air Force (ROKAF) was reduced by some 50 aircraft – mostly shot up on the ground.

However, shortly thereafter USAF pilots actively joined the fray and quickly won air superiority. Air strikes against Seoul and Kimpo were no longer a primary concern of the Yak pilots because they had to intercept Martin B-26 Marauder and Boeing B-29 Superfortress bombers making raids over North Korean territory. According to information from US sources, after a number of successful air raids accomplished between 3rd and 6th July by USAF and US Navy aircraft, the inventory of the North Korean Air Force shrank from 130 to just 18 machines.

Above: A Yugoslav Air Force Yak-9M serialled 2229. The fighter's patchwork appearance is of interest.

Above: North Korean Air Force Yak-9P VK-107As are prepard for another mission against the UN forces. Though the Yak-9 did see action in the opening stage of the Korean war, it was no match for the UN jets.

This North Korean Yak-9P VK-107A serialled 3 Red was damaged by enemy fire, force-landing in a field.

Above and below: A single Yak-9P was captured in North Korea and shipped to the USA for evaluation at Wright-Patterson AFB.

In the same month of July the USAF put most of the Yak-9Ps out of action, and the few that remained intact were redeployed to Chinese territory in Manchuria. North Korean and Chinese Yak-9s based at airfields along the Yalu River performed air defence duties until mid-1951 when they were superseded by MiG-15 jets.

A single example of the Yak-9P fell into American hands and was shipped to the United States for evaluation. Assessing the fighter, US specialists noted that it was the nearest Russian equivalent of the P-51D Mustang. While being superior to the latter in manoeuvrability, the Russian fighter lacked the Mustang's range and altitude performance and was inferior to it in various items of equipment.

The service career of the Yaks abroad arguably lasted somewhat longer than in the Soviet Union; still, by the end of the 1950s they were no longer to be found among the training and combat machines in various pro-Communist countries.

Specifications of the Yak-1 and Yak-7 variants

	I-26-2	Yak-1	Yak-1	Yak-1	Yak-1	Yak-1	Yak-1	Yak-1	I-28 (Yak-5)	I-30	UTI-26	Yak-7	Yak-7M	Yak-7A	Yak-7B	Yak-7-37	Yak-7PD	Yak-7M82	Yak-7B	Yak-7DI
Year of production	1940	1940	1941	1942	1942	1942	1943	1943	1941	1941	1941	1941	1941	1942	1942	1942	1942	1942	1943	1942
Powerplant	M-105P	M-105P	M-105PA	M-105PA	M-105PF	M-105PF	M-105PF	M-106-1sk	M-105PF	M-105PD	M-105P	M-105P	M-105P	M-105P	M-105PA	M105PF	M-105PA	M-105PD	M-82	M-105PF	M-105PF
Power at altitude - (hp)	1,050	1,050	1,050	1,050	1,180	1,180	1,180	1,350	1,180	1,160	1,050	1,050	1,050	1,050	1,050	1,180	1,050	1,160	1,330	1,180	1,180
- (kW)	783	783	783	783	880	880	880	1,007	880	865	783	783	783	783	783	880	783	865	992	880	880
Length - (m)	8.5	8.48	8.48	8.48	8.48	8.48	8.48	8.48	8.48			8.48	8.48	8.48	8.48			8.48	8.37	8.48	8.48
- (ft-in)	27-10.5	27-9.75	27-9.75	27-9.75	27-9.75	27-9.75	27-9.75	27-9.75	27-9.75		27-10.5	27-9.75	27-9.75	27-9.75	27-9.75	27-9.75	27-9.75	27-9.75	27-5.5	27-9.75	27-9.75
Wingspan - (m)	10.0	10.0		10.0	10.0	10.0	10.0	10.0	10.0	10.0	10.0	10.0	10.0	10.0	10.0	10.0	10.0	10.0	9.74	10.0	9.74
- (ft-in)	32-9.5	32-9.5	32-9.5	32-9.5	32-9.5	32-9.5	32-9.5	32-9.5	32-9.5	32-9.5	32-9.5	32-9.5	32-9.5	32-9.5	32-9.5	32-9.5	32-9.5	32-9.5	31-11.5	32-9.5	31-11.5
Wing area - (m²)	17.15	17.15	17.15	17.15	17.15	17.15	17.15	17.15	17.15	17.15	17.15	17.15	17.15	17.15	17.15	17.15	17.15	17.15	17.15	17.15	17.15
- (ft²)	184.6	184.6	184.6	184.6	184.6	184.6	184.6	184.6	184.6	184.6	184.6	184.6	184.6	184.6	184.6	184.6	184.6	184.6	184.6	184.6	184.6
Empty weight - (kg)	2,318	2,364	2,429	2,394	2,412	2,350	2,395	2,257	2,316	2,450	2,550	2,181	2,477	2,638	2,450	2,490	2,694	2,452	2,745	2,528	2,360
- (lb)	5,110	5,211	5,354	5,277	5,317	5,180	5,279	4,975	5,105	5,401	5,621	4,808	5,460	5,815	5,401	5,489	5,939	5,405	6,051	5,573	5,202
Gross weight - (kg)	2,700	2,844	2,934	2,883	2,917	2,780	2,900	2,757	2,884	2,928	3,130	2,750	2,960	3,160	2,935	3,010	3,235	2,904	3,370	3,048	2,835
- (lb)	5,952	6,269	6,468	6,355	6,430	6,128	6,393	6,078	6,358	6,455	6,900	6,062	6,525	6,966	6,470	6,635	7,131	6,402	7,429	6,719	6,250
Speed at sea level - (km/h)	490.0	473.0	468.0	478.0	510.0	526.0	523.0	551.0	531.0	515.0	476.0	500.0	471.0	469.0	495.0	514.0	485.0	500.0	515.0	547.0	505.0
- (mph)	304.4	293.9	290.8	297.0	316.9	326.8	324.9	342.3	329.9	320.0	295.7	310.6	292.6	291.4	307.5	319.3	301.3	310.6	320.0	339.8	313.8
Speed at altitude - (km/h)	585.0	573.0	560.0	563.0	571.0	592.0	590.0	630.0	592.0	650.0	571.0	586.0	560.0	556.0	571.0	570.0	564.0	611.0	615.0	612.0	570.0
- (@ m)	4,800	4,860	4,800	4,850	3,850	3,800	3,850	3,400	4,100	9,000	4,900	4,500	5,000	5,100	5,000	3,650	4,730	7,600	6,400	4,000	3,900
- (mph)	363.5	356.0	347.9	349.8	354.8	367.8	366.6	391.4	367.8	403.9	354.8	364.1	347.9	345.4	354.8	354.1	350.4	379.6	382.1	380.2	354.1
- (@ ft)	15,750	16,000	15,750	15,900	12,000	12,500	12,600	21,000	13,500	29,500	16,000	14,750	16,500	16,750	16,500	12,000	15,500	25,000	20,000	13,000	12,750
Climb to 5,000m (min)	6.0	5.3	6.8	5.9	6.4	4.7	5.6	4.5	5.4	5.2	7.0	5.5	6.8	7.5	6.4	5.8	7.2	5.4	5.6	4.7	5.5
- to 16,400ft (minutes)	6.0	5.3	6.8	5.9	6.4	4.7	5.6	4.5	5.4	5.2	7.0	5.5	6.8	7.5	6.4	5.8	7.2	5.4	5.6	4.7	5.5
Service ceiling - (m)	10,200	9,300	9,900	10,400	11,000	9,500	10,050		10,000	12,000	9,000	9,400	9,250	8,750	9,500	9,900	8,260	11,300	10,000	10,000	10,400
- (ft)	33,500	30,500	32,500	34,000	36,000	31,000	33,000		33,000	39,250	29,500	30,750	30,250	28,750	31,000	32,500	27,000	37,000	33,000	33,000	34,000
Turn time - (seconds)	24	20-21	19-20	19	19-20	17-18	18-19	19	19		19-20	22	24	22	21-22	19-20	23	19-20	24	19-20	17-18
Operational range - (km)	700	700		650	650		700				975	700	643	750	643	645	550	575	700	700	600
- (miles)	434	434		403	403		434				605	434	399	466	399	400	341	357	434	434	372
Take-off run - (m)	300	340		320	320	285	340		320	303	310	375	440	410	435				350	300
- (ft)	984	1,115		1,049	1,049	935	1,115		1,049	994	1,017	1,230	1,443	1,345	1,427				1,148	984
Landing roll - (m)	540	540		530	520	530	500	560	500	525	550	550	650	610	620				540	580
- (ft)	1,771	1,771		1,738	1,706	1,738	1,640	1,637		1,722	1,804	1,804	2,132	2,001	2,034				1,771	1,902
Armament - (mm)	1 x 20	1 x 20	1 x 20	1 x 20	1 x 20	1 x 20	1 x 20	1 x 20	1 x 20	3 x 20	2 x 7.62	1 x 20	3 x 20	1 x 20	1 x 20	1 x 37	1 x 20	2 x 20	2 x 20	1 x 20
	2 x 7.62	2 x 7.62	2 x 7.62	2 x 7.62	2 x 7.62	1 x 12.7	1 x 12.7	1 x 12.7	1 x 7.62	2 x 7.62	2 x 7.62	2 x 7.62	2 x 7.62	2 x 12.7	2 x 12.7		1 x 12.7	2 x 12.7	1 x 12.7

Specifications of the Yak-9 and Yak-3 variants

	Yak-9	Yak-9T	Yak-9D	Yak-9	Yak-9P	Yak-9K	Yak-9B	Yak-9DD	Yak-9M	Yak-9PD	Yak-9U prototype	Yak-9U prototype	Yak-9U production	Yak-9UT	Yak-9U	Yak-9P	Yak-1M 'dooblyor'	Yak-3	Yak-3	Yak-3U
Year of production	1943	1943	1943	1943	1943	1944	1944	1944	1944	1944	1943	1944	1944	1945	1946	1947	1943	1944	1944	1945
Powerplant	M-105PF	M-105PF	M-105PF	M-106	M-105PF	M-105PF	M-105PF	M-105PF	VK-105PF	VK-105PD	VK-105PF-2	M-107A	VK-107A	VK-107A	VK-107A	VK-107A	M-105PF-2	VK-107	VK-108	ASh-82FN
Power at altitude - (hp)	1,180	1,180	1,180	1,350	1,180	1,180	1,180	1,180	1,180	1,160	1,240	1,500	1,500	1,500	1,500	1,500	1,240	1,500	1,800	1,630
- (kW)	880	880	880	1,007	880	880	880	880	880	865	925	1,119	1,119	1,119	1,119	1,119	925	1,119	1,342	1,215
Length - (m)	8.5	8.65	8.5	8.5	8.5	8.87	8.5	8.5	8.5	8.6	8.5	8.6	8.6		8.6	8.5	8.5	8.5	8.5	8.17
- (ft-in)	27-10.5	28-4	27-10.5	27-10.5	27-10.5	29-1	27-10.5	27-10.5	27-10.5	28-2.5	27-10.5	28-2.5	28-2.5		28-2.5	27-10.5	27-10.5	27-10.5	27-10.5	26-9.5
Wingspan-(m)	9.74	9.74	9.74	9.74	9.74	9.74	9.74	9.74	9.74	10.74	9.74	9.74	9.74	9.74	9.74	9.74	9.2	9.2	9.2	9.74
- (ft-in)	31-11.5	31-11.5	31-11.5	31-11.5	31-11.5	31-11.5	31-11.5	31-11.5	31-11.5	35-2.75	31-11.5	31-11.5	31-11.5	31-11.5	31-11.5	31-11.5	30.2	30.2	30.2	31-11.5
Wing area - (m²)	17.15	17.15	17.15	17.15	17.15	17.15	17.15	17.15	17.15	17.65	17.15	17.15	17.15	17.15	17.15	17.15	14.85	14.85	14.85	17.15
- (ft²)	184.6	184.6	184.6	184.6	184.6	184.6	184.6	184.6	184.6	189.9	184.6	184.6	184.6	184.6	184.6	184.6	159.8	159.8	159.8	184.6
Empty weight - (kg)	2,277	2,298	2,350	2,380	2,222	2,291	2,382	2,346	2,428	2,098	2,244	2,477	2,512	2,187	2,593	2,708	2,105	2,346		2,273
- (lb)	5,019	5,066	5,180	5,246	4,898	5,050	5,251	5,171	5,352	4,625	4,947	5,460	5,537	4,821	5,716	5,970	4,640	5,171		5,011
Gross weight - (kg)	2,870	3,025	3,117	3,050	2,820	3,028	3,356	3,387	3,095	2,500	2,900	3,150	3,204	3,260	3,227	3,550	2,660	2,984	2,830	2,792
- (lb)	6,327	6,668	6,871	6,723	6,216	6,675	7,398	7,466	6,823	5,511	6,393	6,944	7,063	7,186	7,114	7,826	5,864	6,578	6,238	6,155
Speed at sea level - (km/h)	520.0	533.0	535.0	531.0	505,0	518.0	507.0	522.0	518.0	503.0	558.0	600.0	575.0	578.0	569.0	590.0	570.0	611.0		
- (mph)	323.1	331.1	332.4	329.9	313.8	321.8	315.0	324.3	321.8	312.5	346.7	372.8	357.2	359.1	353.5	366.6	354.1	379.6		
Speed at altitude -(km/h)	599.0	597.0	591.0	602.0	576.0	573.0	562.0	584.0	573.0	620.0	620.0	700.0	672.0	671.0	672.0	660.0	651.0	720.0		
- (@ m)	4,300	3,930	3,650	3,250	3,950	3,900	3,750	3,900	3,750	10,500	3,850	5,500	5,000	4,900	5,700	5,000	4,300	5,750		
- (mph)	372.2	370.9	348.5	374.0	357.9	356.0	349.2	362.8	356.0	385.2	385.2	434.9	417.5	416.9	417.5	410.1	404.5	447.3		
- (@ ft)	14,000	13,000	12,000	10,750	13,000	12,750	12,250	12,750	12,250	34,500	12,750	18,000	16,500	16,000	18,750	16,500	14,000	18,750		
Climb to 5,000m (min)	5.1	5.5	6.1	5.4	5.4	5.7	6.5	6.8	6.1	5.6	4.8	4.1	5.0	5.2	4.8	5.8	4.1	3.9	3.5	
- to 16,400ft (minutes)	5.1	5.5	6.1	5.4	5.4	5.7	6.5	6.8	6.1	5.6	4.6	4.1	5.0	5.2	4.8	5.8	4.1	3.9	3.5	
Service ceiling - (m)	11,100	10,000	9,100	10,100			8,600	9,400	9,500	13,100	10,400		10,650	10,700	11,100	10,500	10,800	11,800		
- (ft)	36,500	32,750	29,750	33,000			28,250	30,750	31,000	43,000	34,000		35,000	35,000	36,500	34,500	35,500	38,750		
Turn lime - (seconds)	16-17	18-19	19-20	17-18			25-26	26	19-20		19.5	18.5	20	20-21		21	17	18		
Operational range - (km)	660	620	905			850		1,320	950		850	884	675	690	590	1,130	900	1,060		
- (miles)	410	385	562			528		820	590		528	549	419	428	366	702	559	658		
Take-off run - (m)	305	380	370	360		305	440	400	420		320	380	375		375	540	275	345		
- (ft)	1,000	1,246	1,213	1,181		1,000	1,443	1,312	1,377		1,049	1,246	1,230		1,230	1,771	902	1,131		
Landing roll - (m)	450	500	550	530		450	580	500	550		575	535	530		530	582	485	590		
- (ft)	1,476	1,640	1,804	1,738		1,476	1,902	1,640	1,804		1,886	1,755	1,738		1,738	1,909	1,591	1,935		
Armament - (mm)	1 x 20	1 x 37	1 x 20	1 x 20	2 x 20	1 x 45	1 x 20	1 x 20	1 x 20	1 x 20	1 x 23	1 x 20	1 x 20	1 x 37	1 x 20	1 x 20	1 x 20	1 x 20	1 x 23	2 x 20
	1 x 12.7	1 x 12.7	1 x 12.7	1 x 12.7		1 x 12.7	1 x 12.7	1 x 12.7	1 x 12.7		2 x ?	2 x 12.7	2 x 12.7	1x20	2 x 12.7	2 x 12.7	2 x 12.7	2 x 12.7		

Above: This Yak-3 VK-105PF-2 painted to represent Major B. N. Yeryomin's second aircraft was preserved at the Yakovlev OKB museum. It is seen here at Moscow-Tushino during one of the Aviation Day displays.

A Polish Air Force Yak-9P preserved in one of Poland's many aviation museums.

The I-26-1, the first prototype of the Yak-1

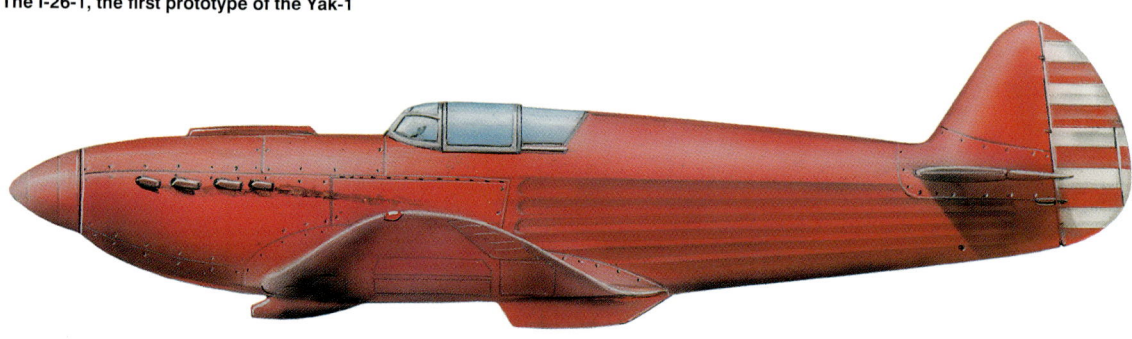

9 Blue, a mid-production Yak-1 with retractable skis, was flown by Lt. Zakharov (Red Banner Baltic Fleet/73rd IAP) in 1942. The serial superimposed on the star insignia is noteworthy.

This early-production Yak-1 (note canopy design) was the mount of Col. I. M. Goosarov in 1942.

9 Black, a winter-camouflaged Yak-1 flown by the 'Normandie-Niémen' regiment. The unit markings were initially limited to an unobtrusive French roundel near the cockpit.

This sharkmouthed Yak-1 '11 White' of the 'Normandie-Niémen' regiment was flown by Albert Durand in April 1943

This colourful Yak-1 sporting ten 'kill' markings was flown by V. Pokrovskiy (Hero of the Soviet Union), 2nd IAP.

Another highly decorated Yak-1; the signboard which the girl is holding reads *Pol'sha* (Poland). This aircraft was the mount of F. Morozov (HSU) of the 31st GvIAP.

Yak-1 '17 Red' of the 'Normandie-Niémen' regiment flown by Yves Bizien is inscribed *To the defenders of the Stalingrad Front from the collective farm workers of the Krasnoyarsk District of the Saratov Region*.

Yak-7A '14 White' was flown by A. V. Chirkov (HSU) of the 29th GvIAP. Note the Order of the Red Banner of Combat painted on the fuselage spine.

This Yak-7B was paid for by donations from Young Communist League members of the Kuzbass region, hence the *Komsomol Kuzbassa* logo. Note the KIM (*Kommunisticheskiy Internatsional Molodyozhi*, Communist Youth International) badge on the star.

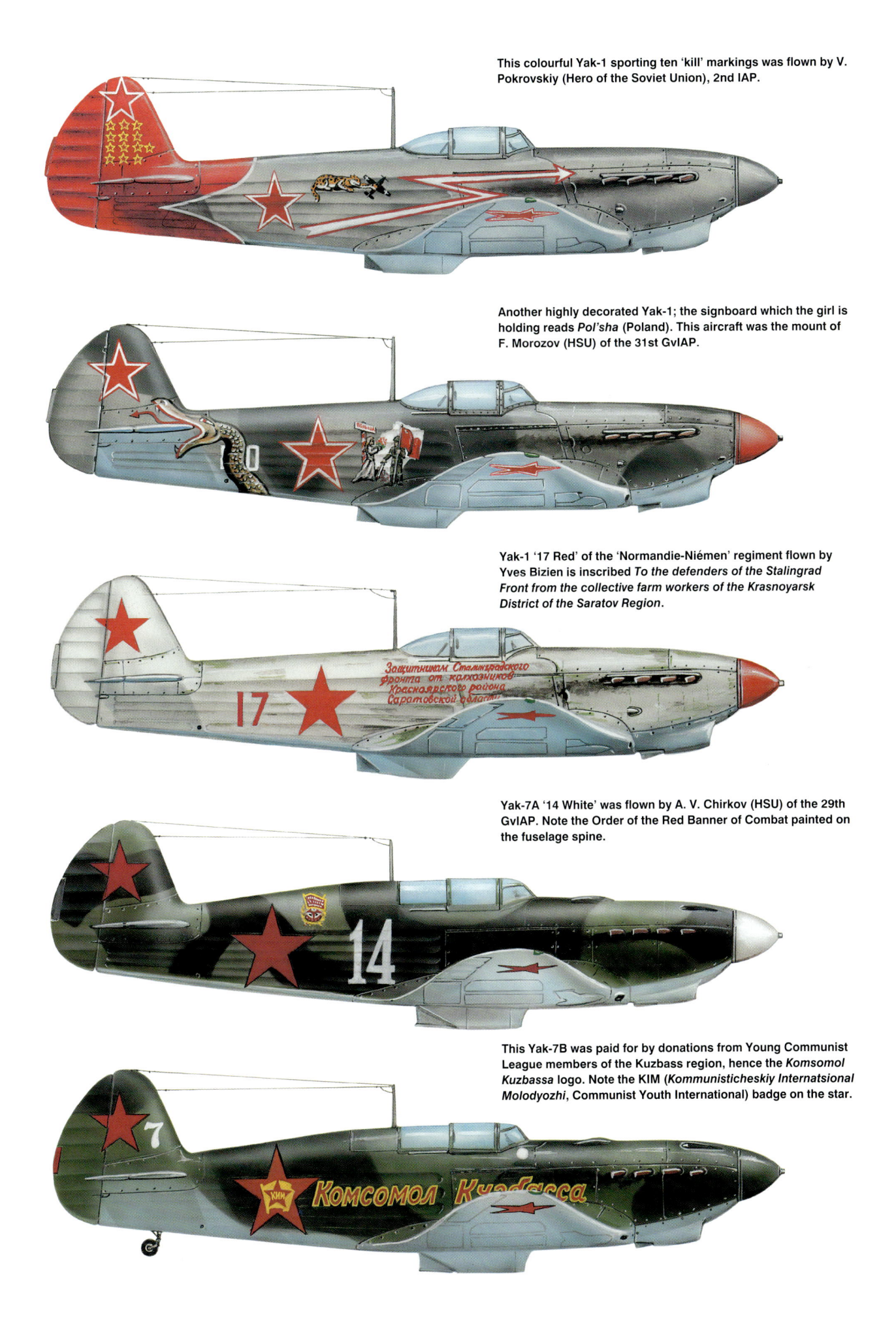

This red-nosed Yak-7B of the 434th IAP was flown by Lt. (sg) V. Orekhov on the Stalingrad Front in 1942. The red nose may have been a quick-identification feature.

Yak-7B '65 Red' inscribed *From the 'Politotdelets'* (Political Section Worker) *collective farm to the defenders of Stalingrad* operated on the Stalingrad Front in the winter of 1942-43.

A late-production 'bubbletop' Yak-7B of the 42nd IAP which operated on the North-Western Front in the autumn of 1942. Note 'ye Scrolle of Honoure' showing four 'kill' markings; surprisingly, these are swastikas instead of the usual stars.

The Yak-7DI development aircraft which was effectively the first prototype of the Yak-9. The titles on the tail read '7-DI'.

Red-nosed Yak-9 '14 White' was flown by Lt. Marcel Lefevre, the CO of the 'Normandie-Niémen' regiment. Note the Cyrillic letter F on the tail, presumably meaning *frantsooz* (Frenchman)!

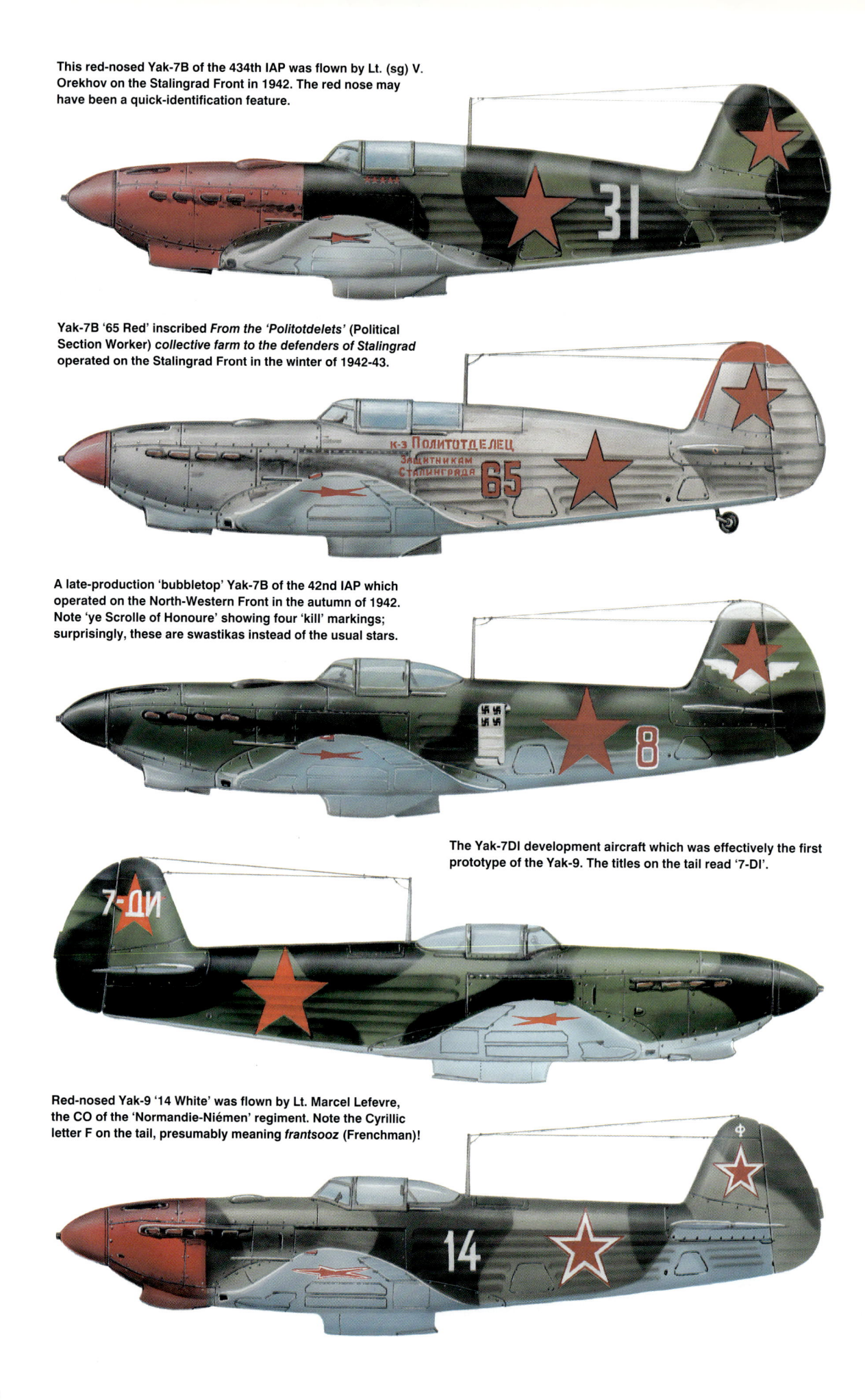

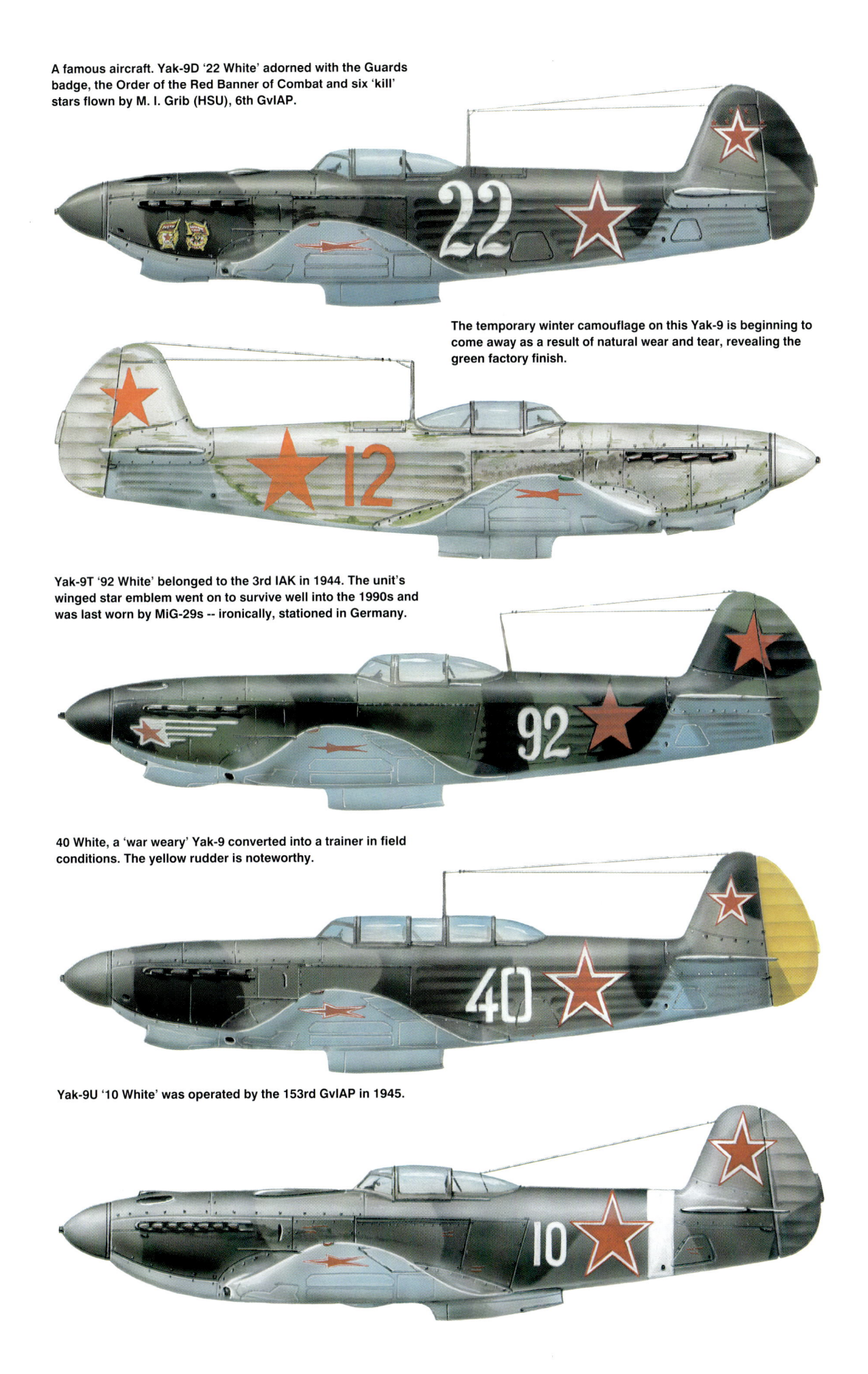

A famous aircraft. Yak-9D '22 White' adorned with the Guards badge, the Order of the Red Banner of Combat and six 'kill' stars flown by M. I. Grib (HSU), 6th GvIAP.

The temporary winter camouflage on this Yak-9 is beginning to come away as a result of natural wear and tear, revealing the green factory finish.

Yak-9T '92 White' belonged to the 3rd IAK in 1944. The unit's winged star emblem went on to survive well into the 1990s and was last worn by MiG-29s -- ironically, stationed in Germany.

40 White, a 'war weary' Yak-9 converted into a trainer in field conditions. The yellow rudder is noteworthy.

Yak-9U '10 White' was operated by the 153rd GvIAP in 1945.

141

Bulgarian Air Force Yak-9D '28 White', 1945.

This Yak-9D was flown by Wg Cdr James A. Storrer (Royal Air Force/239 Wing) as a unit 'hack'.

100 White, A Yak-9D of the Polish Air Force's 1. PLM 'Warszawa' flown by Mikolaj Haustowicz in April 1945.

A North Korean Air Force Yak-9P, 1950.

Ex-North Korean Yak-9T 'T2-3002' was evaluated by the US Air Force at Wright Patterson AFB in 1955

A 150th GvIAP Yak-3 flown by Lt. (sg) V. Orekhov

Yak-3 '100 White' was flown by I. Fyodorov (HSU), 812th IAP.

This Yak-3 is inscribed *To Sergey Luganskiy, HSU, from the Yaoung Communist League members and young people of Alma-Ata*.

This colourful Yak-3 of the 'Normandie-Niémen' regiment was flown by Roger Sauvage in the spring of 1945. Note the 15 'kill' markings.

This is how the Yak-3s of 'Normandie-Niémen' looked in the post-war years.

143

We hope you enjoyed this book...

Midland Publishing titles are edited and designed by an experienced and enthusiastic team of specialists.

Further titles are in preparation but we always welcome ideas from authors or readers for books they would like to see published.

In addition, our associate, Midland Counties Publications, offers an exceptionally wide range of aviation, spaceflight, astronomy, military, naval and transport books and videos for sale by mail-order around the world.

For a copy of the appropriate catalogue, or to order further copies of this book, and any of many other Midland Publishing titles, please write, telephone, fax or e-mail to:

Midland Counties Publications
4 Watling Drive, Hinckley,
Leics, LE10 3EY, England

Tel: (+44) 01455 254 450
Fax: (+44) 01455 233 737
E-mail: midlandbooks@compuserve.com
www.midlandcountiessuperstore.com

US distribution by Specialty Press – see page 2.

Aerofax
MIKOYAN-GUREVICH MiG-15
Yefim Gordon

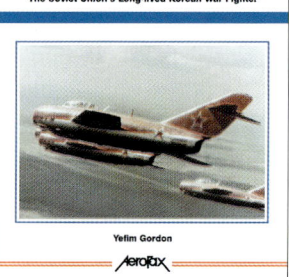

In this Aerofax, compiled from a wealth of first-hand Russian sources, there is a comprehensive history of every evolution of the Soviet Union's swept-wing fighter and its service. Notably in this volume, there are tables listing intricate details of many individual aircraft, a concept which would have been unthinkable in any publications only a few years ago.

There is extensive and detailed photo coverage, again from Russian sources, almost all of which is previously unseen.

Softback, 280 x 215 mm, 160 pages
214 b/w and 21 colour photographs,
7pp col sideviews, 18pp b/w drawings
1 85780 105 9 **£17.95/US $29.95**

Aerofax
YAKOVLEV Yak-25/26/27/28
Yakovlev's Tactical Twinjets
Yefim Gordon

During the 1950s and 1960s the Soviet design bureau Yakovlev was responsible for a series of swept-wing twin-engined jet combat aircraft, known in the west under various names including *Firebar, Flashlight, Mandrake, Mangrove, Brewer* and *Maestro*. All the various models are covered in this Aerofax – as usual with a mass of new information, detail and illustrations from original Russian sources.

Softback, 280 x 215 mm, 128 pages
202 b/w and 41 colour photographs,
plus drawings and 21 colour side-views
1 85780 125 3 **£17.99/US $27.95**

Aerofax
MIKOYAN-GUREVICH MiG-17
Yefim Gordon

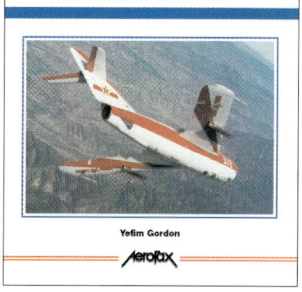

The Soviet Union produced and used around 9,000 MiG-17s. First flown in January 1950, it is an extensively upgraded MiG-15 with a redesigned 'scimitar' wing and lengthened fuselage.

It was built under various designations including the Polish Lim-5P and Lim-6bis and the Czech S-105, and served not only with the Soviet armed forces but with other Warsaw Pact nations, seeing combat in the Middle East, in North Vietnam and in Nigeria.

Softback, 280 x 215 mm, 144 pages
172 b/w and 32 colour photo, 10pp of colour sideviews, 12pp of drawings
1 85780 107 5 **£18.99/US $27.95**

Red Star Volume 1
SUKHOI S-37 & MIKOYAN MFI
Yefim Gordon

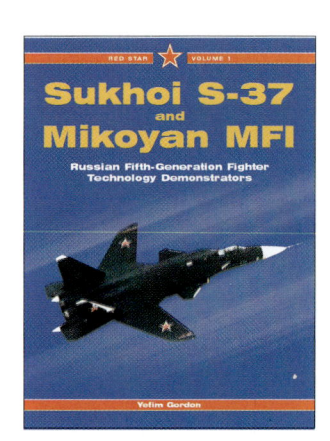

Conceived as an answer to the American ATF programme, the Mikoyan MFI (better known as the 1.42 or 1.44) and the Sukhoi S-37 Berkoot were developed as technology demonstrators. Both design bureaux used an approach that was quite different from Western fifth-generation fighter philosophy. This gives a detailed account of how these enigmatic aircraft were designed, built and flown. It includes structural descriptions of both types.

Sbk, 280 x 215 mm, 96pp, plus 8pp colour foldout, 12 b/w and 174 colour photos, drawings and colour artworks
1 85780 120 2 **£18.95/US $27.95**

Red Star Volume 2
FLANKERS: The New Generation
Yefim Gordon

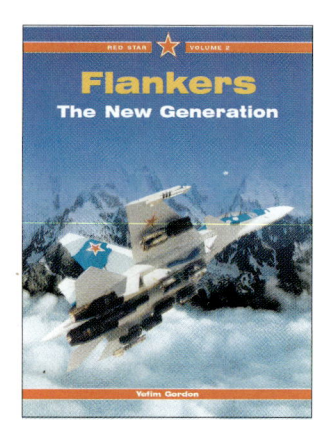

The multi-role Su-30 and Su-35 and thrust-vectoring Su-37 are described in detail, along with the 'big head' Su-23FN/Su-34 tactical bomber, the Su-27K (Su-33) shipborne fighter and its two-seat combat trainer derivative, the Su-27KUB. The book also describes the customised versions developed for foreign customers – the Su-30KI (Su-27KI), the Su-30MKI for India, the Su-30MKK for China and the latest Su-35UB.

Softback, 280 x 215 mm, 128 pages
252 colour photographs, plus 14 pages of colour artworks
1 85780 121 0 **£18.95/US $27.95**

Red Star Volume 3
POLIKARPOV'S I-16 FIGHTER
Yefim Gordon and Keith Dexter

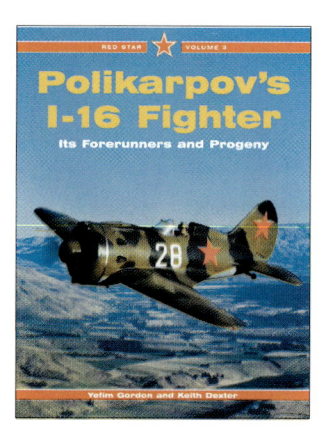

Often dismissed because it did not fare well against its more modern adversaries in the Second World War, Nikolay Polikarpov's I-16 was nevertheless an outstanding fighter – among other things, because it was the world's first monoplane fighter with a retractable undercarriage. Its capabilities were demonstrated effectively during the Spanish Civil War. Covers every variant, from development, unbuilt projects and the later designs that evolved from it.

Sbk, 280 x 215 mm, 128 pages,
185 b/w photographs, 17 pages of colour artworks, plus line drawings
1 85780 131 8 **£18.99/US $27.95**

Red Star Volume 4
EARLY SOVIET JET FIGHTERS
Yefim Gordon

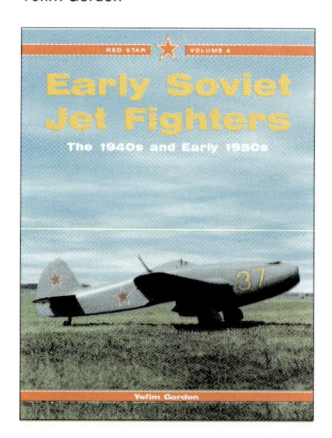

This charts the development and service history of the first-generation Soviet jet fighters designed by such renowned 'fighter makers' as Mikoyan, Yakovlev and Sukhoi, as well as design bureaux no longer in existence – the Lavochkin and Alekseyev OKBs, during the 1940s and early 1950s. Each type is detailed and compared to other contemporary jet fighters. As ever the extensive photo coverage includes much which is previously unseen.

Sbk, 280 x 215 mm, 144 pages
240 b/w and 9 colour photos,
8 pages of colour artworks
1 85780 139 3 **£19.99/US $29.95**